The Evolution of the Hollywood Heartthrob

Sylvia Safran Resnick

The Evolution of the Hollywood Heartthrob
Copyright 2015 by Sylvia Safran Resnick

All Rights Reserved
Printed in the United States of America

The author has made every reasonable effort to contact all copyright holders. Any errors that may have occurred are inadvertent and anyone, who for any reason, has not been contacted is invited to write to the publishers so a full acknowledgement may be made in subsequent editions of this work.

No part of this book may be used or reproduced, stored in a retrieval system, or transmitted in any form or by any means, electronic, mechanical, photocopying, recording or otherwise, without the prior written permission of the author except in the case for brief quotations embodied in critical articles or reviews.

Author has either paid licensing fees or has been granted permission for the use of all photos included in this book.

ISBN - 1-59393-598-6
FIRST EDITION

Published by BearManor Media – Albany, Georgia, USA
www.bearmanormedia.com

To Barry, Scott, and Bryan: The Heartthrobs in my life.
Thanks for your love and support.

PROLOGUE

Hollywood continues to facinate although it has gone through many changes. Once upon a time the mantra of movies was to entrance, titilate and spin dreams that offered relief from everyday problems that plague us. Today romance, laughter and the general uplift moviegoers once experienced has been replaced with overt violence and sexual overtones. Still, today's movies do offer escape, just that of a different kind than in the early years.

From time to time a film illuminates the movie theater, holds the audience spellbound, and generally has a healing effect. These are the times when actors shine, directors feel a sense of pride, and producers revel in what they have had a hand in accomplishing.

If your favorite heartthrob is missing, I apologize. I have to omit some of my personal heartthrobs as well due to space limitations. For now, I want to thank you for reading my book.

Enjoy!

CONTENTS

Chapter One: The Thirties	11
Chapter Two: The Forties	79
Chapter Three: The Fifties	133
Chapter Four: The Sixties	176
Chapter Five: The Seventies	216
Chapter Six: The Eighties	245
Chapter Seven: The Nineties	275
Chapter Eight: The 21st Century 2000-2010	307
Acknowledgements	329
About the Author	330

INTRODUCTION

In a darkened movie theater, a woman leans back in the seat, eyes fastened on the image projected upon a large white screen. The only sound to be heard is that of a piano keeping time with the scene she is watching. As the hero gallops across the desert, there is a burst of loud music. When the hero's lips meet the lips of the lovely heroine in his arms, a sweet melody engulfs the theater. As passions are stirred, a crescendo of sound emerges from the piano and the screen grows dark exciting the imagination .The woman sighs. The other women in the audience sigh too, deep soulful sounds that signify romantic hearts beating in unison. Even before the advent of sound, the motion picture stirred emotions. Eyes fastened with longing on the man on the screen whose brilliant smile embraced them they sat in the dark fantasizing. They could focus their desires on this handsome lover as they wordlessly spun their dreams. It was exciting, but safe.

Thus the object of love and desire on the screen became personified with real romantic longings. A dream for which the female heart throbbed with yearnings and the secret hope that one day she would experience this encompassing love in her real life. The man of her dreams was up there on the big screen; why couldn't he be out there in the world to be hers one day? She fastened her hopes and romantic desires upon a black and white image, waiting patiently for his flesh and blood counterpart to appear in her life. Sometimes she even imagined that the man up on the screen was really hers as she spun the fantasy cloth into her own garment of reality. From this flowed the longings in her heart as she put pen to paper. Fan mail then became the path to love. When movies began to speak to audiences, senses quivered and dreams spun blissfully. In the darkened theater women fantasized that the hero's smile was for her alone; his kiss meant just for her, a promise of fulfillment that over shadowed reality. Each woman convinced the handsome hero belonged only to her.

Even before talkies brought heartthrobs to life, female fans expressed their adoration for the compelling image up on the movie screen. When Rudolph Valentino died suddenly a wave of deep mourning engulfed thousands of his fans who lined up to view his open casket in New York before his official funeral. In Hollywood where a second funeral was held after Valentino's body had traveled there by train, 100,000 mourners mostly women, gathered on the streets around the church to pay tribute to the man who had captured their hearts.

Heartthrobs in the 30's were more than just handsome with perfect profiles and classic, flawless features. It was an era of elegance in both looks and manners. A little over a century ago acting was considered a lowly profession. Today, actors are revered, copied, sought after for everything from product endorsement to appearing at a charity event to insur that as much money as possible is raised. Today actors are often paid as high as 20 million dollars for a single movie. Add that together with the substantial sums earned from DVD's and television and an actor can realize millions from just one film.

Much has changed since the beginning. The romantic screen heartthrob of today is as appealing to women as he was in the '30's when sound brought him to life. Although the romantic hero may have gone through some major changes in the last eighty years, he is still a force in films and in the lives of adoring women who love their movies and their heartthrobs.

Chapter One
THE THIRTIES

Life was difficult, even dismal in the real world, but the reel beckoned with the promise of escape from the harshness of life, even if just for a couple of hours. Scraping together the twenty-three cent price of an adult ticket, women went to the movies to submerge themselves in who was on the white screen. The big as life, beautiful actor may have been unapproachable in reality, but he was completely approachable in their imaginations. Women brought money into the box office just to look at and yearn for the celluloid man, thus creating the image of The Hollywood Heartthrob.

He was sophisticated and charming. The advent of sound brought him even closer to the women who adored him, blissfully drinking in his beauty and the compelling voice that drew them into the pretend world of love and romance. Women felt safe in accepting the sensuality reaching out to them from the screen. In reality, the Heartthrob was unattainable, but feminine dreams were laced with hope. Each woman dreamt that such a man could one day appear on the horizon for her. They were gallant men, well-spoken and well mannered. They were men of an age to enchant, intrigue, and make women in the audience feel safe and protected, perhaps even a little naughty. Heartthrobs offered refuge and escape in a stark and insecure era. In the thirties actors often made movies back to back, sometimes as many as four a year, thus providing their female admirers with plenty of romantic escape from humdrum lives of stark reality.

Actors were never seen in a state of undress on screen. An actor might appear in a scene attired in a dressing gown, usually with a scarf knotted at his throat. On very rare occasions, he might be wearing pajamas.

At the opening of the first drive-in theater in 1932, the screening of a comedy starring dapper Adolph Menjou was well received by the six hundred people who attended one of three showings. The cost for the evening's entertainment was twenty-five cents per car and twenty-five cents per occupant with a maximum charge of one dollar per vehicle.

Early in the decade, Clark Gable caused a furor within the men's undergarment industry when he removed both his shirt and undershirt in a scene from *It Happened One Night*. Sales of men's undershirts dropped dramatically. Women however, especially those who flocked to see his films, were thrilled by his daring. They clung to the emotions stirred within them by an onscreen expressive glance, a passionate embrace, or a fervent kiss. Film kisses could last only a prescribed amount of time set by a censoring board that strongly governed the film industry. Kisses were always closed mouthed. Yet they were as ardent as the more graphic kisses of today. Actors who made hearts flutter in the decade of the '30's were clean shaven except for the few whose mustache was a trademark. You could almost smell the subtle scent of after shave on their smooth skin.

The heartthrob of the 30's may have effortlessly swept a woman off her feet, but it was always in good taste. It was a time of sweet surrender in the most tender and purest of ways. Leading men on screen revered and respected women especially those they loved. Women in the audience reacted to this with a response of their own; a longing to meet and know such a man as the one on screen, a man who made their hearts race.

Sound was new and exciting. Since many actors came to movies from the theater, their voices were trained to resonate. And resonate they did from the big screen right into the titillated hearts of their female fans.

A fan could write to the movie studio and for a quarter be sent an autographed photo to put in a frame on her bedside table. Or she could, and often did, put pen to paper to pour out her feelings, believing that her words would be seen only by the object of her affection. Thus fan mail came to be.

1930's Events

- On March 1, 1932, the kidnapping of the Lindbergh baby from his crib made national news, creating anxiety and fear for parents everywhere.

- Eight days after his inauguration on March 12, 1933, President Roosevelt broadcast the first of his many fireside chats from The White House while a hopeful audience listened attentively.

- August 11, 1934 saw the official opening of Alcatraz, where for dozens of years the most dangerous criminals were housed and a number of movies were made highlighting the Island across from San Francisco.

- In 1935, the Social Security Act was signed into law by President Roosevelt.

- Adorable Shirley Temple was earning $50,000 per picture.

- Disney's first full-length animated classic *Snow White and the Seven Dwarfs* was released to the delight of both children and adults.

- On August 12, 1939, the now classic *The Wizard of Oz* starring Judy Garland made its debut in the town of Oconomowoc, Wisconsin.

- The August 22, 1938 issue of *LIFE Magazine* featured the dancing duo of Fred Astaire and Ginger Rogers on the cover.

LEW AYRES

Vital Statistics

DOB: December 28, 1908 (Capricorn) in Minneapolis, Minnesota
Birth Name: Lewis Frederick Ayres III
Height: 5'9"
Hair: Dark Brown
Eyes: Brown
Physique: Slender and toned

Boyhood Years

Raised by his grandmother (a painter and student of theosophy), Ayres was greatly influenced by her ideals. When he was fifteen, they moved to San Diego, California.

Start of Career

There are two versions of this event.

#1 He was discovered in 1927 playing the banjo with the Henry Halstead Orchestra the Mission Beach Ballroom in San Diego.

#2 Ayres was playing the piano with a Big Band at The Coconut Grove in Los Angeles when a talent scout happened to be in the nightclub. Impressed with the good looks and poise of the young man at the piano, the scout signed nineteen-year-old Ayres to a contract.

The latter seems more plausible since Ayres was an accomplished pianist.

Onscreen Persona

Lew Ayres in *All Quiet on the Western Front* – Universal Pictures, 1930

In 1930, after a number of small parts, Ayres was signed to play the lead in the war drama, *All Quiet on the Western Front,* that of a young soldier in the anti-war film. The film brought him critical acclaim and the attention of studio heads. At the age of twenty two he suddenly gained stature as an actor.

During the years between 1938 and 1941, Ayres portrayed *Dr. Kildare*, the idealistic doctor who quietly put up with Dr. Gillespie, the garrulous head of the department, portrayed by Lionel Barrymore. The good looks and calm, reassuring presence of the young actor in his portrayal of *Kildare* brought women flocking into the movie theatres to spin their dreams of a personal doctor in his image. Handsome, slender, and clean shaven, his well-modulated voice, and calm manner conveyed an inner strength that captured and held the attention of women in the movie theater audience.

Portraying *Dr. Kildare* in nine films, Ayes paved the way for the popular actors who portrayed doctors on the small screen. Many a woman would have feigned illness of only to be examined by this handsome, compassionate doctor and his subsequent counterparts. When *Dr. Kildare's* on screen sweetheart (played by Laraine Day) was killed just before they were to be married, women in the theater wept for his loss.

As a conscientious objector then WWII broke out Ayres refused to go into combat. He did however distinguish himself by accepting dangerous assignments as a medic and was highly commended for his efforts. However for a long time many of his fans turned against him at first, not really understanding what the term conscientious objector actually mean and believed that Ayres just didn't want to fight for his country. Upset with their idol, they boycotted his films in an effort to convince theater owners not to show them.

With news of his exemplary bravery and the care he extended to the wounded, often under fire, Ayres was accepted into the fold as women again embraced his heartthrob image.

Upon returning to his acting career after the war, Ayres appeared in a number of well received films. He developed the character in the syndicated radio show *The Story of Dr. Kildare* that went on to become a series of films romanticizing the white coated heroes of Blair General Hospital.

Lew Ayres in *Dr. Kildare* – MGM, 1939

Personal Life

Ayres had varied interests, astronomy, mineralogy, and meteorology. He also wrote his own piano compositions. One of these, *Wedding Song*, debuted on the Tennessee Ernie Ford night time network. An enthusiast of sketching and painting the actor also attended night classes at a local art school for a number of years perfecting his technique. But the most significant theme of his life was his dedication to the study of the spiritual aspects of religion in various regions of the world.

All Quiet on the Western Front so affected him that Ayres took a firm stand against killing in any form. He became a vegetarian shortly after making the movie. He made no secret of his opposition to war. While at first this did not bode well for his career, Ayres proved himself to be a true hero serving under fire, without a gun, in New Guinea and the Philippines for three and a half years.

After the war, the actor continued his search for spiritual truth and understanding by embarking on a journey that resulted in a Golden Globe winning production, based on his book *Altars of the World*, in which he wrote about his exploration of the philosophies of the Far East.

He was way ahead of the times in his search for spirituality that became so popular in the late twentieth century.

Marriages

A steamy romance with Ginger Rogers was fodder for the fan magazines and Hollywood gossip columnists of that era. Although the couple married, it lasted only six years.

Lola Lane (actress/singer) – 1931-1933 (Divorced)
Ginger Rogers (actress) – 1934-1940 (Divorced)
Diana Hall (airline stewardess) - 1964 until his death in 1996

Children

Justin (with Diana Hall)

Salary

All Quiet on the Western Front - $250.00

Fast Facts

- As a child he wanted to be a doctor.
- Speaking of his career Ayres once told a reporter "Although I have played in a couple of significant pictures, the role I enjoyed most was that of Lana Turner's goofy brother Henry in an unpretentious picture, *Rich Man, Poor Girl*. It was the only opportunity I had on screen to play really broad comedy. I let myself go, even danced the tango with Lana. I had many slapstick scenes in the picture and I loved them."
- Rumor had it at the time that Jane Wyman, his co-star in *Johnny Belinda*, left her husband Ronald Reagan because she was in love with Ayres, but nothing further came of the rumor.
- He made five *Dr. Kildare* films, the first of which debuted in 1938
- Because of his adamant views against smoking, Ayres lost the opportunity to play *Dr. Kildare* in the television series when he persistently requested that the network not accept cigarette sponsorship. Richard Chamberlain was cast instead.

Star on the Walk of Fame

Radio - 1724 Vine St.
Motion Pictures - 6385 Hollywood Blvd.

Date of Death

December 30, 1996 of complications due to coma

Interred

Westwood Memorial Park, Los Angeles, CA

Awards and Nominations

Emmy - 1972 for an episode of *Kung Fu*
Academy Award - Best Actor 1949 *Johnny Belinda*

Lew Ayres and Jane Wyman
Johnny Belinda - Warner Brothers, 1949

JOHN BARRYMORE

Vital Statistics

DOB: February 14, 1882 (Aquarius) in Philadelphia, Pennsylvania
Birth Name: John Sidney Blyth
Nicknames: The Great Profile (professional)
 Jack (to close friends)
Height: 5'10"
Hair: Dark Brown
Eyes: Blue
Physique: Athletic. He was a striking figure.

Boyhood Years

Youngest of the three Barrymore siblings born into an acting dynasty, John life was expected to perpetuate the Barrymore name in the theatre, but he had other ideas. "I tried cartooning. My first job lasted about fifteen minutes. I didn't think it was such a bad sketch, but the editor suggested that I follow in my family's footsteps and become an actor." He took the suggestion and went on to carve out a career that brought him many accolades.

Start of Career

John Barrymore in *Don Juan* – Warner Brothers, 1926

Unlike the majority of his peers who struggled and dreamt of one day getting a job in the theater or in films, Barrymore found the door wide open as he eased into his career with the help of the family name. Ironically, despite his reluctance to be one, he went on to be praised as one of the great actors of his time. He was a Hollywood's tragedy who, for all of his acclaim on stage and in films, spent the last years of his life in a quiet struggle with alcohol. In the end it defeated him.

Onscreen Persona

Starting off in the theater, Barrymore went on to appear in silent films then moved gracefully into talkies. Having developed a voice that resonated from his theatrical experience the transition from silent films to talkies was an easy one for him.

He was nicknamed "The Great Profile" because the left side of his face was remarkably perfect and the only side he allowed to be photographed. Barrymore's chiseled features were perfect from any viewpoint according to his female fans.

As part of the legendary Drew and Barrymore theatrical clan, it was easy for him to enter a field that was usually difficult. To dispel the label of nepotism, Barrymore quickly proved to everyone that he could act with the best of them. At first his career focused on portraying superficial characters in comedic farces. Witty dialogue was Barrymore's forte on and off screen. Many said that the characters he portrayed were more like him in real life. Barrymore delighted in shocking friends with his quick, often cryptic wit.

His remarkable good looks and strong physique together with a natural bent for the ladies in real life came across the screen to captivate feminine hearts in the audience. He was considered one of only a few early romantic leading men whose voice matched that of his appearance; compelling, polished and debonair.

John Barrymore and Greta Garbo in *Grand Hotel* – MGM, 1932

Although he achieved success on screen, Barrymore considered acting in films unmanly and challenged anyone who intimated that he was less of a man because of it. There were incidences of threatened physical response should anyone dare to hint that this was true.

Personal Life

Barrymore bored easily. To ease the boredom of acting he resorted to pulling pranks on co-workers. He began drinking at a very early age to lessen the pain of whatever demons plagued him. Eventually his alcoholic binges became widely known, often fodder for the gossip columnists of his day. Nevertheless Barrymore was beloved for his wit, his quick and frequently self-deprecating quips.

Marriages

Katherine Harris - September 1, 1910-December 6, 1916 (Divorced)
Blanche Oelrichs (actress) - August 5, 1920-November 19, 1925 (Divorced)
Dolores Costello (actress) - November 24, 1928-October 9, 1935 (Divorced)
Elaine Barrie (actress) - November 9, 1936-November 27, 1940 (Divorced)

Children

John Drew Barrymore (actor)
Diana Barrymore (actress, died of overdose of alcohol and sleeping pills at age 38)

Grandchildren

Drew Barrymore (actress)

Fast Facts

- To date, John Barrymore is considered the greatest American actor to play 'Hamlet' and 'Richard III' on stage.
- He is the only one of the three Barrymore siblings never to have been nominated for an Oscar, regarding this omission Barrymore once confided to a friend "I think they were afraid that I would show up drunk embarrassing everyone;" adding in a wistful tone, "I wouldn't have, you know."
- His penchant for women and sharp wit never wavered even as he was dying. A priest came to administer the last rites accompanied by a very homely nurse. When the priest asked if Barrymore if he had anything to confess, he calmly replied, "Father, I am guilty of having carnal thoughts." Astonished, the priest inquired, "About whom?" Pointing to the nurse, a smile flickering on his face, Barrymore replied, "About her."

Memorable Quotes

"Happiness often sneaks in through a door you didn't know you left open."
"A man is not old until regrets take the place of dreams."

Date of Death

May 29, 1942 Los Angeles, of pneumonia and cirrhosis of the liver

Interred

Initially buried in East Los Angeles at Calvary Cemetery but was later moved by son John Drew to Mount Vernon Cemetery in Philadelphia.

Salary

Grand Hotel 1932, $150,000
Rasputin and the Empress 1932, $150,000
Svengali 1931 $30,000 per week

Star on the Walk of Fame

6530 Hollywood Blvd.

John and Ethel Barrymore in
Rasputin and the Empress –
MGM, 1932

JOHN BOLES

Vital Statistics

DOB: October 28, 1895 (Scorpio) in Greenville, Texas
Name at Birth: John Love Boles
Height: 6'
Hair: Black:
Eyes: Dark brown and soulful
Physique: Athletic

Biographical Sketch

Father
  John Monroe Boles (Banker)

Mother
  Jane Love Boles (Housewife)

Boyhood Years

Born into a middle class family John grew up knowing that his parents were hopeful of their son becoming a doctor. Throughout his youth Boles exhibited a penchant for acting as well as having a magnificent singing voice. Although his studies centered around subjects to prepare him for a career in medicine the desire to become a theatrical entertainer eventually won out. Wanting to please his parents Boles enrolled in medical school quickly realizing that medicine was not for him.

Start of Career

John Boles and Gloria Swanson in *The Love of Sunya* – United Artists, 1927

Upon graduating with honors in 1917, Boles accepted an offer to appear in a musical production at The King Opera House. From here it was a step into a Broadway production where he was seen by Gloria Swanson who was so impressed with his breathtaking looks and talent that she went backstage and convinced him to come to Hollywood to star with her in the film *The Love of Sunya*.

Onscreen Persona

Boles' strikingly handsome face and expressive eyes were enough to immediately make him into a matinee idol. Although he did not sing in his early roles his physical attributes were enough to make women take notice.

Swanson's prediction that he had what it took to make it on the silver screen proved right. Possessing a deep and mellow speaking voice Boles easily made the transition from silent-screen to sound. Early on Warner Brothers signed him to star in *The Desert Song*, a musical extravaganza that also showcased his fine singing voice. With the release of the movie, John Boles became a household word. Women were so fascinated by his striking countenance and quiet air of sophistication that they clamored for more of him flooding the studio with fan letters. Sadly throughout his career Boles made few movies that featured his singing ability. His roles mainly centered emotional melodramas that drew women into the theater. His co-stars were luminaries such as Barbara Stanwyck (in the tearjerker *Stella Dallas*), Margaret Sullivan, Paulette Goddard, Rochelle Hudson, and the adorable scene stealer, Shirley Temple who appeared with him in *Curly Top* 1935.

One of his most memorable dramatic roles was in the 1931 version of *Frankenstein* in which he portrayed Dr. Frankenstein, creator of the monster.

He retired in 1952.

Marriage

Marielite Dobbs, 1917 until his death

John Boles and Shirley Temple in *Curly Top* – 20th Century Fox, 1935

Children

Frances and Janet

Happily married and a doting father, Boles shied away from the limelight preferring to live a normal family life. Before making his final decision to become an actor, Boles attempted to fulfill his parents' dream for him by enrolling in medical school. It quickly became apparent to him and to his parents that it was not right for him and never looked back as he went on to succeed in his chosen profession, that of an actor.

Fast Facts

- While his career brought Boles fame and fortune it was tame beside his occupation prior to coming to Hollywood. Rumor had it that for two years during World War I Boles was a spy for the Allies in Germany.

Salary

1935 $117 per week as contract player
1936 *Rose of the Rancho* $50,000

Date of Death

February 27, 1969 a heart attack

Interred

Westwood Memorial Park, Westwood, CA

Star on the Walk of Fame

6530 Hollywood Blvd.

John Boles and Boris Karloff in *Frankenstein* – Universal Pictures, 1931

CHARLES BOYER

Vital Statistics:

DOB: August 28, 1899 (Virgo) in Fiego, France
Name at Birth: Charles Boyer
Height: 5'9"
Hair: Brown
Eyes: Luminous Brown
Physique: Slender and Firm
Outstanding Attribute:
  Sensual Mouth
  Rich, cultured French accent

Biographical Sketch

Father
  Maurice (Farm machinery merchant)

Mother
  Augustine Durand (Housewife)

Boyhood Years

An only child, Boyer was doted upon by his patents. At an early age he exhibited a penchant for entertaining often appearing in plays and concerts put on by the townspeople. Referred to by the people of the town as their prodigy they flocked to see young Boyer perform.

Charles Boyer and Hedy Lamarr in *Algiers* – United Artists, 1938

The death of his father from a stroke when Boyer was ten changed the dynamics of the young boy's life. Mrs. Boyer sold the family business to devote herself to raising her son to be a gentleman. His parents had hoped and planned for Charles to become a philosopher. To that end Boyer earned a degree in philosophy at The Sorbonne before going on to dedicate himself to the his true love, the theater.

Start of Career

While rooming with two actors who were also attending the Sorbonne, Boyer was introduced to a new and exciting world far different from what he had previously known. Auditioning for productions put on by the drama department awakened his imagination, fine-tuned and sharpened his memory so that eventually Boyer was able to memorize dozens of pages of dialogue. In time it served him well as he was asked to step in at the last moment when an actor in the play became ill. Boyer was such a quick study he was able to easily memorize his lines and went on to play the part as if he had rehearsed it for weeks.

Onscreen Persona

Even when portraying a sinister husband determined to drive his wife (Ingrid Bergman) crazy in the 1944 film *Gaslight* something about the Frenchman with the courtly manner and soft eyes made women's hearts throb with yearning. Boyer's lips unusually soft and appealing caused female fans to fantasize about what it would be like to be kissed by him no matter what type of role he was portraying.

Talkies brought even more recognition as his silken accent gave expressive meaning to the words he spoke.

Charles Boyer and Ingrid Bergman in *Gaslight* – MGM, 1944

Dividing his time between France and the U.S. Boyer worked continuously on both continents in films and theater. In a career that successfully spanned thirty years he was considered to be not only charming and handsome but a multi-talented actor. His charisma on screen earned him the title "the last of the great lovers of the cinema."

Personal Life

Marriage

Patricia Peterson (actress) - February 14, 1934 until her death in 1978

Children

Michael Charles Boyer, 1964 (later died of either suicide or an accident)

Fast Facts

- Boyer was a modest man and not at all impressed with his successes and especially not by the female reverence his film image created.
- He was an avid reader and had a long list of books, of every type that he wanted to read.
- Partially bald in his twenties Boyer wore a toupee in films, but never in public.
- He sometimes wore lifts to accommodate those of his leading ladies who were taller than he.

- Friends jokingly referred to him as a stick in the mud because he chose not to be a part of the glamorous life of a Hollywood star. Instead he chose to be with his family living a quiet life at the end of the day.
- He visited his hometown every year enjoying the company of childhood friends. He was often referred to as a book worm because he never stopped studying and reading books. Settled into domesticity Boyer rarely appeared in public emerging only when the studio beckoned him for a film.
- The tragic death of his son created a pall over his life that never lifted.
- Two days after his wife's funeral Boyer took his own life unwilling to go on without the woman he had loved for more than forty years.

Salary

MGM paid Boyer a starting salary of $400 per week upon signing him to a studio contract.

Date of Death

August 26, 1978, in Phoenix, Arizona two days before his 79th birthday from an overdose of barbiturates.

Interred

Holy Cross Cemetery, Culver City, California

Awards and Nominations

Academy/Oscar Best Actor 1937 *Conquest*
Academy/Oscar Best Actor 1938 *Algiers*
Academy/Oscar Best Actor 1941 *Gaslight*
Academy/Oscar Best Actor 1961 *Fanny*

Star on the Walk of Fame

6300 Hollywood Blvd.

Charles Boyer and Margaret Sullavan in *Back Street* – Universal Pictures, 1941

GEORGE BRENT

Vital Statistics

DOB: March 15, 1899 (Aries) in Shannon Bridge, Offaly, Ireland.
Name at Birth: George Brendan Nolan
Height: 6'1"
Hair: Few people knew that his hair had turned prematurely gray at a very early age making it necessary for him to dye it black for the screen.
Eyes: Hazel
Physique: Athletic

Biographical Sketch

Father
  John Nolan (A newspaperman, died when George was seven)

Mother
  Mary (She died four years later)

Boyhood Years

George and his older sister went to live with their maternal grandparents in Dublin after their mother's death. When World War I loomed the two were sent to New York to be raised by an aunt.

A true maverick young Brent joined a radical group in New York when he was only twenty. Soon afterward he returned to his birthplace in Europe enrolling in the National University where he excelled in baseball and football.

Start of Career

George Brent and Bette Davis in *Dark Victory* – Warner Brothers, 1939

While enrolled in a drama class Brent him to join The Abbey Theater after graduation. It was while there that he decided he would become an actor.

Young and spirited Brent had become involved in efforts to make Ireland a free state. It was during the Anglo-Irish war and Brent eventually had to flee for his life. After escaping to Montreal he began a two year tour with a Canadian stage company. Acting was now in his blood and he was determined to succeed. An ability to memorize as many as 25 pages of dialogue in an hour made it easy for him to perform on stage. He once commented ironically that he had appeared in as many as 300 plays in minor and leading roles. Changing his last name to Brent, the young man headed for Hollywood to try for a movie career.

At first he made a very small dent in the movie business appearing in a number of forgettable B pictures.

Actress Ruth Chatterton, viewing a screen test made by Brent, was so impressed by his sophisticated demeanor and good looks that she made him her leading man in a film and later in real life when she became his wife. Warner Brothers signed him to a seven year contract. His acting career had begun.

Onscreen Persona

Self-assured and oozing charm it was Brent who drew women into the theaters despite the fact that his leading ladies were really the stars of the films in which he appeared. His deep, well-modulated voice and magnetic eyes were the catalyst that soon made him a matinee idol.

George Brent and Greta Garbo in *The Painted Veil* – MGM, 1934

Although debonair and charismatic, the sophisticated Brent never achieved the stardom due him despite his innate talent among them *The Painted Veil* (1934) with Greta Garbo, who had personally requested him to play opposite her. Among his other famous co-stars were Bette Davis, Barbara Stanwyck, Olivia de Havilland, Myrna Loy, Loretta Young, and his third wife Ann Sheridan.

In twenty years of acting, Brent never carried a film but that didn't seem to faze him. He is considered to have been the most resilient of leading men.

Being able to memorize as many as seventy five pages of dialogue in an hour was one of his best acting attributes.

He had an agreeable disposition. Leading ladies adored him and the female movie attendees followed their lead.

Women were attracted to this tall, impressive man with the slicked back, patent leather looking hair. A pencil thin mustache seemed to make him even more appealing. His fan mail indicated that he was also considered a friend, sometimes even a father figure to young admirers.

One could say that, to his fans, George Brent was representative of all facets of a man.

Personal Life

While he was a bit of a hermit, shunning parties and nightclubs, even movie theaters because he didn't like to be stared at, Brent was considered quite a ladies man. Four marriages attest to that.

He was a licensed pilot and took to the air whenever he could.

Brent purchased a breeding ranch, raising thoroughbred race horses. In the fifties he semi-retired from Hollywood and devoted himself to his horses full time, returning now and then to appear on the small or big screen.

Romance

A torrid two year love affair with Bette Davis

Marriages

Helen Louise Campbell – 1925-1927 (Divorced)
Ruth Chatterton (actress) - August 1932-1934 (Divorced)
Constance Worth (actress) - May 1937 -December 1937(Divorced)
Ann Sheridan (actress) - January 1942-1943 (Divorced)
Janet Michaels – 1947-until her death in 1974

Children

Barry and Suzanne (with Janet Michaels)

Fast Facts

- He flew his own plane in *The Great Lie*
- He made a number of well received movies with Bette Davis and is said to have had an affair with her during the filming of some of the movies in which they costarred.
- He fled Ireland in 1922 when there was a price on his head due to his radical political involvements.
- In 1931 he suddenly went blind. After surgery in a New York hospital he recuperated at his sister's home.
- His favorite film (in which he costarred with Bette Davis) was *Dark Victory*
- Well into his forties and too old to join up at the start of World War II, but anxious to serve his country, Brent abruptly left his career to become a flight instructor for the duration of the war.
- He played polo, the piano and chess.
- He liked intelligent women who had something to say.
- He was a chain smoker.

- Brent ventured into television in 1956 appearing in the series, *Wire Service*
- In 1978 he made a cameo appearance in the television movie, *Born Again*. That was his last acting job.

Salary

1939 - as a contract player $48,961 annual salary (worth approx. $753,000 in 2010)

Date of Death

May 26, 1979 of emphysema in Solona, CA

Star on the Walk of Fame

Films   1707 Vine Street
TV   1614 Vine Street

George Brent and Yvonne DeCarlo
in *Slave Girl* - Universal International, 1947

RONALD COLMAN

Vital Statistics

DOB: February 9, 1891 (Aquarius) in Richmond Surrey, England
Name at Birth: Ronald Charles Colman
Height: 5' 10'
Hair: Dark Brown
Eyes: Dark Brown
Physique: Athletic
Outstanding Attribute:
  Compelling, Cultured, Highly, Highly Recognizable Voice
  Signature Mustache

Biographical Sketch

Father
  Charles (A silk importer)

Mother
  Marjory (Housewife)

Siblings

There were six children born into the Colman family, three girls and three boys. The first born son died at age five. Ronald was the second son.

Boyhood Years

Ronald Colman and Marlene Dietrich in *Kismet* – MGM, 1944

The family lived in an upper class area in a large two story home with two maids. Born into wealth, Colman planned on attending Oxford hoping to study engineering. When he was sixteen his father died, creating a financial situation that necessitated Colman going to work. Bright and industrious he went from office boy to junior accountant in a short time. By then his plans for the future had changed to an aspiration to enter the Foreign Service.

At the start of World War I young Colman served in London's Scottish Regiment until he sustained injuries that necessitated his being hospitalized and eventually honorably discharged. The shrapnel in his leg left him with a limp that he managed to hide from movie audiences.

Start of Career

While waiting for an appointment with the Foreign Service, a friend offered Colman a small part in a play. At eighteen year Colman volunteered to fight in World War I as a member of the London Scottish Regional Guards. Wounded in France, he was decorated then medically discharged. Barely twenty he went out into the world to make his way. By that time Colman had abandoned plans to become a diplomat and concentrated his attention on acting. He joined The Bancroft Amateur Dramatic Society and became actively involved in the theatre.

Colman migrated to Broadway after struggling to keep his head above water in England. It took two years before he was cast in a hit play thus gaining recognition. During this period, Colman was nearly destitute often hungry and slept in the park. When a clever studio head realized Colman's film appeal, he cast him in the lead in a silent film opposite super star actress Lillian Gish. Afterwards Samuel Goldwyn offered him a contract and his impressive career of thirty years began.

Ronald Colman and Shelley Winters in *A Double Life* – Universal Pictures, 1947

He was young, strikingly handsome, a dignified, elegant figure of a man. However it was with the advent of "talkies" that Colman created the screen idol that made his mark in Hollywood. Because of his melodious voice and theatrical training, Colman moved easily into talkies. He was the epitome of drawing room class, aristocratic, debonair, an actor who played comedy as adeptly as drama .To his female following he was the true romantic.

When actor Colman spoke, women in the audience sat up in their seats and really listened. Some may also have swooned, so seductive was his voice.

He was a private man not given to attending parties and shied away from any display of his stardom.

In his more mature years Colman dedicated himself to the radio series, *The Halls of Ivy* that later became a television series in which he frequently appeared with his second wife, Benita Hume.

Personal Life

Marriages

Thelma Raye - September, 1920 - August, 1934 (Divorced)
Benita Hume - September, 1934 – his death in 1958

Children

Juliet Benita, 1944 (with Benita Hume)

Awards and Nominations

1929 Best Actor in a Leading Role   *Bulldog Drummond* (his first talkie)
1930 Best Actor in a Leading role   *Condemned*
1943 Best Actor in a Leading Role   *Random Harvest*
1948 Best Actor in a Leading Role   *A Double Life*

Fast Facts

- His voice is still instantly recognized.
- The shrapnel in his leg left him with a limp that he strove to hide throughout his acting career.
- Early in his career, Colman endued harsh criticism from reviewers for this limp and his theatrical gestures gleaned from his impressive stage career.
- Many expressed doubts that the silent screen actor would make a successful transition to talkies.
- Quote: (on acting) "One can be someone else in another, more dramatic, more beautiful world."
- His recording of *A Christmas Carol* (1941) was the first version to gain world wide praise.
- The Oscar he won in 1947 for his outstanding performance in *A Double Life* was auctioned off by Christies in 2002 for $174,500. Again in 2012 it sold for $206, 250.
- George Cukor once commented that Colman knew more about performing in front of the camera then any actor with whom he had ever worked.
- Personal quote: "A man usually falls in love with a woman who asks the kinds of questions he is able to answer."
- Met his second wife, Benita Hume, on the set of A Tale of Two Cities
- About his fiercely guarded privacy, Colman remarked "Why should I go to dull parties and say dull things just because I wear greasepaint and make love to beautiful women on the screen?"
- Upon his death The Times referred to him as 'the most complete gentleman of the cinema.'

Salary

Lost Horizon 1937 $162.500

Date of Death

May 19, 1958 of acute emphysema in Santa Barbara, California

Interred

Santa Barbara Cemetery

Star on the Walk of Fame

Motion Picture   6801 Hollywood Blvd.
Television   6150 Vine St.

Ronald Colman in *Lost Horizon* – Columbia Pictures, 1937

GARY COOPER

Vital Statistics

DOB: May 7, 1901 (Taurus) in Helena, Montana
Birth name: Frank James Cooper
Nicknames: Coop
　　　　　　Studs (given to him by Carole Lombard)
Height: 6'3"
Hair: Brown
Eyes: Steel Gray
Physique: Lean, lanky and taut

Biographical Sketch

Father
Charles Cooper (Immigrated to Montana from England at the age of nineteen where he studied law. After a successful law career he became a State Supreme Court Justice in Montana.)

Mother
　Alice (Housewife)

Boyhood Years

When Coop was very young his father bought a 600 acre ranch, originally a land grant, and settled into the life of a rancher. Thus Cooper was a cowboy in the true sense of the word even before he gained fame for portraying one on the screen.

Gary Cooper in *High Noon* – United Artists, 1952

The family migrated to the United States just as World War I seemed imminent, settling in Montana on the ranch purchased by Mr. Cooper.

"Up at 5 a.m. to feed 450 heads of cattle and shovel manure in 40 degrees below was not romantic" the actor said of his life on the ranch. Summers found him working as a guide in Yellowstone Park. After graduating college in Grinnell, Iowa, Cooper returned to Helena with the intention of becoming a political cartoonist. However jobs in that line were scarce. He headed for Hollywood where he felt certain he would have better luck finding a job as a cartoonist. Instead, a couple of his new friends talked him into becoming an extra in (silent) westerns.

Start of Career

An air of laid back casualness and at home in the saddle attitude caught the attention of the right people at Paramount Studios. In 1929 Cooper made his first talkie, *The Virginian*. While in his own comment, he was not much of an actor, his laconic manner of speech and relaxed attitude caught on and his career was launched.

Onscreen Persona

Women in the theater audience were fascinated by this handsome, clean shaven actor who personified the strong, silent type. He won their immediate trust just by appearing on screen in his cowboy gear. Seated confidently astride a horse or pulling a gun from the holster he wore around his waist, he was a true Western hero in a stellar career spanning thirty years.

Even when appearing in more sophisticated roles wearing evening gear or as a World War I soldier, there was something inertly appealing in the actor that tugged at the heartstrings of women.

In 1952 Gary Cooper was voted the country's favorite movie star succeeding even John Wayne. The honor was repeated in 1953.

He had made 80 films by mid-1955 for which the studios take was $250 million while Cooper earned six million in salary plus percentages.

Gary Cooper and Ingrid Bergman in *For Whom the Bell Tolls* – Paramount Pictures, 1943

Paramount studio heads did not want to lose a good thing in the stalwart actor who could play comedy and drama with aplomb. No one was more surprised than Cooper who commented "The general consensus is that I don't act at all." However renowned acting teacher Lee Strasberg proclaimed that Cooper was a natural method actor, but didn't know it.

Raised with the traditional deference to the feminine sex, Cooper carried this into his professional life by always letting his leading lady have the limelight. This very trait may have accounted for the great admiration of his leading ladies, to say nothing of his fans.

A young woman hitch hiked to Hollywood from her home in Pennsylvania just to meet him. It didn't happen and she returned home shattered.

Personal Life

Romances

Cooper was involved in romantic liaisons with a number of Hollywood's beauties. Among them were Clara Bow, Lupe Velez (with whom he lived tempestuously for a while), Carole Lombard, Ingrid Bergman, Grace Kelly, and Marlene Dietrich.

While filming *The Fountainhead* and a married man, he and co-star Patricia Neal fell deeply in love resulting in a three year separation from his wife. Because Maria was a devout Catholic there was no chance of divorce at the time.

In 1951 Gary Cooper had a private audience with Pope Pius XII. Sometime afterward Cooper converted to Catholicism. In 1954 Rocky and Cooper reconciled. His lothario days were over.

Marriages:

Maria Cooper
Veronica (Rocky) Balfe to a New York socialite - December 15, 1933 until his death

Fast Facts

- James Stewart, his closest friend, broke into tears when he spoke of Coop at the televised Academy Awards
- In a 2007 interview, Morgan Freeman said that watching Cooper in films when he was a young man inspired him to become an actor
- Helen Hayes said of Cooper "He is the most beautiful man I have ever met."
- As of June 1955 Cooper had made 80 films earning $6 million from a combination of salary and percentages. The studio made $250 million from these same films
- He played the harmonica and guitar, enjoyed a game of backgammon and bridge and liked nothing better than working in his vegetable garden on the ranch he owned in Encino
- He was a conservative Republican, even to endorsing Thomas E. Dewey in 1944
- Cooper made two movies with Theresa Wright, four with Fay Wray and two with Marlene Dietrich
- He had an insatiable appetite (downing an entire cherry pie and a quart of milk to round out lunch) but remained slender
- Despite being in the early stages of cancer, Cooper performed his own stunts in *The Wreck of the Mary Deare* (1959)
- He was a cowboy actor who actually worked on a ranch
- He often recited Lou Gehrig's farewell speech to soldiers during World War II

Salary

In 1941 it was reported that Cooper was the highest paid salaried actor in America earning $482,820. Translated into 2010 figures this amounts to $7,069,700. While it was a substantial amount of money at that time, it is only a fraction of what current heartthrobs are being paid. He left an estate valued at $9 million dollars

Awards and Nominations

Oscar for Best Actor 1942 *Sergeant York*
Oscar for Best Actor 1952 *High Noon*
Oscar for Best Actor 1943 *Pride of the Yankees*
Oscar for Best Actor 1944 *For Whom the Bell Tolls*
Honorary Academy Award 1961
Inducted into the Western Performers Hall of Fame posthumously

Date of Death

May 13, 1961 from prostate cancer

Interred

Southampton, Suffolk County, NY at Sacred Hearts of Jesus and Mary

Star on the Walk of Fame

6243 Hollywood Blvd

Gary Cooper and Patricia Neal in *The Fountainhead* – Warner Brothers, 1949

CHARLES DAVID FARRELL

Vital Statistics

DOB: August 9, 1902 (Leo) in Onset, Massachusetts
Name at Birth: Charles David Farrell
Height: 6' 2"
Hair: Dark Brown
Eyes: Brown
Physique: Athletic

Biographical Sketch

Father
  David (Talent Agent and lunch counter operator)

Mother
  Estelle (Homemaker)

Boyhood Years

An only child, Farrell spent a great deal of time in the company of adults at the lunch counter managed by his father. He swept the floor, washed dishes and sat awestruck along with the nightly guests who watched silent movies in the room above the lunchroom. It has been said that this may have inspired the young boy to decide upon a career in acting. A handsome, expressive face was what producers of early films sought and Farrell proved to be especially popular with the female sex.

Athletic and strong he came across the silent screen in a way that women couldn't resist.

Charles Farrell and Janet Gaynor in *Seventh Heaven* – Fox Film, 1927

Start of Career

Farrell originally planned on becoming a psychologist but instead joined a theatrical troupe. A vaudeville act brought him to California where friends convinced him to try being an extra at three dollars a day. His classic good looks and lean, muscular build led to his being signed to a film contract.

His role in *Old Ironsides* brought him to the attention of studio heads who cast him opposite Janet Gaynor in *Seventh Heaven*. Farrell tried in hard to be released from this film, but the request was denied. In those days an actor did as he was told or faced suspension without salary. Ironclad contracts made all the difference in those early days.

It was the film *Seventh Heaven* opposite actress Janet Gaynor that raised Farrell to heartthrob status in the early thirties. Farrell and Gaynor went on to make eleven pictures together and became known as the sweethearts of the screen during the decade.

Rumor has it that the couple brought their onscreen romance into their personal lives years prior to Ms. Gaynor's actual marriage.

Many fans were convinced that the two were actually married to each other although it had never been announced. Anniversary gifts arrived for the couple every year in care of the studio.

In a studio biography, Farrell stated that the role of Chico in *Seventh Heaven* was his favorite.

Personal Life

One of Hollywood's most sought after bachelors, Farrell was said to avoid dating because he liked to lounge around unshaven in comfortable clothes and sit on the floor when visiting with friends. In August, 1930 he said in an interview that he was a free spirit who liked to sail, play tennis and make movies. Eventually he changed his mind about remaining a bachelor.

Charles Farrell and Estelle Taylor in *Liliom* – Fox Europa, 1934

Marriages

Virginia Valli (silent film star) February 14, 1931 until her death in September, 1968

Fast Facts

- Farrell arrived in Los Angeles (Hollywood) as manager of a little person with a circus group.
- An explosion on the set of *Old Ironsides* resulted in damage to Farrell's eardrums. Although he lost most of his hearing he managed to hide it for many years.
- In a 1941 poll listing All Time Male Super Stars, Farrell was listed as #16, ahead of Tyrone Power and John Wayne.
- He retired to Palm Springs in the early 40's having fallen in love with the desert area. He became partners with Ralph Bellamy in the Palm Springs Racquet Club (later called The Charles Farrell Racquet Club), a popular private hideaway for movie stars of the era.
- He served as Mayor of Palm Springs from 1950 - 1957

- He played polo with Will Rogers
- He served in the navy during WWII

Salary

As a contract player with Twentieth Century Fox, Farrell was paid approximately $30,000 per year.

Date of Death

May 6, 1990 of heart failure

Interred

Alongside his wife in Wellwood Murray Cemetery, Palm Springs, California

Star on the Walk of Fame

7021 Hollywood Blvd. for Motion Pictures
1617 Vine St. Television

In 1992 he was awarded a star on the Palm Springs Walk of Stars in Palm Springs, CA.

Charles Farrell and Mary Duncan in *City Girl*
– Fox Film, 1930

ERROL FLYNN

Vital Statistics

DOB: June 20, 1909 (Gemini) in Hobart, Tasmania, Australia
Birth Name: Leslie Thomson
Nicknames:
  The Baron
  Satan's Angel (bestowed upon him by Marlene Dietrich)
  Flynny to his close pals
Height: 6'2 1/2"
Eyes: Hazel Brown Mixture
Hair: Brown
Physique: Athletic

Often referred to by women fans as a truly gorgeous man. The thin mustache he wore later in his career served to enhance his chiseled features making him even more strikingly handsome.

Biographical Sketch

Father
  Theodore Thomson Flynn (Biologist)

Mother
  Marrell (Descendant of a midshipman who served on the HMS Bounty)

Sister
  Norah Rosemary (ten years younger)

Boyhood Years

Errol Flynn and Bette Davis in *The Private Lives of Elizabeth and Essex* – Warner Brothers, 1939

As a child young Flynn was prone to getting into trouble. A high spirited boy, he was expelled from every school he attended while living in England with his parents. When he was 17, Flynn adventurously set out to find gold in New Guinea. When that failed he worked at a number of odd jobs to support himself.

Start of Career

A scout from Warner Brothers saw Flynn in a London stage production and brought him to Hollywood for a screen test in 1934.

Another version is that a producer spotting him on a beach in Australia decided that the young man had all of the qualifications necessary to portray the swashbuckling hero that was so popular at the time. He convinced Flynn to appear in a film. Ironically it was the role of Fletcher Christian in *The Bounty*, the forerunner to the American version of *Mutiny on the Bounty*.

Onscreen Persona

Dashing, suave and heroic with finely honed features is the Flynn seen in films. He was the perfect hero who saved the fair lady. He had an edge of the daredevil that reached out from the screen to intrigue women in the audience whatever role he was playing. The thought of being swept up alongside the saddle of this gorgeous man as he sat his horse was enough to set female hearts pounding. Not only was Flynn one of the most popular, highly paid actors of his era, but the sight of his trim figure whether in lavish costume or evening clothes was a thrill that captivated the many women who flocked to see his films.

Personal Life

As he grew into his later teens and early twenties, a devil may care attitude and a penchant for the ladies kept him just ahead of the law, but in the path of jealous husbands. Flynn managed to avoid real trouble until he became careless and allowed his overactive libido to reach out and touch a willing, but underage young woman who went to the mat to bring him down. He was accused of rape and went on trial.

Statutory rape was not only a serious crime, but the fact that this popular actor was accused of such a crime was even more shocking. Through it all Flynn's fans remained steadfast.

He is reported to have received over 10,000 fan letters a week during the trial. The majority of these letters were from adult women, many of them grandmothers. Ninety percent of the letter writers thought him innocent. This included all of the grandmothers. The trial (1942) made daily headlines. Flynn's lifestyle, alcohol, womanizing and drugs was of great concern to his family and friends. He seemed to be bent on scandalous behavior. When asked about his attitude toward his life and where it was heading, Flynn's commented "To hell or to glory. It depends upon your point of view."

Errol Flynn and Olivia de Havilland in *Captain Blood* – Warner Brothers, 1935

It was clear that he was headed for destruction, but with a kind of surreal glory. By the close of the '50's he had dissipated not only his work, but his body as well. His flamboyant days were at an end.

Salary

$150 week for starring role in *Murder at Monte Carlo* (1934). A year later he emerged a star in the film *Captain Blood* for which he received $500 per week. Flynn was said to be at the peak of his career when he appeared in *Elizabeth and Essex* opposite Bette Davis (1939). However his salary did not increase until the filming of *Objective Burma* for which he received $200,000.

Personal Life

Marriages

Lili Damita (French actress with whom he had a tempestuous, Hollywood headline making relationship) May 5, 1935 - April 1942 (Divorced)
Nora Eddington (actress) August 1944 - 1948 (Divorced)
Patrice Wymore October 1950 until his death

Children

Sean (with Lili Damita) 1941-1970. A photojournalist, Sean was assumed killed while on assignment in Cambodia covering the war in Vietnam. His body was never recovered.
Diedre (with Nora Eddington)   January, 1945
Rory   (with Nora Eddington)   March, 1947
Amelia (with Patrice Wymore) December, 1953-September 1998

Fast Facts

- Early on Flynn told everyone that he was Irish thinking that Australia was too little known and he was eager to be accepted by movie audiences. After a screen test from Warner Brothers he left his roots in Australia without a qualm escaping massive tax debts.
- Named #1 on *U.S.Empire Magazine* 100 Sexiest Male stars in film history.
- *Entertainment Weekly* proclaimed him 26th in their list of Greatest Movie Stars
- *Empire Magazine* (UK) ranked him #70 in their list of 100 Top Movie Stars of All Time,
- He was related to a seaman on the real *HMS Bounty* on his mother's side.
- He was considered to play the role of Ashley, Scarlett O'Hara's first love in *Gone with the Wind*. The part went to Leslie Howard.
- He had a vasectomy in 1955.
- Flynn was besieged with various ailments, Berger's disease, thrombosis of the arteries and acute inflammation.
- It was said that Flynn was becoming known as a serious actor with his role in *The Forsythe Saga* co-starring with Greer Garson filmed not long before he died.

- At the time of his death Flynn was accompanied by yet another teenage girl. She had been with him for two years (with her mother's approval) and was just 17 when he died.
- It was during the infamous trial that the phrase "in like Flynn" was coined. While the expression was sexist, it was a sign of the times. The statutory rape trial of Errol Flynn inflamed many upstanding citizens but it also created fodder for Hollywood gossip columnists and plenty of attention from the general public.
- Quotes: "I like my whiskey old and my women young.", "I do what I like.", "It isn't what they say about you, it's what they whisper"

Awards and Nominations

Bambi
   1951   *Silver River*
   1949   *That Forsythe Woman*
   1948   *Adventures of Don Juan*
Hollywood Women's Press Club
Sour Apple for Least Cooperative Actor - 1943 & 1948

Date of Death

October 14, 1959 in Vancouver. B.C. of a heart attack

Interred

In The Garden of Everlasting Peace, Forest Lawn Cemetery in Glendale, CA

Star on the Walk of Fame

Motion Picture 6654 Hollywood Blvd.
Television   7000 Hollywood Blvd.

Errol Flynn and Anthony Quinn in *Against All Flags* – Universal Pictures, 1952

CLARK GABLE

Vital Statistics

DOB: February 1, 1901 (Aquarius) in Cadiz, Ohio
Name at Birth: William Clark Gable
Height: 6'1"
Hair: Dark Brown
Eyes: Brown
Physique: Muscular/Athletic
Outstanding Features:
   Deep Dimple in Right Cheek
   Sleek Mustache

Biographical Sketch

Father
 William Gable (An oil driller)

Mother
 Adeline (Died when Gable was an infant)

Boyhood Years

When his father remarried, Gable found a friend in his stepmother, Jennie, who taught him to play the piano, good manners and how to dress giving him a sense of self confidence. He grew into a tall, shy young man with a booming voice. He was fond of languages and often recited Shakespeare sonnets. At the age of thirteen he was the lone young boy in an all men's band.

Concerned that his son might not be growing up manly, Gable's father encouraged him to hunt and engage in physical work like working in the oil fields with him.

Clark Gable and Norma Shearer in *Idoit's Delight* – MGM, 1939

While Gable was still in high school his father hit upon financial hard times and decided to try his hand at farming. The family moved to Rowena, a small town outside of Akron, Ohio where the older Gable had purchased some farmland. At sixteen Clark quit school to work on the family farm.

When he was seventeen a theatrical performance of *Bird of Paradise* inspired Gable to think about an acting career. His father felt that acting was not a manly pursuit and insisted that his son remain at work on the farm. But Gable did not take to farming and was unhappy living in such a small town. Eventually he left home to work in a tire company in Akron.

Start of Acting Career

At the age of twenty one Clark came into a small inheritance from his grandfather that gave him the opportunity to pursue his dream of becoming an actor. His stepmother, who had always encouraged his ambition, died and his father returned to the oil fields. Clark set off for Hollywood working his way there from Ohio by taking on numerous odd jobs and eventually joining a small theatrical group. An MGM scout had seen Gable in the play *The Last Mile* and believing the young man had potential had encouraged the move.

However there was someone at the studio who was not enthusiastic about the newcomer. His observation upon meeting Gable was that he looked like an ape and his ears were too big. That someone was Darryl F Zanuck.

Somewhere between signing a contract with Irving Thalberg and finally starting to make movies, Gable worked as a tie salesman in a department store.

In time Gable managed to find extra work and bit parts in silent films but the choice roles passed him by. A friend convinced him to try again by joining a more progressive theatrical group. It was this move that led him to work with Josephine Dillon, manager of the group and subsequently Clark's acting coach. Fifteen years his senior Dillon proceeded to create a Pygmalion transformation on young Gable.

She encouraged him to fill out his undernourished body with exercise and good food, oversaw the capping of his teeth, taught

Clark Gable and Claudette Colbert in
It Happened One Night –
Columbia Pictures, 1934

him to carry himself well, worked with him to lower the pitch of his voice thus creating the deep, mellow tone that eventually caused female hearts to flutter unabashedly. Dillon paid for the Gable's complete transformation instinctively sensing his real potential.

Onscreen Persona

He was the epitome of masculinity, inspiring a confidence that women gravitated to in droves. Returning to Hollywood after a brief run in the theater, Gable was signed to a seven year studio contract with MGM and cast in a low budget film.

To the amazement of the studio the film generated a huge amount of fan mail praising Gable for his commanding voice and masculine appeal. Studio heads realized they had a star in the making. What Zanuck thought of that turn of events had been stricken from the records.

Personal Life

Marriages

Josephine Dillon	December 1924-April 1930 (Divorced)
Maria Langham	July 1931-March 1939 (Divorced)
Carole Lombard	March, 1939-January 1942 (her death)
Sylvia Ashley	December 1948-April 1952 (Divorced)
Kay Williams	July 1955-November 1960 (his death)

Children

John Clark - March, 1961 (after Gable's death)

Fast Facts

- Gable confided to his wife Kay that when he died he wanted his casket to be closed. "I don't want strangers looking down at my wrinkles and my big, fat belly when I'm dead" he told her.
- Having gained weight, it was necessary for Gable to crash diet to lose forty pounds before starting production on *The Misfits*.
- He was considered for the role of Tarzan in 1932, but because he was an unknown the part went instead to Johnny Weissmuller.
- In his later years of acting, Gable would only sign contracts that stated he would work no more than an eight hours a day from nine to five. He firmly kept to that schedule leaving the set at five even if it was in the midst of shooting an important scene.
- During WWII rumor had it that Hitler offered a sizable reward to anyone who could capture Gable who along with his cameraman was making combat films. Gable was Hitler's favorite American actor. Luckily Gable escaped that fate.
- He was dyslectic
- Throughout his life Gable yearned for the stability of a real home with wife and children. Sadly, he died shortly before his son was born.
- He never publicly acknowledged his daughter Judy (with Loretta Young)
- Hollywood remembers him as a kind and gentle man.
- He is considered to be one of Hollywood's finest actors.
- He was listed on his birth certificate as "female".
- He is said to have showered numerous times a day.
- A young child admiring the Oscar Gable won for his role in *It Happened One Night* and was overwhelmed when given the statue stating that it was winning the honor, not the statue itself that was important to him. After the actor's death the statue was returned to the Gable family.
- While filming *The Call of the Wild* (1934) Gable and his co star, Loretta Young were passionately involved both on and off screen. The torrid affair resulted in the birth of a daughter, a fact that was hushed up (but whispered about within the Hollywood community) until the publication of Young's posthumous

- autobiography in which she revealed that her daughter Judy was the love child of her affair with Gable.
- In 1938 Gable was dubbed The King of Hollywood. The title became irrevocably his. Even today when someone mentions The King in a Hollywood context, the name and image of Clark Gable comes up immediately.
- A poll conducted by the studio revealed that 98% of the respondents chose Gable to portray Rhett Butler in *Gone with the Wind*.
- He was a gun collector.
- Gable is rumored to have proposed to Nancy Davis in 1948.
- Devastated by the death of Carole Lombard, Gable first went on a drinking spree and is rumored to have tried to kill himself. He finally enlisted in the service as a motion picture specialist at a salary of $7500 per week. Among his duties, his strong and commanding voice was used to make training films.
- Having trained as an aerial gunner, Gable earned the Distinguished Flying Cross. At the end of the war he had acquired the commission of Captain. He refused to make a movie until the war was over with Japan despite having mustered out earlier in the year.
- He is pictured as Rhett Butler along with Vivien Leigh as Scarlett on a 25 cent commemorative stamp issued in 1990.
- He is buried alongside of Carole Lombard

Salary

The Painted Desert 1931 $150 per week
Gone with the Wind 1939 $120,000 per week
The Misfits (1961) $750,000 plus $58,000 for each week of overtime

Date of Death

November 16, 1960 of a massive heart attack, his fourth coronary.

Clark Gable and Vivien Leigh in *Gone with the Wind* – MGM, 1939

Interred

Forest Lawn Cemetery Glendale, CA

Awards and Nominations

Oscar *It Happened One Night* (1934)
Oscar *Mutiny on the Bounty* (1936)
Oscar *Gone with the Wind* (1939)

Star on the Walk of Fame

1610 Vine Street

CARY GRANT

Vital Statistics

DOB: January 18, 1904 (Aquarius) in Bristol, England UK
Name at Birth: Archibald Alec Leach
Height: 6'1"
Hair: Dark brown
Eyes: Brown
Physiqu: Trim
Outstanding Feature:
  Deep cleft in Chin

Biographical Sketch

Father
  Elias Leach (Presser in a clothing factory)

Mother
  Lillian (Housewife)

Boyhood Years

The family lived on the edge of poverty, young Grant always in the shadow of an alcoholic father. When Grant was nine years old he came home from school one afternoon to find his mother gone. He was told nothing about her disappearance, just that she was gone and was left to imagine all sorts of things that he kept to himself.

He learned the truth when he was an adult. His mother had been committed to a mental institution by his father. That was easy to do in those days by a parent or spouse. Years later a law was passed prohibiting it.

Cary Grant and Priscilla Lane in *Arsenic and Old Lace* – Warner Brothers, 1944

After learning the truth about his mother, Grant hired a detective to find her. Little is known about their reunion or what happened to Lillian Leach afterwards.

Start of Acting Career

In 1932, Bud Shulberg, head of Paramount Studios, ordered a screen test for young Leach then signed him to a long term contract. After much discussion it was decided to change the young man's name to Cary Grant. The studios "owned" actors in those days, dictating every phase of their lives including what films they would make, who they dated and the lifestyles they led.

Onscreen Persona

The epitome of sophistication, elegance and easy charm made Grant an immediate hit with movie goers, especially the women. Grant's first film *This is the Night*, a sophisticated comedy became his signature type film although he occasionally took on a serious role.

Today, Grant is best remembered by female audiences for his role in the now classic romantic comedy *An Affair to Remember* opposite Deborah Kerr. It has become a personal favorite of many women.

Cary Grant and Deborah Kerr in
An Affair to Remember –
20th Century Fox, 1957

Personal Life

Romances

He is said to have once been deeply in love with Sophia Loren.

Marriages

Virginia Cherrill (actress) - February 1934–March 1935 (Divorced)
Barbara Hutton (author) - July 1942-August 1945 (Divorced)
Dyan Cannon (actress) - July 1965-March 1968 (Divorced)
Barbara Harris (actress) -April 1981 until his death

Children:

Jennifer (with Dyan Cannon)

Fast Facts

- His ashes are scattered throughout California and the Pacific Ocean as per his wishes in a will drawn up in 1984.
- He was left handed.
- Because of an unusually large head, Grant's suits were custom made with squared off shoulders that were extra wide to balance his appearance.
- He was the first actor to break with a studio and strike out on his own. A very daring and courageous act at the time.
- He changed his name officially and became a U.S.citizen on June 26, 1942.
- He was launched into playing sophisticated light comedy when he chose to portray a ghost in the fantasy *Topper*.
- It has been said that Ian Fleming modeled his James Bond character after the sophisticated splendor that was Cary Grant in dress and manner.

- Although he dropped out of school at fourteen, Grant was self-educated and an avid reader.
- He had one of Jennifer's first baby teeth stored in a Lucite container.
- He gave his entire salary for *The Philadelphia Story* to the British War Effort in 1940.
- Awarded The King's Medal for Service by King George V1 in 1947 for outstanding service to the British War Relief Society.
- He donated his entire salary of $100,000 received for his role in *Arsenic and Old Lace* to the U.S. War Relied Fund in 1944.
- His image is on a 37cent USA commemorative stamp in the Legends of Hollywood series.
- The mole on his cheek was surgically removed between the filming of *Crisis* and *People Will Talk* in the early fifties.
- In order to avoid wearing makeup while filming he kept himself tanned.
- Considered a fashion maven, he had his own ideas about mixing comfort with style in his wardrobe and chose to wear women's nylon panties instead of traditional men's boxer or jockey shorts.
- His third wife, actress Betsy Drake, urged him to try hypnosis and psychotherapy to eradicate his hidden demons that had resulted in a serious inferiority complex. This led to treatments with LSD. It turned out to be the catalyst for what Grant called his "born again" experience. "For the first time in my life I am truly happy" he professed after experiencing sixty psychiatric sessions aided by LSD. He was fifty five at the time.
- Upon the birth of their daughter he gave Dyan Cannon a diamond and sapphire bracelet.
- He secretly longed to make a big screen musical.
- His last film *Walk Don't Run*, 1966 was a comedy with Jim Hutton and Samantha Eggar. Grant did not play the romantic lead.
- Retiring from movies at the age of 60, he continued to be in the public eye as spokesman for the popular Faberge fragrance line.

Salary

Singapore Sue 1932 $150
The Philadelphia Story 1940 $150,000
North by Northwest 1959 $450,000 plus $315,000 for overtime and a percentage of the gross profit

In 1971 *Look Magazine* reported that Grant was worth an estimated $70 million. In 2010 that amount translates to approximately $380 million.

Date of Death

November 29, 1982 in Davenport, Iowa of a stroke while on a speaking tour.

Interred

Per his wishes, he was cremated and his ashes scattered around his home and throughout other areas of California.

Awards and Nominations

Best Actor Drama *Penny Serenade* (1941)
Best Actor Drama *None But the Lonely Heart* (1944)

While he never received an Oscar, he was given a special Academy Award in 1970 for his "unique mastery of the art of screen acting".

In 1981 he was awarded the Kennedy Center Honor for Career Achievement in the Performing Arts joining other honorees, actress Helen Hayes and musician Count Basie.

In April, 1970 Grant was presented a special Oscar by Frank Sinatra at the 42nd Academy Awards ceremony. Inscribed on the statue is the statement 'for his unique mastery of the art of screen acting with the respect and affection of his colleagues.' Sinatra and the audience were moved to tears.

Named #2 on the list of 50 greatest Male Screen Legends by the American Film Institute

Star on the Walk of Fame

1624 Vine Street

Cary Grant in *North By Northwest* – MGM, 1959

LAURENCE OLIVIER

Vital Statistics

DOB: May 22, 1907 (Gemini) in Dorking, Surrey, UK
Name at Birth: Laurence Kerr Olivier
Nickname: His family called him Kim
Height: 5' 10"
Hair: Dark Brown
Eyes: Dark Gray, Intense and Brooding
Physique: Firm & Toned
Outstanding Attribute: Compelling Voice

Biographical Sketch

Father
   Gerald (A clergyman)

Mother
   Agnes (Died when Olivier was twelve)

Siblings
   Two older

Boyhood Years

Olivier's youth was one of culture. Education and the arts were emphasized by his father who made the major decisions in the family. Educated at the (all boys), the young boy made his acting debut at the age of fifteen. Shakespeare was his venue of choice as he learned his craft by studying classical theater.

Laurence Olivier and Merle Oberon in *Wuthering Heights* – United Artists, 1939

Start of Movie Career

Although Olivier starred in a number of films in the early and mid-thirties, his Hollywood career did not succeed until he was cast as the brooding Heathcliff in *Wuthering Heights*, 1939. The film went on to earn him an Academy Award nomination and created a lifelong career as a heartthrob.

When Hollywood beckoned a second time, Olivier responded. American producers knew they had a treasure and devoted their efforts to putting him in front of the movie going public as often as possible.

Onscreen Persona

Olivier lit up the silver screen with a talent and presence that few could resist, especially the women in the audience. He was the personification of culture, brooding sensitivity and a magnetism that drew eager film attendees, even critics into movie theaters. Success called and the actor responded creating a remarkable celebrity that spun around him until his death at eighty two.

Personal Life

Romances

While making a film together Olivier and Vivien Leigh smoldered off screen as well as on resulting in a divorce. Leigh, who was also married at the time, was named correspondent when Esmond sued Olivier on the grounds of adultery. That is the way divorces were processed in those days.

Laurence Olivier and Vivien Leigh in *Fire Over England* – London Film Productions, 1937

Marriages

Jill Esmond (actress) July 1930-January 1940 (Divorced)
Vivien Leigh (actress) August, 1940-January 1961 (Divorced)
Joan Plowright (actress) March 1961-his death

Children

Tarquin (with Esmond)
Richard, Julie, and Tamsin (with Plowright)

Fast Facts

- He was considered for the leading role in *The Godfather* that was eventually played by Brando.
- His ancestry dates back to the Huguenots (Protestants) of France who were ill-treated by the Catholics. The family escaped from this tyranny to England sometime in the 17th century.
- His father is purported to have been a strict disciplinarian who Olivier strive to please.
- Both parents encouraged his acting ambition.
- He was knighted by Queen Elizabeth in 1947. Being knighted by his Queen did not change Olivier who insisted that anyone who wanted to engage him in conversation refer to him as Larry. While proud to have been relegated the status of SIR, he remained down to earth in his relationships.

- Given the title of Baron Olivier of Brighton in 1970 for his services to the theater and therefore able to sit in the House of Lords, a singular honor.
- The American of Motion Picture Arts and Sciences honored Olivier with a special Oscar for the full body of his work in 1981 that encompassed his unique achievement and lifetime contribution to the art of film for the full body of his work.
- He is considered to be the greatest English-speaking actor of the 20th century.
- Years before his death Olivier struggled with ill health but never stopped doing what he loved best in life, acting.
- *Confessions of an Actor* Olivier's autobiography was published in 1984.
  Quotes:
  "I think that I may have gone mad had I not become an actor." "Art is larger than life. It's an exaltation of life" "One probably needs a little touch of madness to act." "Without acting, I cannot breathe."

Salary

The Boys From Brazil	1978	$720,000
Wuthering Heights	1939	$20,000
Rebecca	1940	$50,000
Seuth	1972	$200,000
The Jazz Singer	1980	$1,000,000
Inchon	1981	$1,000,000

Date of Death

July 11, 1989 of renal failure

Internment

Westminster Abbey, London, England UK

Awards and Nominations

Academy/Oscar

Best Actor in a Leading Role	*The Boys From Brazil*	1979
Best Actor in a Leading Role	*Sleuth*	1973
Best Actor in a Leading Role	*The Entertainer*	1961
Best Actor in a Leading Role	*Henry V*	1947
Best Actor in a Leading Role	*Rebecca*	1941
Best Actor in a Leading Role	*Wuthering Heights*	1940

Golden Globe

Best Actor in a Supporting Role *A Little Romance* 1980
Best Motion Picture Actor -Drama *Sleuth* 1973
Best Motion Picture Actor-Drama *Spartacus* 1961

Primetime Emmys

Best Lead Actor in a Drama *The Merchant of Venice* 1974
Best Single Performance by an Actor in a Leading Role *David Copperfield* 1970

Star on the Walk of Fame

6319 Hollywood Blvd.

Laurence Olivier in *Rebecca* –
Selznick International Pictures, 1940

TYRONE POWER

Vital Statistics

DOB: May 5, 1914 (Taurus) in Cincinnati, Ohio
Birth name: Tyrone Edmund Power III
Nickname: Ty
            King of Twentieth Century Fox Studios
Height: 5'10"
Hair: Black
Eyes: Brown

Biographical Sketch

Father
   Tyrone Power II (A brilliant stage actor whose father had also been a renowned actor)

Mother
   Patia Riaume (Actress and drama coach)

Siblings
 Anne (one year younger)

Boyhood Years

Power was a frail, ailing child so when the family doctor advised his parents to move to California for the sake of their young son's health they did so without a second thought. Having divorced her husband because he spent more time in New York pursuing his theatrical career than with his family, Mrs. Powell eventually moved her family back to Cincinnati where they lived with her sister who owned a drama school. During his formative years Ty's mother tutored him in voice as well as drama. He appeared with her in the production of a mission play, *La Golondrina*.

Tyrone Power, Gene Tierney, and John Payne in *The Razor's Edge* – 20th Century Fox, 1946

Start of Career

Power began his acting career when he appeared in a play with his mother. Having outgrown his boyhood maladies, it was natural for the young Power to follow in the footsteps of the acting dynasty that his grandfather had begun.

At the age of seventeen having graduated from high school, Ty moved to Hollywood to live with his father; who had been signed to appear in talkies, the new entertainment medium.

Rumor has it that his father had a verbal agreement with the director of his second film, *The Miracle Man*, that his son Tyrone was to make his film debut by playing a small part in the movie.

In December, 1931 while preparing to shoot a scene, Tyrone Power II collapsed with a heart attack and later died in his young son's arms.

The verbal agreement he had made was quickly forgotten by the director but Tyrone decided to stick around Hollywood and played minor parts in a few films before returning to New York.

The late Katherine Cornell recognized talent in the breathtakingly handsome actor and encouraged him to continue acting in the theater. A scout in the audience during a performance of a Cornell production thought Power was Hollywood material and offered him a screen test. However Cornell encouraged him to wait until he had more experience in the theater and he went along with her suggestion. When the offer was made again in 1936 Power signed a contract with 20th Century Fox.

Despite his amazing good looks and inherent talent, Ty's career had a bumpy start.

Critics were unimpressed with his acting as was the director of Power's first film from which he was fired. His talent was recognized by actress Alice Faye who used her power to persuade a studio head to give the newcomer another chance. This led to a minor role in *Girls Dormitory*. The film created a flurry of interest in young Power from women. But it was influential columnist Hedda Hopper whose comments about Power in her newspaper column brought him the attention needed to help to further his career.

Onscreen Persona

He went on to play a variety of roles, leading man, light comedy, film noir and the romantic swash-buckler in The *Mark of Zorro*. The latter proved to be a highlight in his career, perhaps even a turning point.

Tyrone Power in *The Mark of Zorro* – 20th Century Fox, 1940

It was the film *Lloyds of London* that revealed the talent that led to stardom that lasted until his untimely death.

Power has been described as "startlingly handsome", "classically handsome" and "one of the handsomest men who ever lived" by fans and co-stars. His On screen looks and charisma titillated women in the movie theater audience, causing their imaginations to ignite as the actor seduced them from afar.

The late romance author Barbara Cartland once commented "We don't need blatant sex. We have Tyrone Power".

He received as many as 10,000 fan letters per day.

During his twenty two year reign at Fox, Power played every part available to an actor; drama, musical, period piece, comedy, crime, western, swashbuckler and a memorable noir role in *Nightmare Alley*, now considered to be a cult classic.

Personal Life

Captivating looks and innate charm led to romantic liaisons with some of Hollywood's most popular actresses each claiming he was the love of her life. Among them was Janet Gaynor and Judy Garland.

He was also considered a generous, loyal friend. His longtime stand in was a friend from the early days when he worked as a theater usher while trying out for acting jobs in New York.

In the latter part of the 1930's gossip columns were filled with rumors about Power and his lady love, French actress Annabella. Photographs taken of the two together with accompanying stories of their romance filled the pages of the leading fan magazines of the time.

Marriages

Annabella (actress) 1939-1949 (Divorced)
Linda Christian (actress) 1949--1956 (Divorced)
Debbie Minardos 1958---his death

Children

Romina Francesa 1951 (with Linda)
Taryn Stephanie 1953 (with Linda)
Tyrone Power IV January 22, 1959 (born after Power's death)

Fast Facts

- Darryl Zanuck, head of Fox Studios was concerned that Power's marriage to Annabella would harm Power's career, mainly impacting his female following. Zanuck was wrong. Women continued to respond to Power's smoldering presence onscreen with the same adoration as ever. Power's popularity never wavered, despite his two subsequent marriages.
- On the set of *Witness for the Prosecution* (the actor's last completed film) it was evident that something was amiss with his health. His looks had begun to visibly

deteriorate. Shortly thereafter Powers collapsed and died while on location for his next film. He was just forty-four.

Salary

First contract with Fox $75 per week
Studio contract player $168,250 per year
1957- *Witness for the Prosecution* $300,000 plus a percentage of the gross

Date of Death

November 15, 1958 in Madrid of a heart attack

Interred

Hollywood Forever Cemetery, Hollywood CA. A memorial service is held annually on November 15, marking his death, at Hollywood Forever Cemetery, 6000 Santa Monica, CA to which the public is invited.

Awards and Nominations

1952   Bambi Award   Best Actor   *The Black Rose*

Star on the Walk of Fame

6747 Hollywood Blvd.

Tyrone Power and Marlene Dietrich in *Witness for the Prosecution* – United Artists, 1957

ROBERT TAYLOR

Vital Statistics

DOB: August 5, 1911 (Leo) in Filley, Nebraska
Birth Name: Spangler Arlington Brugh
Nickname: Arly
 The Man with the Perfect Profile
Height: 5' 11 ½"
Hair: Dark Brown
Eyes: Blue
Physique: Firm and Fit
Distinguishing Feature:
  Faint Cleft in Chin
  Thick Arched eyebrows
  Widows Peak
  Resonant Timbre in Voice

Biographical Sketch

Father
  Spangler Andrew Brugh (A farmer who became a doctor in the hope that he would be able to help his invalid wife regain her health)

Mother
  Ruth Adaline (A semi-invalid)

Boyhood Years

An only child, Taylor enjoyed solitary pursuits such as reading, caring for an assortment of animals, and riding his horse. He was not really a loner. He just liked being alone.

Robert Taylor and Greta Garbo in *Camille* – MGM, 1936

In high school he excelled at track and other individual sports. As a prelude to his first ambition for career as a musician Taylor studied the cello and played in the school orchestra. Upon graduating in Pomona College in Los Angeles intending to follow in his father's footsteps and study medicine.

Start of Career

While attending Pomona College, Taylor joined a theater group on campus and was given the lead in a number of productions based upon his stunning looks at first, then because he could act.

75

Taylor was seriously contemplating attending drama school when a scout from MGM saw him in a school production and arranged for him to have a screen test. His extraordinary good looks, compelling voice and innate talent resulted in a studio contract along with a change of name.

Onscreen Persona

Taylor was cast in numerous romantic leads opposite some of Hollywood's most glamorous actresses. However he had to endure the harsh assessment of critics who looked no further than his exceeding good looks labeling him as being "too pretty" to be taken seriously. It was his role in the tear jerker *Magnificent Obsession* (opposite Irene Dunne) that made him a matinee idol. Despite the negativity of the press and film reviewers, Taylor captured the hearts of female fans everywhere. He was now undoubtedly a heartthrob.

Throughout his career Taylor opted for roles that would give him the edge to show a talent that went beyond looks. Notwithstanding the press, Taylor went on to give moving performances in such early romantic films as *Camille* (1936) with the legendary Garbo and with Vivien Leigh in *Waterloo Bridge* (1940). It was the box office success of *Quo Vadis* (1951) opposite Deborah Kerr that established him as a serious actor. His film career took a slight detour with the role of a gangster in *Johnny Eager* (1942) opposite Lana Turner. The rough and tough façade of a gentleman gangster made Taylor more appealing to women.

Robert Taylor and Vivien Leigh in *Waterloo Bridge* – MGM, 1940

When television threatened the movie industry, Taylor made an easy and successful transition into the new media with the television series, *The Detective*.

Personal Life

Romance

The romance of Robert Taylor and Barbara Stanwyck created a stir among fans and the press. They were hot copy. Although Stanwyck was some years older, the two were among a few select duos known as "golden couples". The marriage was rocky at times. Having learned to fly, Taylor spent a great deal of time in the air with his private plane named Missy (Stanwyck's nickname). It is said that Stanwyck often complained that her husband spent so much time polishing his guns and taking care of his plane, that there was little time left for her. They were eventually divorced. Taylor's fans unashamedly mobbed him, pulling bits of clothing from him for souvenirs; fan hysteria was not unusual wherever Robert Taylor showed up.

Marriages

Barbara Stanwyck (actress) 1939-1951 (Divorced)
Ursula Theiss (actress) 1954-1969 (his death)

Children

Terrence, 1955 and Theresa, 1959 (with Theiss)

Fast Facts

- Eleanor Powell was rumored at one time to be a leading candidate to become the second Mrs. Taylor.
- Stanwyck never remarried, but continued to collect alimony in the form of a percentage of Taylor's earnings until his death.
- In 1947 Taylor was among a group of actors who appeared as friendly witnesses, testifying before the House Un-American Committee about communism in Hollywood.
- He was said to have considered remarrying Stanwyck at one time.
- After the death of Clark Gable, MGM bestowed the title of "The New King of Hollywood" upon Taylor. There had always been subtle rivalry for top heartthrob between the two.
- He was made up to look Italian for his role in *Johnny Eager*.
- He spent a great deal of time reading his father's medical books when he was a young boy.
- Katherine Hepburn, his costar in the melodrama *Undercurrent*, said of him, "Robert Taylor is a highly underrated actor with a much bigger talent than suspected"
- "Bob is a really nice guy and it comes through on the screen" is how one producer described the actor.
- During World War II Taylor served as a flight instructor and directed 17 U.S. navy training films
- By the war's end Taylor was commissioned a lieutenant.
- In 1944 he narrated and directed the documentary *The Fighting Lady*.
- A newspaper article once referred to Taylor as Public Dream Man #1.
- Although his first major role was on loan out to Universal, Taylor remained a loyal performer at MGM for thirty years, playing opposite some of Hollywood's most beautiful and accomplished actresses.
- He and Clark Gable were very good friends. Taylor was a pallbearer at Gable's funeral.
- Taylor was fourth in box office appeal in 1936.
- The Hollywood Foreign Press Associates titled him Most Popular Star Abroad in 1954

- A consummate professional he was greatly respected for his dedication to the business of acting. Taylor strove hard to erase his "pretty boy" image by seeking roles that required maturity and went beyond the handsome leading man image.
- He was the first American actor to appear in a movie that was made in England (*A Yank at Oxford*) 1938
- When television threatened to endanger the movie industry Taylor made a name for himself on the small screen in the series *The Detective*.
- His association with MGM Studios was among the longest in Hollywood history.
- Taylor was an enigma in his loyalty to MGM, his home studio.

Salary

$35 per week as contract player, 1934

Date of Death

June 8, 1969 in Santa Monica, CA of lung cancer (Taylor was a chain smoker). Ronald Reagan delivered the eulogy

Interred

Forest Lawn Memorial Park Cemetery in Glendale, CA.

Awards and Nominations

Henrietta Award World Film Favorite- Male (1954) shared with Alan Ladd

Star on the Walk of Fame

500 Vine Street, Hollywood

Robert Taylor and Deborah Kerr in *Quo Vadis* – MGM, 1951

Chapter Two
THE FORTIES

The forties brought uncertainty of another type, War. The European theater was deep into war following the invasion of Poland by the Germans in 1939. While Americans continued to deal with scarcity of money at the start of the decade, they soon found themselves facing scarcity of another kind as they were abruptly drawn into the fight among countries oceans away. Rationing became a way of life. With the war came solidarity among the citizens of the U.S. It was a time of idealism, determination and truth as the country united in a single cause.

In 1943 Los Angeles was the scene of a riot between zoot suit clad Mexican - Americans and American servicemen.

As heartthrobs of the 30's went off to serve their country, a new breed of heartthrob emerged. The beautiful man with the perfect profile evolved into the less perfect but still good looking fellow who could still make feminine hearts throb. Heartthrobs of the 40's often had strong, sometimes irregular features unlike the chiseled perfect profile of the 1930's heartthrob. They were clean shaven except for a few who sported a signature mustache. The appeal of these heartthrobs was evident in the increased number of women who flocked to the movies, often substituting the screen hero for a boyfriend or husband off fighting a war. With the scarcity of flesh and blood men in their lives the on screen heartthrob was an even stronger focus for women.

- The average earnings for a woman went from $17.63 per week in 1940 to $41.86 in 1949. Women working in war plants earned significantly more. They could easily afford the cost of watching their fantasy heartthrob on the Silver Screen.

- Fifty Two year old Charlie Chaplin married nineteen year old Oona O'Neil creating a flurry of gossip. The marriage lasted until Chaplin's death leaving Oona a desolate widow.

- On August 4, 1944 fifteen year old Anne Frank, her family and friends were taken from their attic hideaway by the Nazis into a concentration camp to die.

- On August 6, 1945 America, in an effort to stop the war with Japan, dropped the Atom bomb on Hiroshima.

- November 20, 1945 The Nuremberg Trials began against members of the Nazi party and others accused of murder, crimes against humanity, and a host of other distasteful citations. The world was held spellbound by this momentous trial.

- The notorious gangster Bugsy Siegel was fatally shot in the Beverly Hills home of his lover on June 20, 1947.

- On November 20, 1947 Princess Elizabeth of England married Phillip Mountbatten, Duke of Edinburgh.

- June 25, 1948 marked the date that Joe Louis defeated the then current heavy weight boxer Jersey Joe Wolcott.

- Men wore their hair short and slicked back; sporting fedoras and thick shoulder pads in their suit jackets and sports coats. As the decade advanced so did wages as war time eliminated the financial depression of the previous decade.

- Gossip columnist Hedda Hopper dubbed the era "The Bobby Sox Blitz"

- The price of a movie ticket went from $.29 in 1942 to $.43 in 1949.

- Like their predecessors many of the actors of the '40's had the invaluable experience of having performed in the legitimate theatre before moving on to the celluloid screen.

- There was a shift in acting techniques in the latter days of the decade with the formation of The Actors Studio in New York. Led by famed drama teacher Lee Strasburg, this small group of actors developed an innovative acting technique known as "the method."

DANA ANDREWS

Vital Statistics

DOB: January 1, 1909 (Capricorn) in Doubt, Mississippi
Birth Name: Carver Dana Andrews
Height: 5'10"
Hair: Dark Brown
Physique: Firm/ Muscular

Biographical Sketch

Father
   Charles (Baptist Minister)

Mother
   Annis or Anice (Housewife, mother of thirteen with nine surviving)

Siblings
   Peter Graves (brother, also an actor)

Boyhood Years

When he was of high school age, the family moved to Huntsville, Texas. While attending the Sam Houston State Teachers College in Texas where he majored in business, Andrews became interested in acting. Prior to graduation he worked part time as an accountant for Gulf Oil, but quit this lucrative job to hitch hike to California after graduation with the hope of becoming a screen actor. Taking any job that would pay a decent wage in those lean days, Andrews worked as a school bus driver, orange picker and gas attendant. With the loan of sufficient funds to pay for classes from his employer, Andrews also studied opera while attending the Pasadena Community Playhouse where he appeared in numerous plays. He was very well liked among his peers and his teachers.

Dana Andrews and Elizabeth Taylor in *Elephant Walk* – Paramount Pictures, 1954

Start of Career

It was while appearing in a play depicting the life of composers Gilbert and Sullivan that Andrews was spotted by a talent scout from Samuel Goldwyn Studios. This led to a two year contract during which time the young Andrews attended in-studio classes, but was not cast in any movies. 20th Century Fox bought out half of his contract and he was cast in highly rated movies, although not in any starring roles. *The Westerner* was his first major film.

Onscreen Persona

Whether he was portraying a crusty detective, a disillusioned soldier returning from war or that of a soldier going off to war and leaving behind the girl he tried hard not to love, Andrews engaged his female audience in a powerful way. Not blueprint handsome as some of his predecessors, strong features and a deep steady voice appealed to his female audience in a different way than that of the 30's heart throb. He was strong with an undertone of sensitivity that made his female fans feel protected. Andrews' career moved slowly until 1944 when he played the role of a cynical detective in the film *Laura*, now a classic. His portrayal of the detective who finds himself falling for a woman supposedly murdered tugged at women's heartstrings.

His last romantic film, *My Foolish Heart*, 1949 had women in the audience sobbing.

Dana Andrews and Gene Tierney in *Laura* – 20th Century Fox, 1944

Personal Life

Marriages

Janet Murray   December 31, 1932-1935 (her death)
Mary Todd   November 17, 1939-December 17, 1992 (his death)

Children

David (with Janet Murray) 1934-1964 David died of a brain hemorrhage
Katherine 1942
Stephen   1944
Susan   1948

Fast Facts

- He co-starred in five films with actress Gene Tierney
- He was one of the first actors to be under contract to two studios (Goldwyn and 20th Century Fox) at the same time.
- When his movie career wound down, Andrews moved easily into television's *Bright Promise,* a TV daytime soap opera and Ike, a nighttime TV miniseries.
- With the release of *Laura*, Andrew's fan mail sky rocketed. Women adored the outwardly cynical detective who was smitten with a dead girl's portrait. The popularity of *Laura* found Andrews signing a new and lucrative contract
- His next acclaimed film *The Best Years of Our Lives* furthered the heartthrob image increasing his female fan following.
- In 1947 Andrews was listed twenty third on the list of most popular actors in the country.

- A close friend said of him, "Dana doesn't take himself seriously, just his career".
- He was an ardent Sinatra fan.
- The Hollywood Women's Press Club awarded Andrews a Golden Apple in 1946 for being the most Cooperative actor of the year.
- As President of the Screen Actors Guild, 1963-65 he took a stand against actresses doing nude scenes just to get a part in a film
- Dana Andrews was considered to be one of the major stars of the '40's.
- He overcame a serious alcohol problem and went on to speak out on its dangers to the public for the U.S. Department of Transportation in 1972. He was also spokesman for the National Council on Alcoholism.
- Although he had a fine voice and had studied opera, studio heads chose not to feature his singing voice in a film.
- Toward the end of his life, Andrews was diagnosed with Alzheimer's and spent his later years in a California nursing home.

Salary

A contract player with Goldwyn Studios until the release of *Laura* after which he was signed by the studio to a five year contract for $1.5 million dollars amounting to around $100,000 per film for his next sixteen movies.

Date of Death

December 17, 1992, from pneumonia and congestive heart failure.

Interred

Cremated with ashes held by family

Star on the Walk of Fame

To date, Dana Andrews does not have a Star on the Walk of Fame.

Dana Andrews and Susan Hayward in *My Foolish Heart* – RKO Radio Pictures, 1949

HUMPHREY BOGART

Vital Statistics

DOB: December 25, 1899 (Capricorn) in New York, New York
Birth Name: Humphrey DeForest Bogart
Nickname: Bogie
Height: 5'8"
Hair: Brown
Eyes: Brown
Physique: Slender & Firm
Outstanding Attribute:
  A small diagonal scar on right corner of his upper lip

Biographical Sketch

Father
  Dr. Belmont DeForest Bogart (Prominent surgeon)

Mother
  Maude (Magazine illustrator)

Siblings
  Frances, two years younger
  Katherine, four years younger

Boyhood Years

Born into a wealthy, socially prominent family Bogart was educated in private schools, first at Trinity School, then at Phillips Academy in Andover to prepare for a career in medicine and was expected to go on to Yale. His expulsion from Phillips for an incident involving a faculty member put an end to any hope of his becoming a doctor.

Humphrey Bogart and Katharine Hepburn in *The African Queen* – United Artists, 1951

At 18 he joined the Navy for two years but when he was discharged at the age of 20 he had no idea of what he wanted to do with his life. On an impulse he contacted a family friend who was a theatrical producer and was offered a job as an office boy.

Start of Career

He was working as a stage manager at the World Film Corp. in New York when he was "discovered." The daughter of actress Alice Brady (a friend of the Bogarts) saw potential in him, alerting her mother to that face when he was given a small part in a play in which Brady was starring.

Bogart was just 23. Although he continued to act on stage in small roles, his reviews were rather dismal. One critic referred to Bogart's stage performances as "mercifully inadequate."

Upon moving to Los Angeles, he was signed to a long term studio contract with Warner Brothers. When the studio purchased the movie rights to *The Petrified Forest*, actor Leslie Howard who starred in the film, insisted that Bogart reprise his stage role as Duke Mantee threatening not to appear in the film if the studio refused. It was the break Bogart needed, one he never forgot.

Onscreen Persona

Although not classically handsome, Bogart's looks fit right in with the changing image of the heartthrob of the decade. The tough characters that were Bogart's trademark in the 30's held a certain appeal for many of his feminine fans. It was *High Sierra*, a box office hit that assured Bogart would never play small parts again. While some women appeared to like the tough guy image Bogart portrayed onscreen, it was in 1942 that he finally hit his stride as a recognized heartthrob with the role of Rick in *Casablanca* opposite Ingrid Bergman.

Casablanca revealed a sensitive, romantic Bogart who women understood and adored drawing them into movie theaters in droves. He was a man's man who women prized. It wasn't long before columnists made the public aware that Bogart had gone beyond the On screen romantic leading man into a real life romance right before everyone's eyes. The tough guy image was supplanted by one of a man with a center of tenderness playing to the young woman who was his costar. The woman was Lauren Bacall.

Humphrey Bogart and Ingrid Bergman in *Casablanca* – Warner Brothers, 1942

Personal Life

Romances

Rumor had it that Bogart romanced a number of Hollywood's leading ladies between his first three marriages.

Marriages

Helen Menken (actress) 1926-1927 (Divorced)
Mary Phillips (theatrical actress) 1928-1937 (Divorced)
Mayo Methot (actress) 1938-1945 (Divorced)
Lauren Bacall, (actress) 1945- until his death

A year after his divorce from Phillips, Bogart was introduced to a volatile actress who intrigued him enough to marry again. But Mayo Methot was extremely jealous and had a fiery temper. The two fought in private and in public throughout their seven years of marriage. Their battles blazoned across the theatrical sections of newspapers and in fan magazines. This went on until the film *To Have and Have Not* cast a very young, very attractive actress opposite Bogart. She was quick to win him over with her poise and great sense of humor. Methot began visiting the set daily casting a watchful eye on her husband and his young costar as they played out their scenes in the 1944 film *To Have and Have Not*. It was rumored that Methot was making a last ditch effort to save the battle ridden marriage.

Eventually, both she and the cast members and crew realized that Bogart had gone beyond the onscreen romance of *Casablanca* into a real life romance right before everyone's eyes. The tough guy image was supplanted by one of a man with a heart of tenderness playing to the lovely young woman who was his costar. True love quickly sprang to life.

Lauren Bacall and Bogart were married less than two weeks after his divorce from Methot. It was the first time he had married for love. Bogart was forty-six, his bride just skimming twenty. It proved to be a solid union with the couple gaining popularity not only among fans, but within the Hollywood community.

Children

Both with Lauren Bacall
Stephen (Steve) Humphrey, 1949 named for the character Bogart played in first film they made together
Leslie 1952 (a daughter named for actor friend Leslie Howard who gave Bogart his film start with the role in *The Petrified Forest*)

Fast Facts

- Bogart's first public appearance was at the age of one. His mother had painted a portrait of her son submitting it to an advertising agency. The Mellin Company okayed it for their product and within a short time baby Bogart's face adorned the labels on jars of the popular baby food.
- He was expelled from Phillips Academy where he was studying for a medical career. After that his parents resigned themselves to the fact that their son would not follow in his father's career footsteps
- A chess enthusiast he played chess by mail with GI's during WWII
- A bit in awe of fatherhood, Bogart passed photos of his son around the commissary at lunch proudly stating "He's going to be a great big fella"
- In order to match the height of costars he wore lifts or platforms
- The government honored him with a 32 cent commemorative stamp in their 1997 Legends of Hollywood series

- He and Richard Burton were close friends. He confided in Burton that he aspired to act in a stage production of *Shakespeare*, but thought that he would not be taken seriously by the public due to his onscreen image.
- Only those with whom he was very close were invited to visit him during his illness. Spencer Tracey, with whom he had become close in the early days of both their careers, was among the few.
- He smoked up to five packs of cigarettes a day
- *Entertainment Magazine* ranked Bogart #1 Movie Legend of All Time in 1997
- He was #1 on 1999 list of American Film Institute Greatest Screen Actors
- He loved to golf and did so whenever his schedule permitted
- One of his most significant roles *High Sierra* (1941) was first turned down by George Raft
- Bogart left the studio system in 1948, forming his own film company, Santana Productions
- He was distantly related to the late Princess Diana on her American side. Son Steven Bogart holds an annual Humphrey Bogart Film Festival in Key Largo, Florida
- In 1999 the American Film Institute declared him to be the Greatest Male Star of all Times

Salary

1942 – $114,125

Date of Death

January 14, 1957 in Los Angles of esophageal cancer

Interred

His ashes are interred at Forest Lawn, Glendale, CA in the Garden of Memory (public not permitted) - Just before he was put to rest his widow placed a small gold whistle in the coffin beside him. "If you want me, just whistle," the tag line from their first film together.

Humphrey Bogart and Lauren Bacall in *To Have and Have Not* – Warner Brothers, 1944

Awards and Nominations

Best Actor   *Casablanca*   1943
Best Actor   *The Caine Mutiny*   1951
Best Actor   *The African Queen*   1954

Star on the Walk of Fame

Awarded posthumously on February 8, 1960 at 6322 Hollywood Blvd.

KIRK DOUGLAS

Vital Statistics

DOB: December 9, 1916 (Sagitarius) in Amsterdam, New York
Birth Name: Issur Danelovich Demsky
Height: 5' 9"
Hair: Blonde
Eyes: Blue
Physique: Athletic /Strong
Distinguishing Feature:
   Deep Dimple in Chin

Biographical Sketch

Father
   Harry (Junk dealer)

Mother
  Bryna (Homemaker who assisted her husband in the ragman business as well as caring for her seven children of which Kirk was the only boy)

Boyhood Years

The family lived barely above the poverty line in an era when anti-Semitism was rampant. This led to a strong desire in Douglas to contribute to the Jewish community when his career made it financially possible.

Kirk Douglas as Vincent Van Gogh in
Lust for Life – MGM, 1956

Start of Career

A wrestling scholarship took him to St. Lawrence University where he became intrigued with acting.

His natural talent resulted in a scholarship to the American Academy of Dramatic Arts in New York City.

It was while attending the academy that he changed his name to Kirk Douglas and prepared for a stint on Broadway. However with advent of World War II, Douglas joined the Navy serving as a communications officer. At the suggestion of friend Lauren Bacall, Hall Wallis agreed to screen test the newcomer. Douglas clicked, especially with the women in the audience, and his career took off.

Onscreen Persona

His demeanor on screen was often that of a gruff, hard hearted man who made others sit up and listen. Women movie goers saw beyond that into the tender heart beneath the tough exterior and adored him. He portrayed realism in a way that sustained him throughout a long career playing an assortment of characters with style and aplomb.

Personal Life

Marriages

Diana Dill 1944 - 1951(Divorced)
Anne Buydens 1954 - present

Children

Michael (actor, with Diana)
Joel, Peter, Eric (with Anne. Eric died in July 2004 of a drug overdose)

Grandchildren

Cameron, 1978
Kelsey, 1992
Tyler, 1996
Ryan, 2000
Jason, 2003
Carys Zeta, 2003

Kirk Douglas and Lana Turner in *The Bad and the Beautiful* – MGM, 1952

Fast Facts

- He wrestled in a carnival one summer to earn money.
- Extremely handsome with a voice that commanded attention, Douglas's appeal led to his appearance in a number of diversified films ranging from light comedy to gripping drama. This actor won feminine hearts easily with his charismatic smile and fine honed features. He is said to be one of Hollywood's most resilient actors and a true star in every way.
- Passing up career opportunities at the start of World War II, he joined the Navy as a communications officer.
- In an interview with Mike Wallace in 1957, Douglas stated that his goal was to be a stage actor, not to make movies. Dead broke he agreed to go along when someone invited him to Hollywood.

- He won the admiration of his fellow actors for crediting blacklisted writer Dalton Trumbo as adapting the film *Spartacus* (1960). It has been said that this gesture helped to affect the end of the blacklist still in practice at that time.
- His company Bryna Productions is named for his adored mother
- His charitable foundation has served to support organizations such groups as: Cedars-Sinai Medical Center among others
- He earned $50,000 for speaking only one word in English at the end of a Japanese TV commercial for coffee in 1980.
- He and Burt Lancaster had a playful rivalry but were actually good friends
- In 1996, at the age of eighty, Kirk Douglas was hospitalized with a stroke that robbed him of his speech. It was a long road back, but the same perseverance and determination that has ruled his life from boyhood saw him make a remarkable recovery.
- Creatively Douglas has done it all: acted, authored books, directed, produced.
- He has celebrated his Bar Mitzvah twice, first at 13 and again at the age of 83.
- Douglas devotes a good deal of time to the Douglas Charitable Foundation.
- By passing career opportunities at the start of World War II, he joined the Navy as a communications officer.
- He was close friends with Karl Malden
- There is a greenbelt in Palm Springs named Kirk Douglas Way named for the actor who lived in Palm Springs for many years.
- The Douglas' renewed their wedding vows before a group of close friends and family on their fiftieth anniversary.
- He once thought of becoming a rabbi.
- He is beloved by his peers
- He is considered by his fellow actors to be a true star in every way

Salary:

$15,000 *Champion*, 1949
$400,000 *In Harms Way*
Net worth 60 million dollars

Awards and Nominations

1950 Best Actor in a Leading Role for Champion
1953 Best Actor in a Leading Role for The Bad and the Beautiful
1957 Best Actor in a Leading Role Lust for Life

Special Awards

1957 The George Washington Carver Award of Merit
Man of the Year by Friar's Club for his contribution to humanity
1981 Presidential Medal of Freedom presented by President Carter
1983 Jefferson Award for public service by a public citizen

1984 Inducted into the Hall of Great Western Performers
1991 Chaim Weitzman award in Sciences and Humanities for lifelong service to Israel
1991 Life Achievement Award by The American Film Institute
1995 Einstein Award from the National Dyslexia Research Foundation
 2002 Medal of Honor from UCLA awarded at graduation ceremony for theater, television and film students.

Star on the Walk of Fame

6263 Hollywood Blvd.

Kirk Douglas in *Spartacus* –
Universal Pictures, 1960

GLENN FORD

Vital Statistics

Date of Birth: May 1, 1916 (Taurus) in Quebec City, Quebec, Canada
Birth Name: Gwylln Samuel Newton Ford
Height: 5"11" or 6'1" depending upon which bio one reads
Hair: Dark brown
Eyes: Blue
Physique: Athletic

Biographical Sketch

Father
  Newton (Railway Conductor)

Mother
  Hannah (Homemaker)

Boyhood Years

The family moved to Santa Monica, California to get away from the cold weather when Glenn was eight. Although Ford always wanted to be an actor and worked hard toward that end, he never forgot his father's advice when acting became his primary means of earning a living. That advice was to always have something besides acting to fall back on, something that would insure he would always be able to earn a living. A series of construction jobs while studying acting made Ford proficient at plumbing, air conditioning, wiring, and even the installation of a roof. After achieving stardom and the financial security it brought him, Ford used his handyman skills to work on his home.

Glenn Ford, Ward Bond, and Jean Rogers in
Heaven with a Barbed Wire Fence –
Columbia Pictures, 1939

Start of Career

Participation in the high school dramas grew into Little Theatre productions throughout the West Coast.

Columbia signed him to a contract in 1939. Ironically, the title of his first major role in a movie was *Heaven with a Barbed Wire Fence*.

The studio heads wanted to change his name to John Gower, but the young actor had another idea. Wanting to keep the family name he suggested his screen name be changed to that of Glenford, the town in Quebec where his father was born. Separating the name into two parts and adding an extra n created Glenn Ford, the actor.

Onscreen Persona

Clean cut and boyishly handsome the young actor with the compelling soft spoken voice shot up on the popularity poll from the start creating a career that spanned years of playing a variety of roles from comedy to stark drama.

His appeal to female movie goers was based upon believability. Glenn Ford's appearance in a film created a flurry at the box office among the women of all ages who loved him as a grief stricken, bewildered widower trying to raise his young son alone in *The Courtship of Eddie's Father* as well as in the light comedy in *Tea House of the August Moon*. Ford's innate, seemingly easy, talent made him an actor of many layers. As the young man trying desperately to hide the emotional torment of his love for the dazzling, unavailable Gilda he grabbed the hearts of women in the audience. They saw beneath the façade of wise cracking indifference. He made us laugh, cry and get angry at an injustice. When Glenn Ford appeared on the screen he was completely credible. He was in fact "everyman."

Personal Life

Romance

A steamy romance with actress Hope Lange filled fan magazines and gossip columns with copy in the early 1960's.

Marriages

Eleanor Parker (actress) 1943-1959 (Divorced)
Kathryn Hays (actress) 1966-1969 (Divorced)
Cynthia Hayward 1974-1977 (Divorced)
Jeanne Baus 1993-1994 (Divorced)

Glenn Ford, Marlon Brando, and M Kyo in *Teahouse of the August Moon* – MGM, 1956

Children

Peter Ford (with Eleanor)

Fast Facts

- When asked by Hollywood columnist Hedda Hopper how it felt to be elected Man of the Year by Bobby Soxers, Inc. of America in the mid '40's, Ford replied "grateful."
- His observation at the time of his signing with Columbia, was "the studios wanted actors with perfect profiles. I didn't have one then and I don't have one now."

Author's comment: In fact Ford did have a nearly perfect profile in the symmetry of his slightly turned up nose and well-shaped chin line.

- He modestly refrained from commenting on his appeal to the distaff side of movie audiences. But the appeal was definitely there, perfect profile or not. Throughout his lengthy career, Ford kept a level head in the face of tremendous popularity with his female fans.
- He made five films with Rita Hayworth, but their romantic involvement remained on screen. Although they lived next door to one another in Beverly Hills the two were always just good friends.
- Ford tended to be a bit taciturn on screen. His philosophy was the less said the better.
- He was the fastest gun in Hollywood (beating out veteran John Wayne) as he could draw and fire within 0.4 seconds.
- He and William Holden were two of Columbia's most important actors. They were also good friends.
- Ford made 55 Westerns during his career.
- He was never nominated for an Academy Award to the bewilderment of his fans and many of his peers, but for 52 years the public flocked to see any film with his name in the credits.
- Having once been kicked on the right side of his jaw by a horse, he always opted to be shot from his left profile as he felt it was the only side that was filmable.
- He traveled whenever possible experiencing memorable moments i.e.: climbing Mont Blanc in Europe, hang gliding. His was an adventurous spirit that went beyond mere contemplation. Most inspiring of his experiences meeting some of the greats of the world, Winston Churchill, Somerset Maugham, Noel Coward, Will Rogers (Ford worked as a stable hand for the latter), De Gaulle and Presidents Roosevelt and Truman..
- He spoke seven languages.
- In 1946 the Glenn Ford Scholarship Fund was set up in perpetuity at his alma mater Santa Monica High.
- Although he played many diverse roles, Ford is best known and remembered for his portrayals of the average man caught up in unusual situations.
- His first wife, dancer Eleanor Powell, happily gave up her career when they married to the chagrin of studio heads and fans alike. At the time Ford was hardly known.
- It was the release of *Gilda* (1946), a film that has since become a classic, that the charismatic actor became a box office smash and a true heartthrob.
- During World War II he took leave of his career to serve first in the Coast Guard and then with the Marines. He was also a Captain in the U.S. Naval Reserve.
- He frequently visited American troops in Korea and served with a Special Forces Team during the Vietnam War.
- In the late 70's Ford became intrigued with the occult and was regressed hypnotically to a former life when he was a cowboy in Colorado. Some years later he underwent another hypnosis session and was transported to 1840, during which time he was a teacher of piano in Scotland.

- He was inducted into the Western Performers Hall of Fame in 1978.
- He was an accomplished painter with many of his artistic works displayed in his home.
- In 1992 Ford received the Legion d'honneur medal for his efforts during World War II.

Salary

1946 $1000 per week
Border Shootout 1990 $75,000 per week

Date of Death

August 30, 2006 from a series of small strokes.

Interred

In a Mausoleum at Woodlawn Cemetery, Santa Monica, CA

Awards and Nominations

Golden Globe Best Motion Picture Actor in Musical Comedy 1957 *Teahouse of the August Moon*
Golden Globe Best Motion Picture Actor in Musical Comedy 1958 *Don't Go Near the Water*
Golden Laurel Top Male Comedy Performance 1963 *The Courtship of Eddie's Father*
1948 Golden Apple Most Cooperative Actor by The Hollywood Women's Press Club
1957 Golden Apple Most Cooperative Actor by The Hollywood Women's Press Club
1962 Golden Globe Best Motion Picture Actor in Musical Comedy for *Pocketful of Miracles*

Star on the Walk of Fame

6933 Hollywood Blvd.

Glenn Ford and Ron Howard in *The Courtship of Eddie's Father* – MGM, 1963

JOHN GARFIELD

Vital Statistics

DOB: March 4, 1913 (Pisces) in New York, New York
Birth name: Jacob Julius Garfinkle
Nickname: Julie
Height: 5'7"
Hair: Dark brown, thick and curly
Eyes: Brown
Physique: Muscular

Biographical Sketch

Father
   David (A presser in the garment district)

Mother
   Hannah (Homemaker)

Siblings
   Max, five years younger

Boyhood Years

Born into poverty in the area of New York known as the ghetto on the East Side, his father moved the boys into a tenement in east Brooklyn after Garfield's mother died. He was seven. He lived with a series of relatives until he was a teenager. The relationship between Garfield and his father was strained.

Family members and friends remember him as an outgoing, energetic boy with a quick grin who liked to clown around. Always eager for an audience, he learned how to "perform" early in life.

John Garfield and Priscilla Lane in
Four Daughters – Warner Brothers, 1938

Because he was small for his age, the young boy turned to means of survival by joining a street gang. This resulted in his being sent to a school for problem children where he learned how to box and gained an introduction into the world of acting.

He may have been headed in a very wrong direction if not for the intervention of Angeleo Patri a teacher at Public School 45, who saw beyond the outward show of toughness into a promising hidden talent. It was Patri who was responsible for getting the youngster to shape up. In order to participate in school drama productions, Garfield's grades had to improve. In time he became not only a good scholar, but an admired talent. Patri continued to encourage the potential he saw in his protégée.

Start of Career

A scholarship to Maria Ouspenskaya's School of Drama led him to his first Broadway experience, a walk on when he was seventeen. By 1937 he had caught the attention of someone at Warner Bros.

Soon afterward he drove across country to meet with Jack Warner. The studio head promptly changed Garfield's first name to John and cast him as the melancholy, cynical Mickey Borden opposite Pricilla Lane in *Four Daughters* in 1938.

Onscreen Persona

Garfield presented himself on screen with rugged features and a tough exterior but women in the audience detected the undertone of vulnerability and found it endearing.

Garfield didn't hit his heartthrob stride until the release of *The Postman Always Rings Twice* in 1946. The steamy scenes with costar Lana Turner made women in the audience sizzle. Garfield became a symbol of unrestrained lust. And women eagerly paid the price of a movie ticket to experience it, albeit vicariously. He was the personification of the sensitive, vulnerable guy who hid behind a brusque façade.

John Garfield and Lana Turner in *The Postman Always Rings Twice* – MGM, 1946

Women in the movie theaters responded quickly to the look of pathos in his deep set eyes that overshadowed his rugged good looks. It touched the hearts of women in the audience keeping the actor at the top of his game throughout his film his film history. An inner strength that shone from deep within added to his heartthrob status. On screen he exuded a certain something that told women, he was their protector in any situation. In the days before the women's movement it was an attribute that women aspired to in their men. Rugged yet tender was a combination few could resist.

Personal Life

Liberal politics and involvement in social causes made Garfield a target with the House UN American Witch Hunt of the early 50's. Despite Garfield's testimony before Congress that he had never been involved in Communist activities he was unofficially blacklisted from movies and returned to the theater. Studio heads ran "scared" during those years.

Marriages

Roberta Seidman   1932-1952 (his death)

Children

David   1943-1994
Katherine 1938-1945 (died of an allergic reaction)
Julie 1946

Fast Facts

- A bout with rheumatic fever as a young adult left him with heart damage
- His wife called Garfield's sad smile "Julie's orphan look"
- He is considered to be the First Rebel in Hollywood.
- He was one of the first actors to form his own independent production company in the mid-forties.
- He and Bette Davis opened the Hollywood Canteen providing a friendly environment for service men during the war years.
- Theater being Garfield's first love, he had it written into his contract with Warner Brothers that he be permitted to perform on stage annually.
- He was one of the group of Hollywood actors who protested the HUAC in Washington, D.C. October, 1947 (remember the movie *The Way We Were*).
- After testifying before the HUAC Garfield was followed by the FBI. Rumor has it he was hounded to the point of it affecting his health.
- Although his wife was rumored to be a card carrying Communist, there was never any evidence that Garfield was a member of the party. He was a staunch liberal who spoke the courage of his convictions at a time when it was not considered the smart thing to do.
- His hobby was painting
- His funeral is said to have been the largest in attendance for an actor since that of Rudolph Valentino with more than ten thousand fans mobbing the cemetery.

Salary

While under contract to Warner Bros $82, 291 per year
Net worth, $100,000

Date of Death

May 21, 1952 in New York of a coronary thrombosis

Interred

Westchester Hills Cemetery, Westchester NY

Awards and Nominations

Best Supporting Actor by Academy 1938 *Four Daughters*
Best Actor Award by National Board of Review, 1938
Best Actor by Academy Body & Soul 1947

Star on the Walk of Fame

7065 Hollywood Blvd.

John Garfield, Spencer Tracy, and Hedy Lamarr in
Tortilla Flat – MGM, 1942

PAUL HENREID

Vital Statistics

DOB: January 10, 1905 (Capricorn) in Trieste, Austria-Hungary
Name at Birth: Paul George Julius Henreid Ritter Von Wassel-Waldingau
Height: 6'3"
Hair: Light brown
Eyes: Dark brown
Physique: Slender and toned

Biographical Sketch

Father
  Baron Carl Alphons (Banker in Vienna, Austria)

Mother
  Marie Luise von Hernreid (Socialite)

Boyhood Years

The family was among the nobility of Europe before the war. Henreid grew up in the area of Europe known as Austria-Hungary. Having come from aristocracy, his father was able to provide Paul with many advantages until his death when Paul was only eight. The family finances then fell into the hands of an uncle who mismanaged the Henreid fortune into near depletion.

Paul Henreid and Bette Davis in
Now, Voyager – Warner Brothers, 1942

Start of Career

Studying with Max Reinhardt, Henreid began a career in German films in the 1930's, but moved to Britain in 1935 when war started to rumble. As a Jew, he was an outspoken adversary of the Nazi Party and faced deportation from Britain and possible internment as an enemy alien at the start of WWII. He was saved from this fate by actor Conrad Veidt whose intervention kept Henreid from being sent back to Austria. However he was prohibited from ever returning to his homeland and listed as an enemy of the Third Reich.

It was as minor role in *Goodbye Mr. Chips* (1939) that opened the door to Hollywood. At the time Henreid was broke. On March 6, 1941 he was signed to a freelance contract with RKO Radio Studios.

Onscreen Persona

His urbane demeanor appealed to the female audiences during the somber years of war. They responded eagerly to his onscreen charm and sophistication. In *Now, Voyager* (1942) opposite Bette Davis when Henreid lit the those two cigarettes at once for the first time in the film, the heartbeat of women in the audience quickened and thereafter raced whenever Henreid appeared on screen. The gesture was at once intimate and loving. It was this film that launched him as a romantic heartthrob.

Personal Life

Marriages

Elizabeth Gluck 1936 until his death

Children

Monica
Mimi

Paul Henreid, Ingrid Bergman, and Humphrey Bogart in *Casablanca* – Warner Brothers, 1942

Fast Facts

- At his mother's suggestion Henreid attended medical school for a year.
- Unwilling to give up his love of acting he saved every spare bit of money he could so he could attend theatrical events from plays to opera.
- While attending the Graphic Academy in Austria to study for a promised position upon graduation, he continued with his true ambition by taking night classes in acting.
- A longtime theatrical background easily evolved into a movie career.
- He was blacklisted from acting by the HUAC in 1952 and turned his career around by becoming a successful director.
- He was buried with a fan letter sent to him before he became a household name. Although he never divulged the contents, Henreid claimed that the letter meant more to him than any of his awards.

Date of Death

March 29, 1992 of pneumonia.

Interred

Buried Woodlawn Cemetery Santa Monica, CA

Star on the Walk of Fame

6366 Hollywood Blvd

WILLIAM HOLDEN

Vital Statistics

DOB: April 17, 1916 (Aries) in O'Fallon, Illinois
Birth Name: William Franklin Beedle, Jr.
Nickname: Golden Boy
            Bill
Height: 5'11"
Hair: Dark blonde (sometimes lightened for films)
Eyes: Hazel
Physique: Slender and athletic

Biographical Sketch

Father
  William Franklin Beedle (Industrial chemist)

Mother
  Mary (School teacher)

Siblings:
  Robert Westfield 1921-1944, (plane shot down in World War II)
  Richard (1925)

Boyhood Years

Reports state that Bill Holden was an energy packed young boy given to mischievous deeds and prone to seek adventure. The family being financially comfortable, Holden grew up privileged experiencing none of the struggles of some of his actor peers. Holden is remembered by all who knew him as a kind, caring man. He grew up to personify the handsome boy every girl longs to know. Participating in sports activities while in school directed his innate energy in a positive way.

William Holden, Gloria Swanson, and Eric von Stroheim in *Sunset Boulevard* – Paramount Pictures, 1950

Start of Career

A trip to New York at the age of 18 was the impetus that led to an interest in acting. Holden became intrigued by the idea of an acting career after attending a number of theatrical productions. When he returned home, he enrolled in Pasadena College to study chemistry as he was expected to follow in his father's professional footsteps. However he also joined a drama club that performed at the Pasadena Playhouse. One of his performances caught the attention of a talent scout who was in the audience. Holden was offered a contract. He didn't resist nor did his parents try to dissuade him.

Onscreen Persona

Twenty year old William Holden was so handsome; women fell in love with him at first sight. In those days movies were classified as A and B, with the latter being mostly trite. While cast in B films at the start of his career, Holden managed to capture a following among female movie fans. He was adored not only for his charismatic looks but because there was a warm strength about him that made women feel protected. It was the film *Golden Boy* that catapulted him to the top of the charts and to heartthrob status.

Although the picture was released in late 1939, Holden's popularity among women fans actually began to peak in 1940 when the film arrived in neighborhood theaters.

World War II interrupted his career. Holden joined the Air Force not long after the war began, serving as a lieutenant in a special service unit. He returned to civilian life and a burgeoning movie career. His look had undergone a subtle change. The bloom of boyishness had worn off just enough for him to be considered for substantial roles in *Sunset Boulevard* and *Born Yesterday* giving audiences an opportunity to see a multi-talented William Holden. No longer considered just a handsome, affable young man, but an actor who could wrench tears, draw laughter and earn disdain from movie goers as the roles he played required. When television beckoned Holden wooed a new female audience on his TV series *The Blue Knight*.

Personal Life

Earlier, in 1941 he married actress Brenda Marshall. The couple was considered by everyone to be ideal. Their divorce after thirty years of marriage created a bit of a stir among his female fans, puzzled and saddened by the divorce. At the same time, Holden admitted that he had lost his zest for acting and began drinking in earnest.

William Holden and Audrey Hepburn in *Sabrina* – Paramount Pictures, 1954

His drinking continued while his looks faded with little resemblance to his *Golden Boy* looks remaining. Still he had enough influence to continue to be selective about the roles he chose to play. And he chose well. Following his time in the service, Holden went on to create a solid female fan following.

As a bachelor he dated a number of Hollywood's top actresses but none captured his heart. Among the beauties he romanced were Grace Kelly and Audrey Hepburn. After meeting Stefanie Powers, things changed. The two fell in love and were together for many years, working as a team to build the Mount Kenya Safari Club, a wild animal sanctuary that Holden and a friend founded in the '70s.

Romance

Long term relationship with actress Stephanie Powers

Marriage

Brenda Marshall, 1941 – 1971 (Divorced)

Children

Peter
Scott (Died in January 2005 of cancer)
Virginia (Brenda's daughter by a previous marriage was adopted by Holden)

Fast Facts

- While his looks dissipated due to years of heavy drinking, William Holden's appeal to female en fans remained constant. Mention his name to a woman of a certain age and she will likely respond with a dreamy smile and a nostalgic gleam in her eye, remembering.
- He was a dedicated collector of Asian art. The collection was donated to the Palm Springs Museum of Art after his death.
- He loved fireworks displays.
- He is reported to have had a compelling singing voice, having sung in the choir as a young boy, but he never sang in films.
- He played the piano, clarinet and guitar.
- He favored poker as a card game and was reputedly good at it.
- By his own description, he was a very conventional fellow.
- He was a descendant of George Washington on his mother's side.
- He was the best man at the wedding of Ronald Reagan and Nancy Davis in 1952
- It has been rumored that he showered four times daily.
- He advocated for wildlife conservation in Africa that led the formation of the wildlife reserve that still exists.
- Rumor had it that Holden acted as an undercover agent for the CIA to deliver messages during his travels to leaders throughout the world
- His ashes were scattered in the Pacific Ocean.

Salary

Contract salary upon signing with Warner Brothers in 1939 was $50 a week for first three months increasing to $400 per week (when he worked on a film) after the first year.

Sunset Boulevard (1950) $30,000
Stalag 17 (1952) $48,535

Date of Death

November 16, 1981 from a hemorrhage caused when he fell, striking his head on the corner of a table. It is said that it took some time for him to bleed out. He was alone in his apartment at the time.

Awards and Nominations

Oscar (1952) *Stalag 17*

Star on the Walk of Fame

1651 Vine St.Hollywood.CA

William Holden and Kim Novak in *Picnic* – Columbia Pictures, 1955

VAN JOHNSON

Vital Statistics

Date of Birth: August 20, 1916 (Leo) in Newport, Rhode Island
Birth Name: Charles Van Dell Johnson
Height: 6'1"
Hair: Reddish blonde
Eyes: Blue
Physique: Athletic

Biographical Sketch

Father
   Charles E. Johnson (An athlete who performed on the parallel bar and did tumbling exhibits for the fun of it. His real job was as gymnastic instructor)

Mother
    Loretta (Housewife)

Boyhood Years

  The family dynamics provided a tense, strict atmosphere due to his father's philosophy that discipline and self-control were the watchwords of life. Loretta's rebellion led to alcoholism and eventual abandonment when Van was just three years old. While his father never applied corporal punishment he had only to give his only child a look to make him toe the line. Raised by his paternal grandmother who moved into their home after Mrs. Johnson left, Van's memory of his boyhood revolved around the smell of delicious Swedish cooking, a sparse but neat home and the affection of his grandmother. At an impressionable age, the young boy, realized he was expected to hold back his emotions never displaying feelings of joy, sorrow or anger. Van grew up wondering if he was loved despite the affection shown by his grandmother.

Van Johnson and Esther Williams in
Easy to Wed – MGM, 1946

Part of his success as an actor may have been due to the fact that he was able to adeptly express the emotions that he'd suppressed when he was growing up.

Onscreen Persona

  More than just the boy next door, he became the epitome of the high school sweetheart, the serviceman on leave and the Prince Charming of her dreams to female movie goers. It was his smooth movie voice, the smatter of freckles on his face and the genuine sparkle in his blue eyes that captivated feminine hearts.

Johnson made the screen light up as though bathed in sunshine with his warm smile and easy charm.

Personal Life

Rumor had it that in real life he was moody, often intolerant of any difficulty that might arise. Even minor incidents such as the lack of ice in a bucket or one of the children misbehaving at the dinner table could find him getting up from the table to silently seek solace in his bedroom according to his stepson Ned. Friends correlated this behavior with Johnson's emotionally repressed upbringing by a strict, no nonsense father and lack of nurturing from his mother.

In the forties, the studio was master. An actor under contract did as he was told in every facet of his personal life. Thus Van Johnson was coupled with any number of glamour gals of that era, his smiling face photographed at many Hollywood events with a beautiful actress on his arm. A strong friendship developed between Johnson, actor Keenan Wynn and his wife Evie who tooled around together on their motor cycles. It was a threesome of note as fan magazines displayed photos of the threesome relating stories of their strong bond of friendship.

Those who were close to Johnson were not too surprised when Johnson married Evie within hours of her having obtained a Mexican divorce from Wynn. Johnson had spent several weeks recuperating at the home of the Wynn's after three months in the hospital after a much publicized motorcycle accident. The friendship between the two men understandably ended as the threesome merged into the twosome of Van and Eve

Van Johnson, Katharine Hepburn, Spencer Tracy, and Angela Lansbury in *State of the Union* – MGM, 1948

Actress June Allyson, who made musicals with Johnson, remembered him as being very down to earth and often funny.

Marriages

Eve Wynn, January 1947-1968 (Divorced)

Children

Daughter, Schuyler January 6, 1948
Stepfather of Ned and Tracy Wynn

Fast Facts

- Shortly after his movie debut Johnson was involved in a near fatal accident that left him with a plate in his head.
- He always wore red socks, even with formal wear.
- He was a dancer on Broadway.
- He made a number of musicals during his reign at MGM.
- There was a rumor circulated that his female fans wore their bobby sox at half-mast upon learning of his marriage.
- He was nicknamed MGM's Golden Boy
- He signed a seven year contract with MGM in 1942 and was one of the studio's major stars for 15 years
- Doctors saved his life after the car accident caused by a drunk driver who ran a red light. A metal plate was placed in his head
- He was diagnosed with skin cancer, undergoing surgery in his forties and a second time a few years later.
- He was second at the box office after Bing Crosby in 1945.
- He was nicknamed The Voiceless Frank Sinatra at a time when Sinatra brought his female fans to screams. Johnson sang in some of his musical films, so the nickname was a kind of good natured ribbing.
- 1950 he debuted in Las Vegas as a song and dance man.
- His career continued for many years even after the war when heartthrobs of earlier years returned to the studios. Johnson had carved a niche into the hearts of his fans that that remained steadfast.
- Because his talent was versatile Johnson turned to writing as well making frequent guest star appearance on TV when the focus of his career changed.
- His also became active in summer stock and dinner theater.
- At the age of 75 he was still performing.
- Although the majority of his peers balked at the control of the studio contract, Johnson liked the structure of being a contract player. He thought of it as one big happy family.
- He had close friendships with Rosalind Russell, Lucille Ball and Spencer Tracey
- He was estranged from his daughter for many years.
- Johnson and his father's relationship remained strained even after Van was an adult.
- Upon retiring from acting, Johnson lived out his life in an assisted living facility in Nyack, New York

Salary

MGM contract paid him $350 a week

Date of Death

December 12, 2008 in Nyack, N.Y. of natural causes. He was cremated.

Awards and Nominations

The film *Two Girls and a Sailor* in which Johnson co-starred with June Allyson and Gloria De Haven was nominated for an Oscar, a rarity for a musical.
Nominated for an Emmy in 1976 for outstanding single performance in a television series, *Rich Man, Poor Man.*

Star on the Walk of Fame

6600 Hollywood Blvd.

Van Johnson and Elizabeth Taylor in
The Last Time I Saw Paris – MGM, 1954

PETER LAWFORD

Vital Statistics

DOB: September 7, 1923 (Virgo) in London, England
Birth Name: Peter Sydney Ernest Aylen
Nickname: His mother called him Pierrot.
    Frank Sinatra dubbed him brother-in-law when Lawford joined The Rat Pack in 1960
Height: 6'
Hair: Brown
Eyes: Blue
Physique: Slender & Firm

Biographical Sketch

Father
   Lt. General Sydney Lawford (A war hero who was knighted soon after the end of the WWI. He was also a part time actor.)

Mother
   May (A journalist whose columns appeared in London papers, she became an actor in later years. Sir Sydney was her third husband. He was also the father to her son (Peter) conceived while she was married to Major Ernest Vaughn Aylen who was under Lawford's command at the time. The scandal eventually forced the family to take refuge in the United States. It has been said that Peter did not find out about his true paternal parentage until he was a mature adult.)

Boyhood Years

Peter Lawford and Elizabeth Taylor in *Little Women* – MGM, 1949

Because he traveled the globe with his parents, Lawford had no formal education, but was tutored. He developed a complex about this and always felt inferior to other boys because his education was what he considered to be limited. Nevertheless he was fluid in French, Spanish and Italian and could hold his own in any conversation with his peers. By the age of 15, he had traveled the globe a number of times. In his early teens, Peter ran through a glass door sustaining severe injuries to his right arm and hand. Although doctors managed to save the arm, it was slightly deformed causing the youngster to develop yet another complex. In later years the injury resulted in his being exempt from the draft during World War II. A boon to both the actor and the industry. Around the same time the family found their funds depleted when the UK entered the war in 1939. Having moved to Palm Beach, Florida around that time Lord and Lady Lawford held the social position of a kind of royalty within the community.

Onscreen Persona

Movies were the lure enticing women into movie theaters. With his clipped, British accent and aristocratic good looks, he went on to become a major force on the Silver Screen. One of the few actors available to fill the many roles that rolled out of writers, Lawford at that time, he made his screen debut in the film *A Yank at Eton* and later gained critical praise for his role in *The White Cliffs of Dover* in his role as a young WWII soldier. He always came across as a refined, highly educated Englishman with impeccable manners. One of his most endearing roles was that of Laurie in the 1949 remake of *Little Women*. He was considered the romantic lead at MGM. The forties were Lawford's claim to fame.

Personal Life

Romances

Lawford parlayed his onscreen roles into his off screen life with many romantic escapades. The youthful actor was romance personified. A pert messenger on the MGM lot spent a summer being courted by the twenty three year old actor who showered her with roses and attention. He grew into a "man about town" reputation as he courted some of the most glamorous beauties of the decade, ie: Ava Gardner, June Allyson, and Lana Turner, (with whom he had a relationship of many months). But he could not to marry his one true love due to studio pressure and the narrow thinking at the time.

Peter Lawford and Bette Davis in *Dead Ringer* – Warner Brothers, 1964

Lawford and beautiful African American actress Dorothy Dandridge fell deeply in love and planned on getting married at a time when racial intolerance was widespread. In the end, much like a melodramatic movie script, the two parted ways realizing that it would end both their careers if the relationship continued.

Marriages

Patricia Kennedy, 1954 -1966 (Divorced)
Mary Rowan, October 30, 1971- January 2, 1975 (Divorced)
Deborah Gould, June 24, 1976-1977 (Divorced)
Pat Seton, July 1984 until his death (They'd been together since 1976)

Children

All with first wife Pat Kennedy
Christopher, March 29, 1955
Sydney (daughter), August 25, 1956
Victoria Frances, November 4, 1958
Robin Elizabeth, July 2, 1961

Fast Facts

- In his lean days before his career took off, Lawford worked as a parking lot attendant in West Palm Beach, Fla. and as an usher in a Westwood, CA movie theater.
- He became a U.S. citizen so he could vote for his brother in law John Kennedy in the 1960 presidential election.
- He was a year old when his biological parents married. Lawford did not learn the truth about his parentage until he was in his late twenties.
- In 1945 he won a poll conducted by fan magazine *Modern Screen* as the most popular actor in Hollywood and his fan mail increased by thousands a week.
- Rumor had it that Marilyn Monroe and President Kennedy often had clandestine liaisons in Lawford's beach front home
- After severing ties with MGM, Lawford went on to form his own company, producing a number of popular TV series.
- He named his production company Chrislaw after his firstborn, Christopher Lawford.
- His mother occasionally appeared in *The Thin Man* series in which Lawford starred.
- Once close buddies, the friendship of Lawford and Sinatra was severed due to Sinatra's jealousy over Ava Gardner and Lawford having lunch together one afternoon. They patched it up after a few years, but the relationship hit a final impasse when Lawford was a guest in the home of Bing Crosby (a staunch Republican). Sinatra, an avowed Democrat, could not forgive Lawford for what he considered a breach of their friendship.
- Lawford was the first one of the original Rat Pack to die.

Salary

His contract with MGM called for him to be paid $100 per week with guarantee of 40 weeks for one year.

Date of Death

December 24, 1984 in Los Angeles of cardiac arrest complicated by kidney and liver disease

Interred

Cremated and interred in Westwood Village Memorial Park Cemetery until a dispute with his widow and the cemetery resulted in the removal of his ashes that were then dispersed in the Pacific Ocean. A plaque with his name remains at the interment site.

Star on the Walk of Fame

6922 Hollywood Blvd.

Peter Lawford, Frank Sinatra, Dean Martin, and Sammy Davis, Jr. in *Sergeants 3* – United Artists, 1962

ROBERT MITCHUM

Vital Statistics

DOB: August 6, 1917 (Leo) in Bridgeport, Connecticut
Birth name: Robert Charles Durman Mitchum
Nicknames: Mitch
           Old Rumple Eyes
Height: 6'1"
Hair: Brown
Eyes: Blue
Physique: Broad shoulders muscular arms, slightly barrel chested
Outstanding Feature:
  Deep dimple in chin, hooded eyes

Biographical Sketch

Father
  James Thomas Mitchum (A railroad worker killed on the job when Mitchum was barely two)

Mother
  Harry Anniette Gudnerson (Line O Type Operator)

Siblings

John younger by 2 1/2 years (actor)
Julie, four years older

Boyhood Years

Robert Mitchum and Burgess Meredith in *The Story of G.I. Joe* – United Artists, 1945

Having lost his birth father when he was just two, Mitchum was raised by his mother and stepfather, a major in the British army. As a teenager he showed disdain for all authority figures. This created a discipline problem for his parents while giving Mitchum a sense of daring adventure. He was sent to live with his grandparents in the hope that they would cast a good influence on him. Instead he was expelled from school after getting into a scuffle with the principal. At 14, Mitchum ran away from home, He was later sent to a chain gang for vagrancy, having been found riding the rails.

While working at Lockheed Aircraft in California, his sister coaxed him into joining an amateur theater group during which time he played small parts in a number of films. It was in 1945 as Lt. Walker in *The Story of G.I. Joe* that his talent finally gained recognition. Following the release of the film, his career zoomed upwards. Suffice it to say that in his acting roles Mitchum tended to play convincingly as a rebellious nonconformist drawing from his life experience.

Onscreen Persona

Despite what appeared to be a laid back approach it was this very ability to make seeming effortlessness. Fans of the female persuasion fell for the bad boy attitude. As women often do they wanted to change him, confident that all he needed was the love of a good woman. An icon in the '40's he moved easily into super stardom by the early 1950's. Mitchum appeared to accept his stardom lightly, but there are those who stated that the actor pretended nonchalance for effect. Perhaps it was a leftover from his prankster days.

Personal Life

Marriage

Childhood sweethearts, Robert was sixteen and Dorothy fourteen when they met. They were married in 1940. Although rumors persisted that the very private, taciturn actor often had romantic liasons with costars, he and his wife remained married for fifty seven years at the time of his death.

Children

James (actor)
Christopher (actor)
Trina

Grandchildren

Bentley
Price
Carrie   actress
Kian   model

Great Grandchildren

Cappy
Grace

Robert Mitchum and Jean Simmons in *Angel Face* – RKO Pictures, 1953

Fast Facts

- Served as a medic in WWII for received the Victory Medal
- Shirley MacLaine spoke candidly of her three year affair with Mitchum on the Joy Behar show in 2011, stating that he was a very brilliant man

- He continued to smoke pot throughout his life
- In 1968 a group of teenagers declared him to be the coolest of celebrities
- He was a big fan of Elvis
- He was a chronic insomniac all of his adult life
- Collected quarter horses, housing them on a 76 acre ranch near Los Angeles
- It was rumored that Mitchum made it a practice to plant a kiss on the cheek of any woman who asked for his autograph.
- His song lyrics and the poetry he wrote revealed a soft side few people knew about.
- He played the saxophone

Salary

Undercurrent 1946 $25,000
Out of the Past 1947 $10,400
Home From the Hill 1960 $200,000 plus % of gross
Ryan's Daughter 1970 $870,000

Date of Death

July 1, 1997 in Santa Barbara, CA of cancer

Interred

He was cremated, his ashes sent to sea by his wife and neighbor Jane Russell. As he wished, no memorial service was held.

Awards and Nominations

1945	Best Supporting Actor *Story of G.I. Joe*
1958	BAFTA (Best Foreign Film Actor)
1960	Golden Laurel (Top Male Star)
1960	Golden Laurel (Top Male Dramatic Performance)
1962	Golden Laurel (Top Male Star)
1963	Golden Laurel (Top Action Performance)
1950	Sour Apple (Hollywood Women's Press Club) Least Cooperative Actor
1978	Sho West Convention, USA Lifetime Achievement.
1980	Los Angeles Film Critics Association
1950	Sour Apple by Hollywood Women's Press Club for Least Cooperative Actor
1960	Best Actor *Home from the Hill*
1960	Best Actor *The Sundowners*
1967	Best Actor
1978	Sho West Convention, USA, Lifetime Achievement
1980	Los Angeles Film Critics Association, Career Achievement

1991   NBR USA, Career Achievement
1992   Cecil B. DeMille Award
1993   San Sebastian International Film Festival, Donostia Achievement

Star on the Walk of Fame

South Side of 6200 block of Hollywood Blvd.

Robert Mitchum and Marilyn Monroe in
River of No Return – 20th Century Fox, 1954

GREGORY PECK

Vital Statistics

Date of Birth: April 15, 1916 (Aries) in La Jolla, California
Name at Birth: Eldred Gregory Peck
Height: 6'3"
Hair: Black
Eyes: Brown.
Physique: Well proportioned & Firm

Biographical Sketch

Father
  Gregory Peck, Sr. (Pharmacist)

Mother
  Bernice Mae Ayres (known as "Bunny")

Boyhood Years

Peck's parents divorced when he was five years old. An only child Peck was raised by his paternal grandmother in La Jolla until he was ten. Of his young boyhood the actor often said that his fondest memories were of being taken to the movies by his grandmother and of his dog.

At the age of ten he was sent to a Roman Catholic Military School. At fourteen he went to live with his father in San Diego where he attended high school. After graduation he enrolled in what was then Teachers College (now San Diego State University). A sports enthusiast Peck joined the track team. He also enrolled in theatre and public speaking courses but after a year switched to Berkeley where he was a pre-medical student. Strong and athletic Peck joined the university rowing crew.

Start of Career

Gregory Peck and Maria Palmer in *Days of Glory* – RKO Radio Pictures, 1944

Peck's dramatic teacher encouraged him to join the University Little Theater. It was then that he became interested in an acting career. In his senior year he was cast in five plays by the director of The Little Theater on campus. During that time, Peck worked as a hasher for a sorority in exchange for meals. Graduating with a BA in English he took off for New York to study acting at the Neighborhood Playhouse. A scout saw him perform one night and persuaded Peck to join the group of young actors at Selznick studios. His career was launched with the film *Days of Glory* in 1944. That same year *The Keys to the Kingdom* in which he had a leading role was also released, His career was firmly established at that time. He was the epitome of quiet charm, but even when he deviated to more sinister on screen roles, his popularity did not diminish.

Onscreen Persona

Tall, dark and exceedingly handsome Peck spoke in a voice that commanded attention. This combination proved to be fodder for the romantic imaginations of female movie goers who couldn't get enough of the young actor.

Due to a back injury Peck was exempt from the service during World War II thereby was offered a number of choice roles.

Personal Life

Marriages

Greta Kukkonen October, 1943- December 30, 1955 (Divorced)
Veronique Passani December 31, 1955 until his death

Children

Stephen, Carey, Jonathan (with Greta)
Anthony, Cecilia (with Veronique)

Fast Facts

Gregory Peck and Audrey Hepburn
in *Roman Holiday* –
Paramount Pictures, 1953

- 1941 David Selznick lamented about the newcomer, "I'm sorry to say that I don't see what we could do with Gregory Peck. He photographs like Abraham Lincoln. If he has personality, I can't see it."
- Four years later, 1945, Peck was one of Selznick Studio's hottest actors, sought on loan by major studios for leading roles in their films.
- In 1946 Peck and friends actor Mel Ferrer and actress Dorothy McGuire founded the La Jolla Playhouse that is still thriving at the University of California at San Diego.
- In July, 1951 Sid Skolsky stated in his column that Peck had been nominated for an Oscar more times than any other actor
- He slept in an extra wide and low bed
- He was a good dancer
- He thought of becoming a priest when he was an adolescent
- He was for gun control legislation.

- Although raised a Catholic, Peck did not see eye to eye with many of the Catholic doctrines. As a liberal Catholic he supported gay rights and was pro-choice on abortion.
- On June 12, 1975 Peck's son Jonathan committed suicide. He was thirty. Peck was deeply affected by Jonathan's death and was never the same afterward.
- In 2003 Atticus Finch, the character portrayed by Peck in *To Kill a Mockingbird* was named by the American Film Institute as the #1 Hollywood hero of the century.
- In later years upon hearing that an actor was being paid 30 million dollars per picture, Peck commented "I was born too soon."
- A U.S. commemorative stamp honoring Peck was issued On April 28, 2011 in Beverly Hills, CA.

Salary

Days of Glory   1944 $10,000
The Purple Plain 1954 $250,000

Ironically Peck took a big cut in salary plus a percentage to make *The Omen*. He made the most money of his career from this film that eventually earned 60 million dollars at the box office.

Date of Death
June 12, 2003 of cardio respiratory arrest complicated by bronchial pneumonia

Interred
Cathedral of Our Lady of the Angeles, Los Angeles, CA

Academy Awards, Best Actor

Keys of the Kingdom   1945
The Yearling   1947
Gentlemen's Agreement   1949
Twelve O'Clock High   1951
To Kill a Mockingbird   1962

Other Awards

Golden Globe *The Yearling* 1947
Golden Globe *To Kill a Mockingbird* Best Actor 1963
Henrietta Award for World Film Favorite, Male 1955
The Jean Hersholt Humanitarian Award 1968
Presidential Medal of Freedom by President Lyndon B. Johnson 1969
Cecil B. DeMille Award 1969
SAG Life Achievement Award by Screen Actors Guild 1971
AFI Life Achievement Award given by the American Film Institute 1989

Crystal Globe award for outstanding artistic contribution to world cinema 1996
National Medal of Arts 1998
Emmy /TV mini series *Moby Dick* 1999
2000 The National University of Ireland made him a Doctor of Letters.
Founding Patron, University College Dublin School of Film

Star on the Walk of Fame

Originally located at 6100 Hollywood Blvd in 1955, the plaque was one of a dozen "Stars" stolen in a rash of burglaries. It was replaced in November, 2005.

Gregory Peck and Mary Badham in
To Kill a Mockingbird –
Universal Pictures, 1962

Chapter 3
THE FIFTIES

Best remembered by many as the last decade of sanity It was an era when people could leave their doors unlocked, family values were prime and children could still walk home from school and play out front without fear of being abducted or harmed. It was also the decade when television was introduced with families gathered around their sets after dinner to watch whatever was programmed instead of going to the movies.

Competition with the small screen created a marked decline in attendance at movies forcing many theaters throughout the country to close. Hollywood suffered outside the box office as well.

The hunt for communists and sympathizers descended upon the community creating a climate of fear and suspicion. A special committee formed and led by Senator Joe McCarthy sought the Red Menace in movie land with all of the zealousness of earlier witch hunts.

While the majority of actors remained mum, some stepped up to the plate to report what they thought of as communist infiltration within the Hollywood community. It became a time of darkness and strife especially as the interrogation of film actors, writers and directors about alleged communist activities was daily fare on television.

The film *The Way We Were*, produced decades later, touched on this committee and the consequences of the investigation that resulted in the loss of work and ultimately the devastation of lives for many within the Hollywood community.

1950's Events

- The Opening of Disneyland, The hip swiveling appearance of Elvis on the *Ed Sullivan Show*, Cuba under the dictatorship of Castro.

- The average income in 1950 was $3200, a new car $1500 with a gallon of gas going for eighteen cents. By the close of the decade income had risen to around $5,000 and the price of a new car was $2200.

- The Cold War overshadowed family life as bomb shelters sprang up in many back yards with the spread of rumors of possible nuclear attack. The good and the bad seemed to coexist at a time when family life struggled to remain wholesome and hopeful.

- It was also the decade when the term "brain washed" came into use. The release of the film *The Manchurian Candidate* staring Frank Sinatra gave us a glimpse of what brain washing actually entailed.

- This is the decade that produced the mothers and grandmothers of today.

- The price of a movie tickets was around $.50 at the start of the era.

- On screen a unique mix of heartthrobs emerged. Actors displayed an inner core of sensitivity that calmly embraced female fans. These were men who women felt genuinely cared about women but without obvious sentimentality. Actors were handsome, exuding an air of inner strength in place of the near beauty of other decades.

- Closed mouth kisses were as ardent as the tongue swallowing kisses of recent decades.

- Women went to the movies seeking a kind of affirmation of themselves as they accepted the changing image of the heartthrob On screen.

- There was prosperity in the wake of the Cold War.

- It was also the decade that finally saw the demise of the "studio system" as actors were freed from a kind of bondage, no longer under the thumb of studio moguls dictating personal aspects of their lives. Many actors sought further independence by forming their own production companies.

- Cinerama, Todd-AO and Vista Vision generated expansive films enticing people back into the movie theaters.

MARLON BRANDO

Vital Statistics

DOB: April 3, 1924 (Aries) in Omaha, Nebraska
Name at birth: Marlon Brandeau
Nicknames: Bud
    Mumbles (bestowed upon him by Frank Sinatra)
Height: 5'10"
Hair: Dark Brown
Eyes: Dark Brown
Physique: Toned and Muscular in early years

Biographical Sketch

Father
  Marlon Brando, Sr. (Salesman)

Mother
  Dorothy Pennebaker (An actress in amateur theatricals and mentor of Henry Fonda)

Siblings

  Jocelyn (actress)
  Frannie (artist)

Boyhood Years

Rumor has it that both parents were alcoholics. His father was also remote. Brando was a restless, difficult child sent to military school in Minnesota by his father. Ever rebellious, he was expelled prior to graduation. Brando continued to "search for himself" eventually moving to New York where sister Jocelyn enrolled him in a Dramatic Workshop. At last he felt that he had found his niche and devoted himself to a career as an actor from that time on. As an aspiring actor he felt a purpose in life. Something he had never experienced before.

Marlon Brando and Teresa Wright in
The Men – United Artists, 1950

Start of Career

He first gained recognition in the film *The Men* (1950).

When John Garfield turned down the offer to play Stanley Kowalski in the film version of *A Streetcar Named Desire*, Brando went on to reprise his stage role in the movie.

Streetcar brought him an Academy Award nomination along with accolades from critics and fans alike. It is considered to be one of the best films ever made. The affirmations and acceptance Brando had sought throughout his young life was his at last. Although many scouts offered to have him screen tested, Brando chose to continue as an independent talent unwilling to keep within the parameters of the still prevailing studio contract.

Onscreen Persona

Brando dug deep into the core of his being as he morphed into what has been called one of the greatest actors of all time. Even as the chauvinistic, roughhewed Stanley Kowalski there was a subtle appeal that made women gravitate to him Although Brando was frequently cast as a kind of anti-hero his "soft center" was revealed in films like *On the Waterfront* and as the romantic lead in *Sayonara*. He was young, well built and openly sensual. Women longed for him. He may have been rough on the outside, but women fans saw beneath the crusty top layer into the tender layer beneath

Brando played against the establishment whether on screen or off.

Personal Life

The true core of Brando emerged as a frequent supporter of the "little" guy. He had a penchant for lost causes. In real life Brando was probably a rebel with a cause. It was this underbelly of compassion that shone through on the screen lending credence to his reputation of being one of the most brilliant actors in film history. However, his innate rebellion spilling over into his personal life was often the source of much consternation.

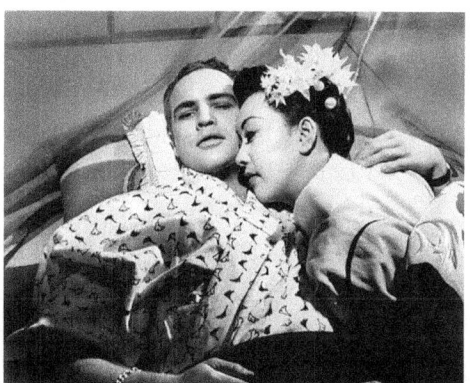

Marlon Brando and Miiko Taka in *Sayonara* – Warner Brothers, 1957

Marriages

Anna Kashfi (actress) 1957- May, 1958 (Divorced)
Movita Casenada (actress) 1960-1962 (Divorced)
Tarita Terpia (Tahitian actress) August 10, 1962-July, 1972 (Divorced)

Children

He has been reputed to have fathered eleven children, some by his housekeeper.

Grandchildren

Tuki Brando, 1990 and rumored to be twenty nine others

Fast Facts

- Frances Ford Coppola, author of the bestselling book *The Godfather* wanted Brando to play the part of Don Corleone but had to fight the studio heads until at last Brando was given the part.
- He owned an island atoll in Tahiti
- He contributed a large sum of money to Michael Jackson to help him launch his Heal the World Foundation.
- He often spent time at Michael Jackson's Neverland to rest and recuperate.
- He was described by female fans as having basic animal magnetism
- He was the second actor to turn down a Best Actor Award (for *The Godfather*), boycotting the ceremony and sending instead an American Indian Rights activist wearing full Apache dress who gave Brando's reasons for the boycott in front of an astounded audience of his peers.
- Elia Kazan said of Brando "his sexuality was rooted in a duality; an ambivalence between a gentle yearning and a dangerous dissatisfaction."
- Unlike his contemporaries, Brando did not arouse the hue and cry of teenagers. Instead his fans were mature, adoring women who were drawn to that animal magnetism he naturally exuded.
- Although it is said that he gave one of his greatest performances in *Last Tango in Paris* (1973) there was much controversy over the film's erotic nature so while he deserved the nomination, the Oscar went to another fine actor.
- He was a champion of the underdog.
- In the 60's Brando's career took a downward spiral as one by one of his films were met with a dismal audience response.
- Brando confided in a friend that he and Marilyn Monroe had been good friends as well as lovers.
- The debut of *The Godfather* (1972) re-established Brando's career with his portrayal of the title role. While no longer a Hollywood Heartthrob, he remained an icon and a Hollywood legend on his own terms.
- He was respected for his acting genius.
- His innate talent astonished such notables as George Englund and John Huston.
- With the filming of *Superman*, Brando was chosen to portray Superman's father. Once again resurrecting a dimming career.
- Prior to his death Brando recorded his voice for *The Godfather: The Game* reprising his role of Don Corleone.

Personal quotes

"Never confuse the size of your paycheck with the size of your talent."
"The only thing a actor owes his public is not to bore them."
"If we are not our brother's keeper, at least let us not be his executioner."
"I don't mind that I'm fat. You still get the same money."

Salary

$40,000 *The Men*
$3 Million for *Superman*
Net worth $100 Million

Date of Death

July 1, 2004 at UCLA Medical Center of respiratory failure.

Interred

His body was cremated and ashes scattered in Death Valley and Tahiti.

Awards and Nominations

8 times for Oscar
4 times for the BAFTA Awards
Best Actor *On the Waterfront* (1954) Golden Globe
Best Actor *The Godfather* (1972)

Star on the Walk of Fame

1765 Vine Street

Marlon Brando and Al Pacino in
The Godfather – Paramount Pictures, 1972

ROSSANO BRAZZI

Vital Statistics

DOB: September 18, 1916 (Virgo) in Bologna, Italy
Name at Birth: Rossano Brazzi
Height: 5'10"
Hair: Sandy Brown
Eyes: Blue
Physique: Athletic

Biographical Sketch

Father
  Aldemo Brazzi (Shoe manufacturer)

Mother
  Maria Ghedini Brazzi (Shoe designer)

Siblings

  Younger brother Oscar
  Younger sister Franca

Boyhood Years

Having lost two children before he was born, Mrs. Brazzi sheltered Rossano fearing he might also be taken from her. It has been said that he was much overprotected and catered to, young Rossano delighted in the attention he received from his family and friends, often entertaining then by reciting poetry. He had a strong singing voice, appearing in the leading role in a school operetta when he was in junior high. It was his first experience of audience acceptance outside of family and friends. A lover of opera Brazzi often sang his favorites around the house.

Rossano Brazzi, Humphrey Bogart, and Ava Gardner in *The Barefoot Contessa* – United Artists, 1954

In his mid-teens Brazzi experienced the pressures of politics under the dictatorship of Mussolini. While outwardly it didn't appear to affect him, he joined the Resistance as soon as he was of age.

A lover of sports, he was on his college soccer team for two years and slated for professional boxing matches in Florence and Rome. However after seriously injuring his opponent, Brazzi threw his gloves in the ring and never boxed again.

At the age of eighteen, his father convinced him to study law at San Marco University in Florence. It was there that his interest in acting was piqued. Friends talked him in to trying out for a part in a little theater production. At the time Brazzi was intent upon fulfilling his father's wish that he become a lawyer. Upon receiving his law degree, young Brazzi was apprenticed to a friend of his father's in Rome. A series of tragic events resulting from the political climate of the country struck the family.

Rumors have circulated about the reasons for the demise of Brazzi's parent, one that they were murdered by members of the Facist party, the other that his father suffered a fatal stroke politics the family was closely watched and close members brutalized during the reign of Mussolini.

When WWII erupted in the European theater Italian actors were exempt from entering the military service. The government decided that actors were needed to make the movies that built national morale and entertained the troupes as well. He was strongly anti-facist due to the afterward.

Start of Career

Rossano Brazzi and Katharine Hepburn in
Summertime – United Artists, 1955

In 1949 he moved to the U.S. and was immediately cast in the technicolor remake of *Little Women*. A few years later he gained International notice for his role in *The Barefoot Contessa*. But his most memorable role, one that stirred the hearts of women everywhere, was that of Katherine Hepburn's lover in *Summertime*, now a classic film. Next came the much celebrated *South Pacific* in which the actor wooed Mitzi Gaynor. Despite his having a fine singing voice the studio in its infinite wisdom had his singing voice dubbed. The surge of popularity as a romantic lead in the '50's, led Brazzi's career well into the 80's after which he played mostly character roles.

Onscreen Persona

In the decade of the 50's Brazzi popularity was rated high in Italy and in the U.S women readily surrendered to his innate charm and good looks.

Personal Life

While attending the University he met and fell deeply in love with Lidia Bertolini, a young woman from a titled family who was majoring in literature. They planned to have a church wedding with family and friends in attendance, but Lidia's aristocratic parents did not take to Rossano as their son-in-law. After dating for two years, the couple eloped to Rome over all parental objections.

Brazzi's parents felt that marriage would hamper his career and also thought they were too young. On January 25, 1955 they couple celebrated their fifteenth anniversary by renewing their vows at a church in Florence with both sets of parents and other family members in attendance. The Pope sent a special benediction the marriage lasted forty-one years, ending sadly with Lidia's death.

Marriages

Lidia Bertolini January 25, 1940 until her death in April, 1981
Ilse Fischer (former housekeeper) 1984 until his death

Fast Facts

- Brazzi believed that he had ESP having experienced two very prophetic dreams during his young adult years. One was the prediction of the illness and death of his youthful love, the other the prediction of the illness and eventual death of his first wife before she was diagnosed with pancreatic cancer by a doctor. Throughout his life he experienced flashes of knowing.
- Unlike the suave sophisticated playboy he portrayed On screen. Brazzi enjoyed the quiet life of a solid marriage.
- During the run of *South Pacific* the actor received 30,000 fan letters a week
- He has been described by a family member as a very handsome, kind natured, a spiritually evolved man.
- He was a Freemason
- As a young girl, his second wife Isle, told her mother that one day she would marry Brazzi.

Salary

Three Coins in the Fountain $25,000

Date of Death

December 24, 1984 in Rome, Italy of a viral infection

Interred

Buried in Rome, Italy

Rossano Brazzi and Mitzi Gaynor in
South Pacific – 20th Century Fox, 1958

Star on the Walk of Fame

Brazzi does not have a Star on the Walk of Fame

RICHARD BURTON

Vital Statistics

DOB: November 10, 1925 (Scorpio) in Pontrhydyfen, Wales
Name at Birth: Richard Walter Jenkins
Height: 5'9"
Hair: Dark Brown
Eyes: Blue
Physique: Firm & Wiry

Biographical Sketch

Father
   Richard Walter Jenkins (Coal miner)

Mother
   Edith (Housewife)

Siblings
Burton was the twelfth of thirteen children

Boyhood Years

Because his mother died giving birth to her thirteenth child, two-year-old Richard was sent to live with his married sister Cecilia and her husband. He adored his sister who became his surrogate mother.

Richard Burton and Olivia DeHavilland in *My Cousin Rachel* – 20th Century Fox, 1952

As he grew into young manhood he was mentored by a tutor, who took charge of his education. It was Philip Burton, the tutor, who encouraged the young boy's interest in the theater having recognized a latent talent. He taught the Burton manners and guided his upbringing. It is said that Richard's father wanted one of his sons to "live in sunshine," so encouraged his youngest son to lead a normal life rather than go into the mines. In school Richards excelled in sports, playing rugby and cricket. He had a penchant for literature. To earn spending money, the youth delivered newspapers, hauled manure, and was a messenger. He left school at the age of sixteen to work full time. In Burton's late teens he joined a dramatic group. It was at that time that Richard became Phillip Burton's ward. The schoolmaster and the young man developed a close father/son relationship. Philips Burton encouraged his ward to seriously consider an acting career. Encouraged by his mentor, Richard gained notice performing in school productions. However he decided to quit school at the age of sixteen to start earning a living. Later,

Richard submitted to intense studying in school subjects as well as those that were to prepare him for his future acting career.

In 1943 he was allowed to enroll in Exeter College, Oxford for six months. At that time he had joined the RAF, however he could not become a pilot due to poor eyesight so served his country as a navigator.

Upon making the decision to seek a career he changed his name to Richard Burton to honor his mentor. Young Burton went on to gain critical acclaim as a theatrical star in the late '40's and early 1950's. Discharged from the service, he signed with a theatrical agency. He had gone to London by then hoping to make his fortune. He was soon admired by British critics who considered him to be leading man material. But his first reviews were for theatrical performances. Burton's dulcet tones and his innate ability to charm came across the stage effortlessly. In time word of this special talent reached Hollywood film makers and he was wooed by Hollywood agents At first was cast in roles that the public failed to notice, it was the lead in *My Cousin Rachel* that made producers and audiences sit up and take notice. Author Daphne du Maurier had urged the studio to cast the young Burton in the lead of the film based upon her book. And a star was recognized at last.

Onscreen Persona

Although he seldom smiled on screen, women loved his brooding look. Charismatic and compelling, the Burton spell was cast upon every woman in the movie theater audience. His melodic voice alone held them in a hypnotic spell of adoration. No matter rumors of his womanizing, drinking or other "naughty" habits, when Burton appeared on screen women sat back and dreamed.

The vibrant tone of his voice sending shivers up and down their spines.

Richard Burton and Elizabeth Taylor in *Cleopatra* – 20th Century Fox, 1963

In My Cousin Rachel (1952), his first role of note, Burton's quiet but strong demeanor tugged at the hearts of women in the audience. It continued to draw women into the movie houses as Burton starred in other notable films throughout the decade. He went on to enchant until his untimely death at age 58.

Personal Life

It has been said that this actor slept with every woman with whom he co-starred except for actress Julie Andrews, who did not succumb to his charms.

Romances

The most torrid and notorious relationship was the one that emerged during the making of *Cleopatra* between Elizabeth Taylor and Burton. Both were married to other people at the time, but that did not curtail the intensity of desire they felt for one another. Years before *Cleopatra*, Elizabeth Taylor had made a somewhat negative comment about Burton who she met briefly at a Hollywood party. "He seems so full of himself and he never stops talking." she is reputed to have said.

The dynamic love duo of Taylor and Burton created copy in dozens of magazines, filling gossip columns during the filming of *Cleopatra* in London and Rome. Their passion had been ignited and continued to grow. Despite the fact that Elizabeth's husband, Eddie Fisher, was on the set almost every day, once the affair had begun it became obvious to everyone within vision of the two lovers. They were soon the "in" couple. Speculation had it that the affair created added interest to movie goers who flocked to see *Cleopatra*, vicariously enjoying the love scenes between Taylor and Burton on screen. They fact that fervent kisses were for real, not just for the camera, made it all the more intriguing to women.

The couple bought property in the quiet little town of Puerta Vallarta, Mexico that soon burgeoned into the thriving, hustle and bustle of a small city as tourists sought out the place where the two lovers fled for privacy. Today Puerta Vallarta continues to bear the aura of Taylor and Burton's love affair.

Marriages

Sybil Williams February 5, 1949-December 5, 1963 (Divorced)
Elizabeth Taylor March 15, 1964-June 26, 1974 (Divorced)
Elizabeth Taylor October 10, 1975-August 1, 1976 (Divorced for second time)
Susan Hunt August, 1976-1982 (Divorced)
Sally Hay July 3, 1983 until his death

Children

Kate Burton (actress) and Jessica Burton (with Sybil Williams)
Maria Burton adopted (with Elizabeth Taylor)

Fast Facts

- He was buried in a red suit in honor of his Welsh ancestry. A copy of Dylan Thomas' poems was buried with him according to reports.
- Burton was considered by many in Hollywood to be a theatrical actor second only to Laurence Olivier.
- He was known as a womanizer, rumored to woo women to bed by reciting soliloquies from Shakespeare.

- He quit Oxford after only six months to seek a career in Hollywood.
- He was nominated seven times for an Oscar, but never won.
- He put his career aside to enlist in the RAF during WWII.
- His first love being theater, he continued to perform on stage for many years even after achieving success in Hollywood.
- He was an avid book reader and had a much-admired command of English poetry.
- He taught English poetry at Oxford in the early 1970's.
- He loved to do crossword puzzles.
- He was an insomniac.
- Ignoring his family's objections, Burton married Taylor on Sunday, March 15 1964 in Montreal, Canada
- As they entered a hotel in Boston fans ripped Burtons coat off in their zealousness to touch him.
- Burton created a national flurry of excitement when he gifted Elizabeth Taylor with a 69 carat diamond ring. Cost was $1.5 million.
- Burton on Burton: "I've done an awful lot of rubbish in order to have somewhere to go in the morning.
- The more I study religions, the more I am convinced that man never worshipped anything but himself."
- Women on Burton: Elizabeth Taylor (early) on the set of *Cleopatra* "he is a devious snake pit." Suffice it to say she changed her opinion of him.
- Actress Lee Remick "He has this marvelous way of making a woman feel as if she is the only one in the world. And it is bliss."
- Tammy Grimes "He makes a woman feel beautiful."
- He once tried his Shakespeare seduction technique on Lauren Bacall, but failed because her heart and love was always with Bogart.

Salary

My Cousin Rachel $50,000
Wagner   (1983) $1,000,000
Net Worth $50 million

Date of Death

August 5, 1984 in Switzerland of a cerebral hemorrhage

Interred

Vieux Cemetery, Celigny Geneva, Switzerland

Awards and Nominations

Six Academy Award nominations for Best Actor

Five Nominations for Golden Globe for Best Actor
One time by the Academy for Best Supporting Actor

Golden Globe for Most Promising Newcomer 1953
Golden Globe for Best Actor Equus 1978

Star on the Walk of Fame

Posthumously in 2012 alongside that of Elizabeth Taylor's Star at 6336 Hollywood Blvd.

Richard Burton and Robert Goulet in the stage production of *Camelot* - 1960

MONTGOMERY CLIFT

Vital Statistics

Date of Birth: October 17, 1920 (Libra) in Omaha, Nebraska
Birth Name: Edward Montgomery Clift
Nickname: Monty
Height: 5' 10"
Hair: Dark Brown
Eyes: Light Gray
Physique: Wiry

Biographical Sketch

Father
  William Brooks Clift (Banker)

Mother
  Ethel Anderson Fogg (An heiress in her own right, known as Sunny)

Siblings
Older brother Brooks
Twin sister, Roberta (born minutes before Monty)

Boyhood Years

Early years spent in Europe as mother strove to expose her children to the culture and sophistication of European society. The "Crash" of 1929 changed the family's financial status and Sunny was forced to return to the States with the children to deal with the effects on the family finances due to the depression. Because of the accents and mannerisms cultivated while living abroad, the Clift children often found themselves teased by their peers. This may have accounted for Monty's ultimate sensitivity. He had a strained relationship with his father who, it was said, was often violent and abusive as well as a bigot.

Montgomery Clift and Olivia DeHavilland in *The Heiress* – Paramount Pictures, 1949

Start of Career

As many of his predecessors, Clift was a theatrical actor for ten years. Rumor had it that he often drew upon the dynamics of his own family, that the ignorance and the violent behavior of his father, when a part cast him up against an adversary displaying these same attributes. This ability lent a quality to Clift's innate talent that made him an exceptional actor.

Onscreen Persona

Exceedingly handsome with a gentleness that stirred a combination of compassion and tenderness in women, Clift was the vulnerable, young man for whom feminine hearts clamored. He was the fragile young man they wanted to take care of. Feminine hearts softened at the sight of Clift on screen.

His signature as an actor was in his dedication to researching whichever role he portrayed, making each part come to life with seeming ease.

Personal Life

A tormented closet homosexual, it was rumored that he had experienced a heterosexual relationship with Libby Holman, an affluent Broadway actress and his mentor, sometime during the 1940's. Throughout the '50's Clift was plagued with health issues. While filming *Raintree County,* a horrific automobile accident on the way home from a party may have been the incident that finally brought him down.

Montgomery Clift and Elizabeth Taylor in *Raintree County* – MGM, 1957

Plastic surgery did not restore his good looks. Coupled with continuing poor health and the dark secret he tried to keep from the public, Clift's life was far from easy. The fact that he was gay was something he tried very hard to hide, but rumors persisted within the community leaking out into the public who refused to believe it.

One saving grace was his close friendship with Elizabeth Taylor. They remained devoted friends until his death.

Fast Facts

- He spoke fluent French, Italian and German,
- Rumor has it that his ghost visits the Hollywood Roosevelt Hotel where he lived during the filming of *From Here to Eternity* (1953)
- He is referred to as a "friend" in Marlon Brando's autobiography.
- He nicknamed Elizabeth Taylor, "Bessie Mae".
- He loved caviar and ate it whenever he could.
- Lee Remick said of Clift, "He inspired in me the feeling of wanting to look after him.
- He was like a wounded bird, so vulnerable."
- He modeled Arrow shirts for the John Robert Powers Modeling agency in 1933
- His mother, Ethel died just a few weeks before her 100th birthday.

Salary

$ 50,000, *Raintree County* (1947
$ 60,000, *Red River* (1948)
He waived payment for his role in *Judgment at Nuremberg* (1961)

Date of Death

July 23, 1966 coronary artery disease

Interred

Buried in Quaker Cemetery outside of New York City

Nominations Academy/ Oscar

Best Actor in Leading Role   *The Search* 1949
Best Actor in Leading Role   *A Place in the Sun* 1952
Best Actor in Leading Role   *From Here to Eternity* 1953
Best Actor in Supporting Role   *Judgement at Nuremberg* 1962
BAFTA Awards
Nominated 1962 Best Foreign Actor   *Judgment at Nuremberg*
Laurel Awards 1962 Top Male Supporting Performance *Judgment at Nuremburg*

Star on the Walk of Fame

6104 Hollywood Blvd.

Montgomery Clift and Donna Reed in
From Here to Eternity – Columbia Pictures, 1953

TONY CURTIS

Vital Statistics

Date of Birth: June 3, 1925 (Gemini) in Bronx, New York
Birth Name: Bernard Schwartz
Height: 5' 9"
Hair: Thick, black and curly
Eyes: Blue
Physique: Toned & Muscular

Biographical Sketch

Father
  Emanuel (Tailor)

Mother
  Helen (Housewife)

Siblings
Julius and Robert, both younger

Boyhood Years

Tony Curtis and Piper Laurie in
Son of Ali Baba –
Universal International Pictures, 1952

His parents migrated to America from Hungary. For the first years of his life the only language Tony spoke was Hungarian. They lived in cramped quarters in the back of his father's tailor shop in the tenement district of Brooklyn. Curtis' memories of his childhood were not pleasant. His mother's behavior was erratic. It was rumored that she often beat her sons. When Tony was about eight, his mother was diagnosed with schizophrenia. Later in life his brother, Robert, was also diagnosed with this devastating mental illness and eventually institutionalized. At an early age Tony and Julius were sent to an orphanage because their parents were unable to provide them with food. Julius was killed by a truck leaving Tony virtually alone in the world. He joined a street gang specializing in cutting school and stealing from the dime store. A caring neighbor intervened when Curtis was eleven and sent him to camp where the young boy was able to expend his energy in a positive way. The lessons he learned at this camp turned his life around setting him on a positive path.

Start of Career

Following his discharge from the Navy when World War II ended, Curtis studied acting under the G.I. Bill. Among his schoolmates were Elaine Stritch, Walter Matthau, and Rod Steiger. A talent scout saw Curtis in an off-Broadway production of *Golden Boy* and signed him immediately to one of the standard studio contracts. Studio publicists went to work immediately to create his star image.

Onscreen Persona

His looks were a reminder of the matinee idol of the 30's. His perfect profile and beauty drew a new wave of women into movie theaters. Tony Curtis was a matinee idol in the true sense of the word. Women adored his looks. At one time studio heads were so concerned that his beauty was a detriment that they nearly overlooked his true potential. But by the end of the 1950's Curtis was no longer identified by his exceptional good looks, but for his talent as an actor in whatever role he portrayed.

Tony Curtis and Janet Leigh in *Houdini* – Paramount Pictures, 1953

Tony Curtis became a name that graced the screen. His versatile talent became known throughout the movie industry in comedy, romantic and serious drama earning him a prominent place among other Hollywood icons as he proved his talent for nearly sixty years.

Personal Life

At the start of the fifties the romance of starlet Janet Leigh and heartthrob Tony Curtis produced reams of copy for fan magazines. They were the "Love Couple" of the times. Their marriage in 1951 created fervor among fans who adored them. With the birth of their daughters, Kelly and Jamie Lee the family completely captured the hearts of movie goers. Unfortunately, the end of this love fest came in 1962 when Leigh filed for divorce. Fans were devastated. Undaunted, Curtis went on to marry again many times.

Marriages

Janet Leigh 1951-1962 (Divorced)
Christine Kaufman 1963-1968 (Divorced)
Leslie Allen 1968-1982 (Divorced)
Lisa Deutsch 1993-1994 (Divorced)
Jill Vandenberg 1998 until his death

Children

Kelly Curtis 1956 (with Leigh)
Jamie Lee Curtis (actress) 1958 (with Leigh)
Alexandra Curtis 1964
Nicholas Curtis 1970 died 1994
Benjamin Curtis 1973

Granddaughter

Helen Claire Boyer

Fast Facts

- Curtis dated starlet Marilyn Monroe before both became famous.
- When his film career began to dwindle in the 60's, Curtis created to a modicum of success in television but in the 80's he focused his talent on painting as a second career. Some of his canvases have been sold for upwards of $25,000.
- His son Nicholas died of an overdose of heroin at the age of 23, leaving Curtis with a sadness that he carried with him for the rest of his life.
- Early in his career, Curtis shared an apartment with Marlon Brando.
- The first name Universal gave him was Antonio Cortez. However studio big wigs realized that Cortez might be too Latin and changed it to Curtiz that eventually morphed into Curtis. The first name of Tony evolving from Antonio seemed to suit him best.
- He was a confirmed hypochondriac. Fearing he would catch cold when filming a rainstrom scene, the studio had to heat the water that fell upon him. By the mid '50's he was on the psychiatrist's couch three times weekly dealing with his fears, one of which was that of flying. Because of this he insisted upon sailing to France rather than flying for the filming of *Trapeze*.
- Curtis readily admitted to being hooked on uppers, downers, dope, heroin and cocaine throughout his younger years.
- In 1984 he was admitted to the Betty Ford clinic after being rushed to the hospital with cirrhosis of the liver. At the end of his life Curtis had reconciled with all of his children and grandchildren after years of alienation. "I want to have a dynasty that lasts forever," he said at the time.
- A collection of his art is on exhibit permanently in The Museum of Modern Art in New York.
- Elvis Presley is said to have adapted Curtis's duck tail he was so impressed by it.
- It was said of Curtis that he had vanity but no ego.
- "When I was a child, I was enthralled by the movies, believing I could fence, ride a horse and kiss girls. Just as in the movies."
- He was privileged to watch the Japanese sign the article of surrender in Tokyo Bay in September, 1945. It took place a mile away from the top deck of his submarine where he viewed this historic event through a pair of high powered binoculars.

- A renewed interest in their heritage inspired Curtis and his daughter, Jamie Lee to help finance the rebuilding of the Great Synagogue in Budapest as a tribute to their Jewish-Hungarian heritage. It is now the largest synagogue in Eastern Europe.
- His will read shortly after his funeral left his entire 60 million dollar estate to his widow as trustee. While a bequest was made for the education of his grandchildren, his five children were left out of the will.
- He was buried, according to his wishes, with his favorite Stetson hat, an Armani scarf, driving gloves, an iPhone and a copy of the book, *Anthony Adverse* that is said to have been the inspiration for the first name he adopted for the screen.

Salary

$75 per week   *Criss Cross* (1949)
$300,000   *Black Commando* (1982

Date of Death

September 10, 2010 of cardiac arrest in Henderson, Nevada

Awards and Nominations

1958 Golden Globe   *The Defiant Ones*
1958 Academy Award *The Defiant Ones*
1968 Golden Globe   *The Boston Strangler*
1957 Henrietta Award World Film Favorite
1958 Henrietta Award World Film Favorite
1960 Henrietta Award World Film Favorite

Star on the Walk of Fame

North side of the 6800 block on Hollywood Blvd.

Tony Curtis and Marilyn Monroe in
Some Like it Hot – United Artists, 1959

JAMES DEAN

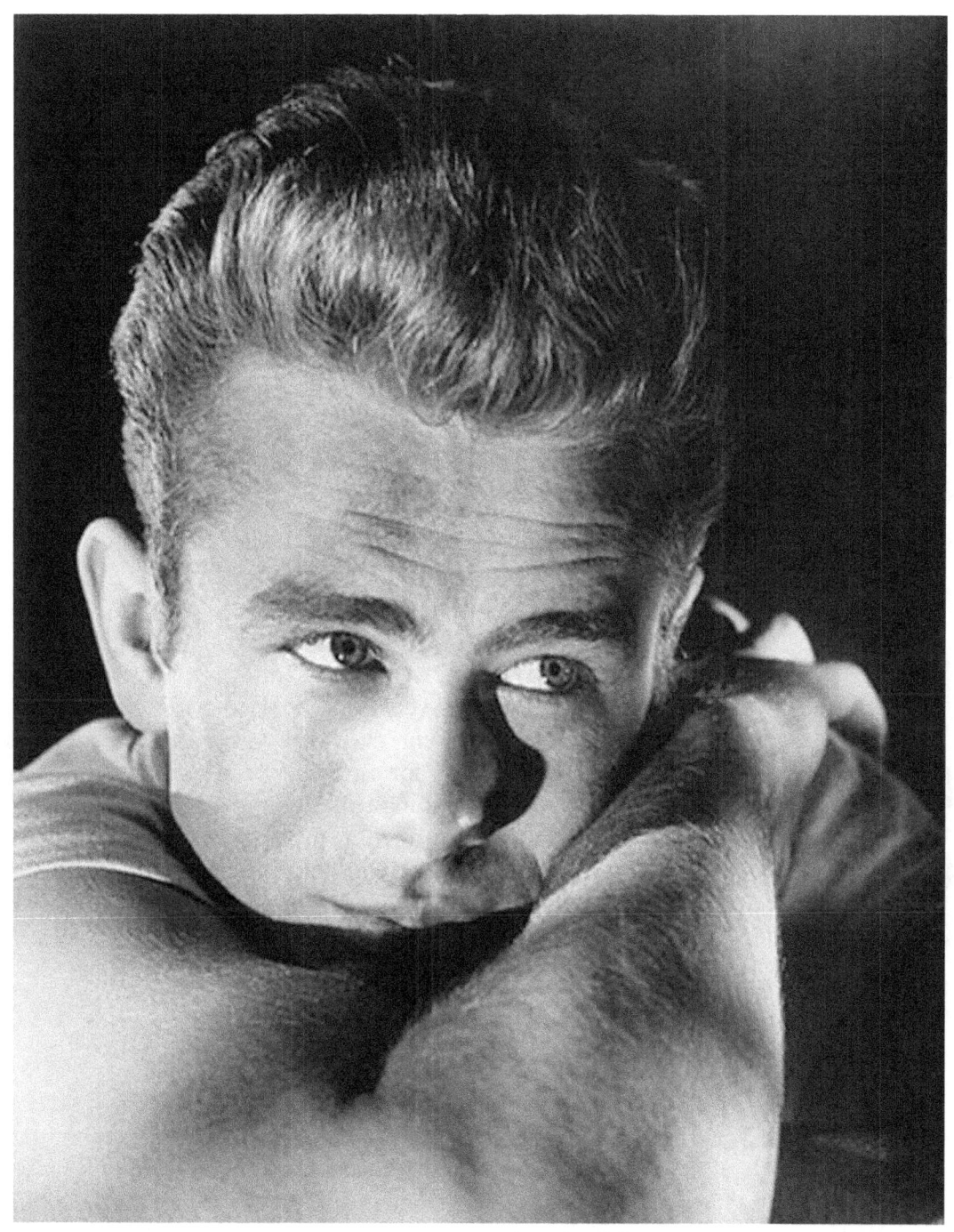

Vital Statistics

DOB: February 8, 1931 (Aquarius) in Marion, Indiana
Name: James Byron Dean
Height: 5'8"
Hair: Brown
Eyes: Blue
Physique: Wiry

Biographical Sketch

Father
   Winton Dean (Dental technician)
Mother
   Mildred (Housewife)

Boyhood Years

When his mother died of lung cancer, nine year old Jimmy was sent to live with a paternal aunt and uncle in Fairmount, Indiana.

James Dean and Julie Harris in
East of Eden – Warner Brothers, 1955

Start of Career

His performance in a Little Theater production of *The Immoralist* first in Fairmont and then New York so impressed Elia Kazan that he signed the young man for a major role in *East of Eden*. Prior to that defining role Dean appeared in minor roles in a variety of films that included a musical, a war movie and a comedy before being cast in the three epics that zoomed him to the top of the charts creating the dedicated fan following that has lasted now for sixty years.

Onscreen Persona

Dean has been equated with the youthful rebellion of the '50's, described as being a young man who displayed a range of emotions combining shyness and sensuality with an expressive face of classic beauty. His very special acting technique deftly cajoled female audiences into a response of sublime adoration. He was at once vulnerable, rebellious, and natural.

Personal Life

Romances

Dated Ursula Andress during her starlet days

It was rumored that he was very much in love with actress Pier Angeli, but she was Catholic, he was not. Her mother intervened, blocking any hope of their marrying.

James Dean and Elizabeth Taylor in
Giant – Warner Brothers, 1956

Fast Facts

- It is said he was a practical joker,
- Loved to read.
- Ronald Reagan called Dean "America's Rebel"
- Before his tragic death Dean signed a nine-picture contact with Warner Bros for $900,000.
- His estate at the time of his death was valued at $96,438 after taxes. Because he did not have a will, the estate went to his father from whom Dean was estranged most of his adult life.
- The fast lane was one Dean traveled effortlessly. He was young and enthusiastic about life.
- Although rumor had it that Dean was speeding when the fatal accident occurred, a test done by Failure Analysis Associates indicates that he was not going faster than the 55 to 56 m.p.h. at the time. The accident was therefore not his fault.
- He studied dance with Katherine Dunham for a short time.
- He was named one of the 100 Sexiest Stars in the history of films (1995) by *Empire Magazine*
- #33 in the *UK Magazine Empire* listing of 100 Movie Stars of All Time (1997)
- He is buried at Park Cemetery, Fairmount, Indiana
- He was at the time of his death to be the only actor to be awarded more than one Oscar nomination posthumously (*East of Eden*, 1955 and *Giant*)
- He was a heavy smoker
- Was once told he was too short to be a serious actor

Salary

1956 *Giant* 1956 $21,000
1956 *Rebel Without a Cause* (1956) $10,000
1955 *East of Eden* (1955) $1,000 week

Date of Death

September 30, 1955 fatal car crash outside of Paso Robles, CA

Interred

Park Cemetery, Fairmount, Indiana

Awards and Nominations

East of Eden (1955) Posthumously for Lead Role
Giant (1956) Posthumously for Lead Role
BAFTA Best foreign actor, *Rebel Without a Cause*
BAFTA 1956 Best foreign actor *East of Eden*

1957 Golden Globe World Film Favorite (Male) Henrietta Award
1956 Golden Globe Best Foreign Actor (*East of Eden*)

Star on the Walk of Fame

1719 Vine Street

James Dean and Natalie Wood in
Rebel Without a Cause –
Warner Brothers, 1955

ROCK HUDSON

Vital Statistics

DOB: November 17, 1925 (Sagitarius) in Winnetka, Illinois
Birth name: Roy Harold Scherer, Jr.
Nickname: Mr. Beefcake
Height: 6'4"
Hair: Black
Eyes: Dark brown
Physique: Athletic

Biographical Sketch

Father
   Harold (Auto mechanic)

Mother
   Katherine (Telephone operator)

Boyhood Years

Rock Hudson and Jennifer Jones in *A Farewell to Arms* – 20th Century Fox, 1957

An only child, life was good for Roy until his parents separated when Roy was just a young boy. Later abandoned by his father, Roy took on a paper route and delivered groceries to help out financially. When his mother lost her job, the two moved in with Roy's grandmother. After his mother remarried life took on a different hue. Wallace Fitzgerald adopted the boy, who took his stepfather's last name. Although he was shy, his voice blended well as a member of the school's glee club. In an effort to earn his own way, Roy was delivered newspapers and ran errands in the neighborhood. In his early teens he worked as a golf caddy.

Start of Career

After serving with the Navy in the Philippines as an aircraft mechanic during World War II, Hudson migrated to Los Angeles where his mother resided.

Although he had failed to land parts in school productions because of a poor memory, young Hudson was so enamored of movies he decided it was his destiny to become an actor. Hanging around the studio gates he was soon distributing head shots to studio personnel. One of them, Henry Wilson, a highly respected talent scout, saw in this tall, strikingly handsome young man the potential for the silver screen.

His teeth were capped , his name changed to Rock Hudson and the studio proceeded to give him lessons in dance, fencing, riding and elocution. Wilson helped to create an actor whose outstanding good looks and affable smile captured the hearts of the female movie attendee throughout the country.

Onscreen Persona

Smooth, sophisticated, and with a smile that captivated all women, Hudson was the shining star of Universal Studios where he was a contract player. A versatile actor, Hudson played a variety of roles ranging from romantic comedy to stark drama and did them all well. Considered to be a classic actor he was once referred to as a young 'Rhett Butler.' One description of him was "raw" masculinity. He hit another stride with the long running television series, *McMillan and Wife* in the 1970's. The soothing timbre of his voice sent women in the audience into blissful sighs. He was all that a movie idol should be.

Personal Life

The public was not ready to accept a homosexual love icon. In the mid 50's when rumor had it that Hudson's secret life was going to be revealed in a scandal sheet, a marriage was arranged for by the studio to his agent's secretary. The reason for the marriage was vehemently denied by all concerned. But those in Hollywood knew the real reason.

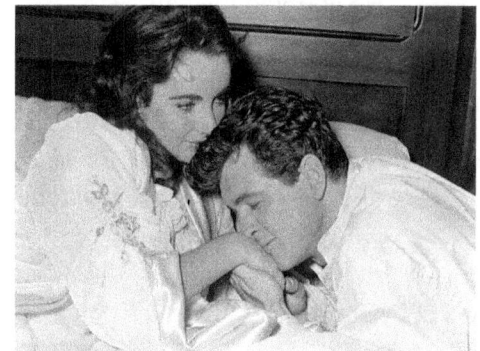

Rock Hudson and Elizabeth Taylor in *Giant* – Warner Brothers, 1956

The truth of his homosexuality came out many years later in a statement by Hudson when he was dying of AIDS.

Romances

He was often photographed on the town with a beautiful actress on his arm. When Hudson dated actress Vera Ellen for three years, fans eagerly waited for them to announce their engagement.

Marriage

Phyillis Gates, November 1955-1958 (Divorced)

Fast Facts

- He had his eyelids lifted
- He called his home Castle

- He was the first the first in the Hollywood community to publicly acclaim that he had AIDS.
- A heavy smoker throughout his lifetime, Hudson underwent quintuple bypass surgery in 1981
- There was speculation that Hudson may have contracted AIDS from a transfusion during heart surgery.
- He graced the screen for nearly forty years
- Although the film was not a box office success, *Seconds* was a Cannes Film Festival favorite in 1966. Upon speaking with a Hollywood journalist at a sneak preview of the film Hudson confided he was disappointed that it had not gained more attention in the U.S. Hudson expressed pride in the movie that bordered on what may have been considered science fiction at the time.
- He was among of the last stars under the "studio system"
- He adopted his half sister
- He was left handed
- He flew to Paris to seek treatment for his illness
- He donated $250,000 to research in AIDS before his death.
- Hudson's revelation of his sexual identity and a donation to AIDS research opened the door to awareness of this insidious disease, especially within the Hollywood community.

Salary

$100,000 for *Giant*.

Hudson is said to have been the highest paid actor in television when he appeared in the series, *McMillan and Wife*

Date of Death

October 2, 1985 of AIDS in Beverly Hills, CA

Interred

Forest Lawn, Riverside, CA
.

Awards and Nominations

1956 Academy Award Best Actor in a Leading Role, *Giant*

1959 Golden Globe (Henrietta) World Film Favorite Male Actor
1960 Golden Globe (Henrietta) World Film Favorite Male Actor
1961 Golden Globe (Henrietta) World Film Favorite Male Actor shared with Tony Curtis
1963 Golden Globe (Henrietta) World Film Favorite Male Actor

1963 Bambi
1960 Bambi
1958 Bambi

Star on the Walk of Fame

6104 Hollywood Blvd.

Rock Hudson and Doris Day in Pillow *Talk* – Universal Studios, 1959

PAUL NEWMAN

Vital Statistics

DOB: January 26, 1925 (Aquarius) in Cleveland, Ohio
Name at Birth: Paul Leonard Newman
Height: 5' 9 1/2"
Hair: Sandy Brown
Eyes: Startling Blue
Physique: Slender and Athletic

Biographical Sketch

Father
   Arthur (Owner of sporting goods store0

Mother
   Theresa (Worked in his father's store)

Boyhood Years

Life for young Newman was just what a boy would want. His father owned a successful business, the family lived in upscale Shaker Heights where Paul and his brother Arthur went to school and hung out with other boys in the affluent neighborhood. Newman showed a penchant for acting as young as the age of seven when he appeared in a school play. His mother, a liberal thinker encouraged Paul's interest in acting.

Paul Newman and Elizabeth Taylor in *Cat on a Hot Tin Roof* – MGM, 1958

Start of Career

After graduating from Kenyon College, Newman honed his craft with a year at Yale Drama School then took off for New York for further studying at the New York Actors Studio. A Warner Brothers scout in the audience when Newman appeared in the Broadway production of *Picnic* in 1953 was impressed enough to sign him to a contract. However he was miscast in his first film *The Silver Chalice* a year later and nearly saw the end of his career before it had hardly begun. Being the man he was Newman apologized to his movie fans in an ad that appeared in the trades.

After that his roles were more carefully chosen for him and his heartthrob status never wavered.

Onscreen Persona

Hot and sizzling is the only way to describe Newman's movie image. He held women entranced whenever he appeared on the silver screen, radiating heat across the screen with just an expression or a few words of dialogue. Newman became a Hollywood icon early in his career and continued to excite female hearts by just the mention of his name. He is one of the few actors of yesterday whose name is recognized by young women of the 21st century.

Personal Life

Marriage

Jackie Witte 1949-1958 (Divorced)
Joanne Woodward 1958 until his death

Children

Alan Scott 1950 (died of an accidental overdose in 1978) (with Jackie)
Stephanie   1951(with Jackie)
Susan   1953 (with Jackie)
Claire   1955 (with Joanne)
Elinor   1959 (with Joanne)
Melissa   1961 (with Joanne)

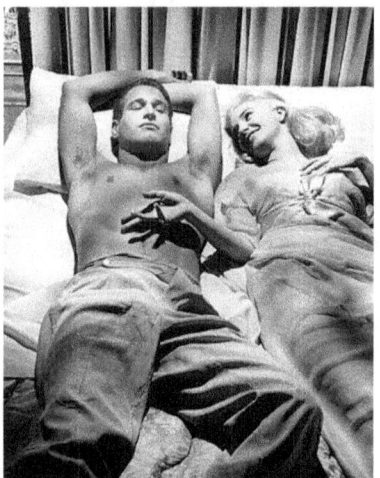

Paul Newman and Joanne Woodward
In *The Long, Hot Summer* –
20th Century Fox, 1958

Fast Facts

- He was color blind
- He sometimes ate watermelon while in the shower
- He liked drinking beer chug a lug style
- He was an ultra liberal lending his political support to liberal candidates
- Personal quote "People stay married because they want to, not because the doors are locked"
- He was in demand for more than fifty years and never lost his appeal to women of all ages
- He and Joanne slept in a bed they purchased from a brothel in New Orleans
- He opened the Scott Newman Center for drug abuse prevention to honor his deceased son.
- He was an enthusiastic race car driver
- He burned his tuxedo on his 75th birthday stating that he was through with formality
- He established the Hole in the Wall Gang summer camp for children with cancer related diseases.
- Critics have said that Newman was one of the finest actors of The Golden Age of Hollywood
- All of the profits from the Paul Newman's Own business go to charity.

Salary

Cat on a Hot Tin Roof   1958 $ 17,000
The Sting   1973 $500,000 + plus profit participation
The Towering Inferno   1974 $1,000,000 + 10% of profit
Blaze   1989 $5,000,000

Date of Death

September 26, 2008 lung cancer

Awards and Nominations

Nominated for nine Academy Awards but never won
While Newman never won an Oscar he was honored in other venues including The Golden Laurel and BAFTA
In 2006 Newman received a Life Achievement Award from the Academy

Star on the Walk of Fame

7060 Hollywood Blvd.
.

Paul Newman and Piper Laurie in
The Hustler – 20th Century Fox, 1961

SIDNEY POITIER

Vital Statistics

Date of Birth: February 20, 1927 (Pisces) in Miami, Florida
Name at Birth: Sidney L. Poitier
Height: 6' 2 1/2"
Hair: Black
Eyes: Brown
Physique: Slender well toned

Biographical Sketch

Father
   Reginald James Poitier (Farmer)

Mother
   Evelyn

Sibling
Cyril, older brother

Boyhood Years

Sidney Poitier and Diahann Carroll in *Paris Blues* – United Artists, 1961

Born in Miami two months premature, when his parents had journeyed from Cat Island, the Bahamas to sell produce from their small farm in the Bahamas, Poitier was not expected to survive. Nursed by his parents who opted to stay in Miami for the first three months of their son's life, he became a U.S. citizen by default having been born stateside. The family moved to Nassau when he was ten.

Because Poitier was a bit of a rebel, feared to be headed for delinquency he was sent to live with his older brother in Miami when he was fifteen. At seventeen he moved to New York on his own and worked at whatever job he could get before joining the U.S. Army.

Start of Career

Rejected by the American Negro Theatre, Poitier then spent several months honing his diction and perfecting his acting. It was while performing a small role during a Broadway production of "*Lysistrata*" that he gained recognition. Impressed by Poitier's great reviews, Darryl Zanuck offered the young man a role in the movie *No Way Out* (1950). Afterwards, Poitier unhesitatingly turned down offers that he considered not right for his career until he was given the opportunity to play a leading role in the film *The Defiant Ones* (1958). This led to his first Academy Award nomination for Best Actor.

Onscreen Persona

A gentle demeanor belied a hidden strength that appealed to women in the audience. Poitier's portrayals onscreen commanded attention no matter what part he played. Many were breakthrough roles, removing some of the barriers that had existed between blacks and whites, His integrity blending with a powerful talent created a following in stardom that still brings accolades. Mention the name Sidney Poitier to any movie goer and the response is one of admiration and respect.

Sidney Poitier and Dorothy Dandridge in *Porgy and Bess* – Columbia Pictures, 1959

Personal Life

Marriages

Juanita Hardy   April, 1950–1965 (Divorced)
Joanna Shimkus 1976

Children

Beverly, Pamela, Sherri, and Gina (with Juanita Hardy)
Anika and Sydney (with current wife Joanna Shimkus)

Fast Facts

- He was so poor that he had to sleep in the men's room of the bus station when he first arrived in the U.S,
- On April 15, 1967 Poitier was made Ambassador of the Bahamas to Japan
- In 1974 he was knighted by the Queen. However he has never used the title Sir Sidney Poitier.
- He is of Haitian ancestry on his father's side.
- He was given an Honorary Doctorate degree from Shippensburg University of Pennsylvania
- Poitier speaks fluent Russian.
- He is tone deaf
- Once told by a casting director that he should stop wasting people's time and get a job as a "dishwasher or something," Poitier decided then and there to devote himself to becoming an actor.
- He is the first black actor to win an Oscar (*Lillies of the Field*) 1963

- In 1967 he was the first black actor to place his hand and footprints in cement in the forecourt of Grauman's Chinese Theater.
- He and Harry Belafonte are lifelong friends
- Poitier and Gary Cooper share honors as the most represented actors named by the American Film Institute for having made the Most Inspiring Movies of All time.
- He is the recipient of the Screen Actor's Guild Life Achievement Award
- He is a survivor of prostate cancer
- He is the author of "*The Measure of a Man: A Spiritual Autobiography* (2000) and *Life Beyond Measure: Letters to my Great Granddaughter*."
- In 1997 Poitier was appointed the Bahamian Ambassador to Japan

Salary

No Way Out (1950) $3,000
Porgy and Bess (1959) $75,000
Guess Who's Coming to Dinner (1967) $200,000 plus a percentage of the gross profits

Awards and Nominations

Sidney Poitier and Katharine Houghton in *Guess Who's Coming to Dinner* – Columbia Pictures, 1967

1958   Oscar for *The Defiant Ones*
1958   British Academy Film Award Best Foreign Actor, *The Defiant Ones*
1958   Silver Bear Best Actor, Berlin Film Festival, *The Defiant Ones*
1963   Academy Award for Best Actor in a Leading Role, *The Defiant Ones*
1963   Golden Globe Award for Best Actor in a Leading Role, *Lilies of the Field*
1974   Knight Commander of the Order of the British Empire
1992   AFI Life Achievement Award
1995   SAG Life Achievement Award
1995   Kennedy Center Honors
2000   NAACP Image Award for Outstanding Actor in a Television Movie. Mini-Series or Dramatic Special for *The Simple Life of Noah Dearborn*
2002   Honorary Oscar from The Academy "for his extraordinary performances and unique presence on the screen and "for representing the industry with dignity, style and intelligence."
2009   Presidential Medal of Freedom, the highest civilian honor in the United States given to him by President Barack Obama.

Star on the Walk of Fame

7065 Hollywood Blvd.

Chapter Four
THE SIXTIES

Walter Cronkite called the 60's the most turbulent decade of the century. Baby Boomers were growing up unwilling to allow life to continue status quo. They demanded changes.

The sixties were about defying convention. This is the decade best known as the age of youth. These 70 million teenagers and young adults demanded radical change. They were openly defiant of generations before them and made no secret of their disdain of the idea of following in the footsteps of their fathers, grandfathers, and prior generations. Protests, sit-ins and riots were the result of a youth oriented rebellion against society's complacency as they saw it.

Still some young people maintained their ideals looking to their vibrant new president to help them effect change. The televised debate between Kennedy and Nixon took center stage as the two men challenged each other in front of millions of enrapt viewers watching and listening in their homes.

- Rock and Roll continued to influence music.

- Women emulated our first lady, wearing perky hats atop bouffant hairdos. Elegance returned to fashion as they copied Jackie's elegant style.

- October 16, 1960 Walt Disney Company was established.

- On January 10, 1961 Dashiell Hammett creator of Phillip Marlowe, the hard-boiled detective in a series of mystery novels, passed away.

- Although the fear of communism lingered, it no longer took center stage.

- For a while the country was in a safe mode. Youngsters could play outdoors without fear of being harmed.

- On August 13, 1961 The Berlin Wall went up dividing East and West Berlin.

- On February 4, 1964 The Beatles stepped out of a plane to the tune of 3000 enraptured fans loudly voicing their approval of the four multi-talented young Britain's. Beatle mania swept quickly through the country.

- On July 30, 1965 President Johnson signed Medicare into law.

- The twist was the dance of the times.

- On the big screen Robert Redford's affable smile wooed women into the theaters.

- Marilyn Monroe's mysterious death shocked the nation early in the month.

- On the small screen the bad boy charm of Ryan O'Neal in the TV series *Peyton Place* captivated hearts. Chad Everett's good looks enthralled female viewers of TV's *Medical Center*, his dimpled grin and solid performance as a charm laden doctor winning over female viewers of the series.

- Women sought the warmth and friendliness of the 60's heartthrobs. They exuded assurance beyond their handsome faces, making women feel secure in a world that was moving too fast. Change was unsettling. An agreeable smile on a good looking young countenance was the comfort women sought for the $1.22 they paid at the box office. Being able to see their heartthrobs on television every week in the privacy of their homes was even more appealing.

- By 1967 more than half of movie audiences were age 24 or younger. Viewers were fascinated with the medical series that sprang up on television. Actors who had not yet made it on the big screen became overnight sensations on the small screen. There was no reason to leave home for this type of entertainment.

- However we were not to experience continued serenity. The country was spun into havoc with the advent of the Civil Rights movement and eruption of the Vietnam War. Demonstrations abounded.

- Women found themselves enamored of the handsome hero with a charming manner and accent as the foreign heartthrob appeared on the Silver Screen. The Berlin Wall went up, the Peace Corps was founded and Russia was first to put a man in space. The Japanese Bullet Train began its' long awaited run.

- The Beatles invaded the U.S.,

- Cassius Clay (Muhammad Ali) became the new heavyweight champion boxer.

- Neil Armstrong landed on the moon.

- Woodstock's festival of love drew in 500,000 people.

- With the assassination of President Kennedy in 1963, we were reminded of how fragile our world had become. Innocence and hope began to slip away.

- While the country was financially solvent and with many families able to afford homes of their own, there was also the reality of political unrest and war to put a shadow on American life.

- 1968 has come to be known as the bloodiest year of the Vietnam War.

- April 14, 1969 beloved icon Katherine Hepburn passed away

- October 24, 1969 Richard Burton showed his devotion to his lady love, Elizabeth Taylor with the gift of a 69 carat point pear shaped diamond ring. It was the talk of Hollywood and under the hair dryer in salons throughout the world.

- The blatant use of drugs emerged as a perceived antidote for young people struggling to make sense of their world. Displaying little to hide their scorn for the older generation disrespect became a mantra for many of our youth in their rebellion against the establishment.

- Not even the landing of a man on the moon in 1969 could overshadow the anti-establishment behavior of some of our more rebellious young people.

- Toward the end of the decade, men were letting their hair grow to shoulder length while romance on the screen was replaced with violence and stark realism.

- It was a time of great uncertainty, especially for the female gender.

- So women went to the movies for comfort and escape.

WARREN BEATTY

Vital Statistics

DOB: March 30, 1937 (Aries) in Richmond, Virginia
Name at Birth: Henry Warren Beatty
Nickname: Pro
               The Chief
Height: 6' 2"
Hair: Dark Brown
Eyes: Blue-green
Physique: Athletic

Biographical Sketch

Father
  Ira (Professor of Psychology and School Principal)

Mother
  Kathryn (Drama teacher)

Sibling
Shirley MacLaine (actress)

Boyhood Years

An athlete in high school, Beatty was offered a number of football scholarships, but declined them.

Warren Beatty and Natalie Wood in
Splendor in the Grass –
Warner Brothers, 1961

Raised by encouraging, supportive parents he was drawn to acting and was determined not to be left behind by his older sister Shirley (MacLaine) who had already begun to carve out a brilliant career as a dancer and film actress.

He attended Northwestern University for a year before dropping out to study acting.

Start of Career

Renowned acting teacher, Stella Adler, furthered Beatty's ambition when she became his acting coach after recognizing his potential. Taking her encouragement to heart Beatty accepted a role on a television show, *The Many Loves of Dobie Gillis*. In it Beatty showed his lighter side. He was charming and appealing. Disappointed in what he termed a "ridiculous" part, Beatty turned his talents to off Broadway. After numerous performances on stage he returned to the screen. As Bud, the fervent young suitor of Natalie Wood in *Splendor in the Grass*, he began a love affair with his female public. A box office success, the movie quickly launched Beatty as a heartthrob. From there a series of varying roles brought good reviews, but it was the release of *Bonnie and Clyde* that established him as an actor of substance.

The clamoring of his female audiences never stilled. His appeal onscreen never wavered. This upsurge of adoration from female fans was enough to elicit an increase in his fan mail, magazine covers, and interviews in the popular fan magazines.

Beatty continued to strive for critical favor by appearing in a series of movies roles ranging from quirky comedies to more serious parts such as *Bonnie and Clyde*. The latter finally showed him as an actor of substance.

Onscreen Persona

Beatty exhibited a vulnerability that made women want to both nurture and to bed him, the latter in conflict with the former. Few female movie fans could resist his smashing good looks and strong, athletic body. Imaginations flared and hearts raced whenever this hottie appeared on screen.

Personal Life

Warren Beatty and Faye Dunaway in *Bonnie and Clyde* – Warner Brothers, 1967

A flamboyant love life brought Beatty more attention at times then his acting as he made the rounds with an array of Hollywood beauties. Among them was Leslie Caron (with whom he is reputed to have had an affair while she was still married), Goldie Hawn and Madonna. Early on in both of their careers Beatty was engaged to Joan Collins and they lived together for a while. The engagement was broken soon after he began filming *Splendor in the Grass*. While that relationship fizzled out, one with co-star Natalie Wood sizzled as the two were swept up in a fervent romance.

This was no surprise to Beatty watchers or studio heads as rumor had it that an affair with his female co-star in whatever film he was currently shooting was par for the course. Fans never knew which actress he would be romancing from one press release to another. The "playboy actor" could very easily describe Beatty as he was during those years. When he finally married, it came as a shock not only to his fans, but to the many Hollywood women he had romanced at one time or another. All of Hollywood had been convinced that Beatty was a confirmed bachelor.

Marriages

Annette Benning, his co-star in the film *Bugsy* broke the love'em and leave'em cycle as the two fell deeply in love. Two month old daughter Kathlyn was present at their secret wedding ceremony on March 3, 1992. The public announcement of their marriage on March 12, 1992 stunned a great many. Since then Beatty has been a settled family man.

Children

Kathlyn	1992
Benjamin	1994
Isabel	1997
Ella	2000

Fast Facts

- Eldest child daughter Kathlyn is currently considering gender surgery and goes by the name of Stephen Ira.
- He is allergic to oysters
- Has a photographic memory for phone numbers
- In 2005 *Premiere Magazine* ranked him #29 on the list of Greatest Movie Stars of All Time
- Member of Sigma Chi fraternity
- He and Natalie Wood dated for a short time after her split with Robert Wagner in 1962
- He made *Bonnie and Clyde* with a special financial arrangement with Warner Brothers. Having little faith in the film, the studio heads agreed to give the actor 40% of the gross proceeds instead of a pre-set salary. The picture made 70 million dollars in the first six years. This made Beatty a very wealthy man.
- A political liberal, Beatty campaigned for McGovern in the New Hampshire Democratic Primary in 1972

Personal Quotes

"You've achieved success in your field when you don't know whether what you're doing is work or play".

"I'm old, I'm young, I'm intelligent, and I'm stupid. My tide goes in and out."

"For me, the highest level of sexual excitement is in a monogamous relationship."

Salary

Ishtar	(1987)	$500,000
Bonnie & Clyde	(1967)	$200,000 + a percentage of the gross sales
Splendor in the Grass	(1961)	$15,000

Awards and Nominations

Golden Globe   1961   Best Motion Picture Actor-Drama, *Splendor In the Grass*
Golden Globe   1962   Most Promising Newcomer-Male (shared with Bobby Darin)
Golden Globe   1968   Best Motion Picture Actor-Drama *Bonnie and Clyde*
Golden Globe   1999   Best Performance by an Actor in a Motion Picture-Comedy/Musical *Bulworth*
Academy Award 1968   Best Actor in Leading Role *Bonnie & Clyde*
Golden Globe   1968   Best Motion Picture Actor Drama *Bonnie & Clyde*
BAFTA   1968   Best Foreign Actor *Bonnie & Clyde*
Academy Award 1979   Best Actor in a Leading Role, *Heaven Can Wait*
Academy Award 1981   Best Actor in a Leading Role, *Reds*
Academy Award 1992   Best Actor in a Leading Role, *Bugsy*
Golden Globe   1992   Best Performance by an Actor in a Motion Picture Drama, *Bugsy*
Golden Apple 1962 Sour Apple, Least Cooperative Actor (Hollywood Women's Press Club)
2000 Irving Thalberg Award
2007 Cecil B.DeMille Award

Star on the Walk of Fame

To date Beatty does not have a Star on the Walk of Fame

Warren Beatty and Julie Christie in
Heaven Can Wait – Paramount Pictures, 1978

JAMES BROLIN

Vital Statistics

DOB: July 18, 1940 (Cancer) in Los Angeles, California
Name at Birth: Craig Kenneth Bruderlin
Height: 6' 4"
Hair: Brown
Eyes: Brown
Physique: Athletic

Biographical Sketch

Father
   Henry (Building contractor)

Mother
   Helen Sue (Homemaker)

Siblings
Sue
Barbara
Brian

Boyhood Years

James Brolin and Joanna Cameron in
Marcus Welby, M.D. –
ABC Television, 1969-1976

Brought up in the upscale suburb of Westwood, California, Brolin recalled in a 2011 *Parade* interview: "I was raised in a family where no one had a serious bone in their body. Family dinners were filled with laughter. Every answer was a riddle, a joke or a prank."

His acting ambition was to play comedy. However Brolin's main focus as a youngster was on building model airplanes with the hope of one day flying his own plane.

As with many teenagers of his generation Brolin was an admirer of James Dean. He had an ambition to direct or be a cinematographer. Becoming an actor was not on his agenda then when family friend, William Castle (director/producer) came to dinner one night he was so impressed with Brolin's good looks and composure that he arranged for an audition for a role in an upcoming movie.

Start of Career

Brolin was clean cut, handsome, personable and seemed to have just what the movies were looking for in a new talent. While he did not land the part he originally tested for,

Brolin decided that he wanted to be an actor and proceeded to log in hours of study toward achieving that goal. Along the way he became friends with many young actors who received their academic education while attending acting classes. By the time of graduation, Brolin's family was cheering him on to follow his dream. A contract with 20 Century Fox came soon after graduation. His career was launched.

Onscreen Persona

His innate reserve appealed to women who found the calm, inner strength Brolin exuded made them feel that he was a man who they could count on. Brolin made the ladies in the audience feel protected and appreciated at a time when the world's insecurity abounded. A number of parts on the big screen and television led to a major breakthrough in his career. As 'Dr. Steve Kiley' assistant to 'Marcus Welby' (Robert Young) led to seven years of adoring fans who breathed in his bedside manner. 'Dr. Kiley' rode a motorcycle to work further enhancing the image of someone who could be counted upon. It was an era when women thought men who rode motorbikes were equivalent to a strong protector. Women had not found the thrill of riding a motorcycle for themselves.

The composed and capable manager and then owner of a luxury *Hotel* in the series of the same name further endeared the actor to women of all ages. He was the perfect example of class, calm, and efficiency while romantic and considerate at the same time.

James Brolin and Connie Sellecca in *Hotel* – ABC Television, 1983-1988

Personal Life

Marriages

Jane Cameron Agee 1966-1984 (Divorced)
Jan Smithers (actress)   1986-1995 (Divorced)
Barbara Streisand (singer, actress, director, producer) July 1, 1998

Children

Josh Brolin (with Jane)
Jess Brolin (with Jane)
Molly Elizabeth (with Jan Smithers)

Grandchildren

Trevor
Eden

Fast Facts

- Debuted in series *Bus Stop* 1961
- Directed son Josh in *My Brother's War*
- Brolin is a staunch Democrat
- An avid pilot, he has owned three planes in forty years as a licensed pilot making one of his childhood dreams come true.
- Former father in law of actress Diane Lane
- Supported John Kerry in 2004 election
- Listed among 25 Most Intriguing People in *People Magazine* (1998)

Salary

Hotel $50,000 per episode
Net worth $50 Million

Awards and Nominations

Emmy 1971, 1972, 1973 Outstanding Performance by an actor in a supporting role, Drama for *Marcus Welby M.D.*
Golden Globe 1972 Best Supporting actor, Television for *Marcus Welby M. D.*
Golden Globe, 1984 & 1985 Best Performance by an actor in a TV series, drama for *Hotel*
Emmy 2004 Outstanding Lead actor in a Miniseries or Movie *The Reagans*
Golden Globe 2004 Best Performance by an actor in a Miniseries or Motion Picture *The Reagans*
Emmy Outstanding Performance by an Actor in a Supporting Role in Drama for *Marcus Welby M. D.*
Golden Globe 1971 & 1972 Best Supporting Actor, Television for *Marcus Welby M. D.*

Star on the Walk of Fame

7030 Hollywood Blvd.

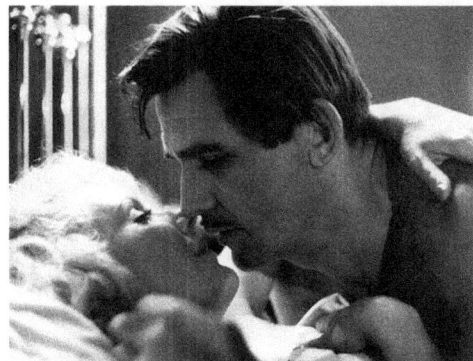

James Brolin and Jill Clayburgh in *Gable and Lombard* – Universal Pictures, 1976

RICHARD CHAMBERLAIN

Vital Statistics

DOB: March 31, 1934 (Aries) in Beverly Hills, CA
Name at Birth: George Richard Chamberlain
Height: 6'1"
Hair: Light Brown (blond in mid-career)
Eyes: Blue
Physique: Washboard abs.

Biographical Sketch

Father
  Charles (Salesman)

Mother
  Elsa (Housewife)

Sibling
  Bill, six years older

Boyhood Years

Richard Chamberlain in *Dr. Kildare* – NBC Television, 1961-1966

Although the family address was in Beverly Hills, it was not the posh section, but one where hard working middle class families lived. Chamberlain's father had a penchant for alcohol that was disruptive to his home life. Young Richard was painfully shy. In time the senior Chamberlain authored a book that led to a nationwide lecture tour sponsored by AA, but Richard was never able to come to terms with the persistent feeling of not measuring up to his father's expectations of him. Art and sports in high school helped to ease life. It was the starring role in a school production of *The Pied Piper* when he was eight that may have planted the seed that led him into the acting profession. Although he majored in art while attending Pomona College, Chamberlain also participated in school theatrical productions. It was during that time period that he realized his true calling and began devoting himself to honing his craft in anticipation of pursuing an acting career after graduation.

Due to sign with Paramount Studios Chamberlain was called up to serve in the Korean War. Discharged with the rank of Sergeant nearly two years later he devoted the next few years to the study of acting. Exceedingly handsome and talented, Chamberlain was soon appearing in guest roles on television. In time he was able to create a resume impressive enough to warrant auditioning for bigger parts. It was the starring role in the *Dr. Kildare* television series that shaped his rise to stardom. Lew Ayres, who had made *Kildare* famous in the movies, turned down the role in the television series when the network insisted upon having it sponsored by a cigarette manufacturer. At the time Ayres was adamant about smoking being a health hazard. The part went to Richard Chamberlain who adoring teenagers soon made their pin up guy.

Onscreen Persona

Classically handsome, he exuded refined charm. Teen aged girls and young women easily responded to Chamberlain. He may have been the boy next door with a light layer of sophistication but he was, after all, portraying a doctor on television. To most women, actors personified their onscreen roles. As *Dr. Kildare*, Chamberlain paved a smooth foundation for a doting fan base. In later years his roles brought a new dimension to his acting as he became a steamy sex symbol in his role as Father Ralph de Bricassart in *The Thorn Birds*. Ensuing roles in *Shogun* and *The Bourne Identity* established him as an actor of substance and staying power.

Richard Chamberlain and Rachel Ward in *The Thorn Birds* – ABC Television, 1983

Having always had a good singing voice Chamberlain was persuaded to record a few singles in his *Dr. Kildare* days that were popularized by his thousands of fans. But Chamberlain's ambition leaned toward deeper acting roles causing him to move to England to concentrate on other acting venues after the demise of *Dr. Kildare*. To the delight of his fans his career has never faltered. Fans faithfully followed him in any acting role no matter where he was. Chamberlain's onscreen versatility has sustained an enviable career well into his mature years.

Personal Life

Columnists often linked Chamberlain with lovelies in Hollywood, but he remained an elusive bachelor until his biography, *Shattered Love* (published in 2003). In it the actor revealed the secret he had kept for many years; that he had been in a long standing homosexual relationship for much of his adult life. His fans have been openly supportive, adoring and loyal as the climate surrounding being gay changed to a more positive one.

Partnered with producer-director Martin Rabbett for over thirty years.

Fast Facts

- Young girls besieged radio stations in the 60's with requests for the song "*All I Want to Do is Dream*" sung by Richard Chamberlain
- He ranked #6 in *TV Guide's* 50 Sexiest TV Stars of All Time

- During the five years *Dr. Kildare* aired, Chamberlain received upwards of 50,000 fan letters a month of which letters contained marriage proposals, request for invitations to visit the actor in Hollywood among its contents.
- One fan wrote to say that she had named her new son Chamberlain
- He was supposedly named a beneficiary in an older woman's will.
- Local fans often gathered to greet him outside of the studio gate when he arrived for work at 6 a.m.
- A young woman in her mid-twenties hid in his apartment surprising him when he arrived home after work. He has never figured out how she got into the apartment.
- There were numerous Richard Chamberlain fan clubs in the U.S. and in England where the actors also caused female hearts to go pitter patter.
- He is a talented painter
- He is the second actor to play *Hamlet* on stage. The first was John Barrymore
- A day has been named after him in Hawaii
- *The Thorn Birds* was the second most watched mini-series of its time. (*Roots* was #1)
- Chamberlain was known in Hollywood as "The King of the Mini-Series")
- While starring as *Dr. Kildare*, Chamberlain received as many as 12,000 fan letters a week.

Salary

Dr. Kildare $1500 per week

Awards and Nominations

AFI   Best Actor in a Leading Role   1978
Emmy   Outstanding Lead Actor/ Special Program, Drama or Comedy 1975 *The Count of Monte Cristo*
Outstanding Lead Actor/Limited Series or Special, 1981 *Shogun*
Outstanding Lead Actor/Limited Series or Special   1983 *The Thorn Birds*
Outstanding Lead Actor/ Limited Series or Special   1985 *Wallenberg, A Hero's Story*
Golden Globe   Best TV Actor-Drama 1980 *Centennial*
Golden Globe Best Performance/Actor/Mini-series made for television 1989 *The Bourne Identity*
Won
Golden Globe   Best TV Star/Male 1963 *Dr. Kildare*
Golden Globe   Best TV Star/Male 1964 *Dr. Kildare*
Golden Globe   Best Performance/Actor/TV-Series 1981 *Shogun*
     Best Performance/Actor/Mini-Series   1984 *The Thorn Birds*
 Golden Apple
 Golden Apple Nominated
     Most Cooperative Actor Hollywood Women's Press Club 1962
Award Golden Apple
Most Cooperative Actor 1963

Golden Apple   Male Star of Year 1980

Star on the Walk of Fame

7020 Hollywood Blvd.

Richard Chamberlain and Yoko Shimada in
Shogun – Paramount Television, 1980

SEAN CONNERY

Vital Statistics

DOB: August 25, 1930 (Virgo) in Fountainbridge, Scotland
Name at Birth: Thomas Sean Connery
Nickname: Tommy as a youngster,
            Big Tan when a teenager
Height: 6' 2"
Hair: Dark brown
Eyes: Brown
Physique: Athletic

Biographical Sketch

Father
  Joseph (Factory worker and trucker)

Mother
  Euphamia (Effie) (Housekeeper)

Siblings
Neil, eight years younger

Boyhood Years

Sean Connery and Lois Maxwell in *You Only Live Twice* – United Artists, 1967

Growing up in the depression era gave Connery a stark look at the world. The family was so poor that he went to work at the age on nine delivering milk and in a local butcher shop to help the family out financially.

A few years later he ended his formal education so he could continue working full time. Among the many jobs he held, was that of an artist's model, body builder, a coffin polisher and a truck driver. At the age of twenty he was a third place winner in the Mr. Universe competition for strength.

Start of Career

Connery loved both sports and acting choosing to follow the advice of actor friend Richard Henderson who encouraged him to choose acting.

One of his earliest low budget films was *Tarzan's Greatest Adventure* in 1959. At the time he offered the starring role in James Bond, he was undecided about doing a film series. However friends in the business convinced him that the series could be a real boost of his career. Writer Ian Fleming was not totally agreeable with the selection of Connery for his popular character, commenting that the actor did not have the refinement the author envisioned for the character. It was Fleming's girlfriend who convinced him otherwise insisting that Connery was sexually charismatic and would do the part justice. Film director Terence Young played *Pygmallion* to Connery by teaching him Bond mannerisms, how to walk and how to talk like a secret agent. As a result a finely honed character was formed that together with Connery's innate acting ability created one of the most memorable and popular characters in films.

Onscreen Persona

Connery's intense good looks and strong features caused feminine hearts to beat faster in whatever role he portrayed.

Sean Connery and Catherine Zeta-Jones in *Entrapment* – 20th Century Fox, 1999

He is considered the personification of suave displaying a polished gentleman persona in films such as *Marnie* as well as the elegant, sophisticated Bond. A versatile actor, Connery has proven himself to be many faceted. Regardless of what character he portrays on screen the appeal to women is always there. Age appears not to have any effect upon his popularity.

Personal Life

Marriages

Diane Cilento (actress) 1962-1974 (Divorced)
Micheline Roquerbrune (artist/painter) 1975

Children

Jason (actor, with Diane)

Fast Facts

- He was responsible for making Richard Gere cry on the set of First Knight, 1995.
- Although Connery appeared in a number of low budget films early in his career, it was as James Bond in 1960 that he gained movie star stature and the status of heartthrob.
- He was thirty two at the time of his rise to the top.
- Prior to his decision to become an actor, he was considering an athletic profession as a soccer player.
- In order to audition for a role in *South Pacific* Connery took lessons in voice and dance.

- Because of a legal matter that disillusioned him, Connery took a hiatus from movie making for two years.
- He does voice overs while waiting for the right script.
- He and his wife make their home in The Bahamas
- Japanese and South African news bureaus erroneously reported him dead from throat cancer in 1993.
- A report by Connery in the magazine *Wine Spectator* revealed that he had been diagnosed with a heart condition.
- He has been named "The Greatest Living Scot".
- Estonia displays a bronze bust sculpture of the actor.
- Famous quote "Love may not make the world go round, but I must admit that it makes the ride worthwhile."
- Upon completion of his farewell Bond film, *Diamonds Are Forever* Connery donated his considerable salary to the Scottish International Education Trust.

Salary

1962 $20,000 *Dr. No*
1963 $250,000 *To Russia With Love*
1964 $500,000 + 5% US gross salary *Goldfinger*
1983 $5,000,000 + 5% of net US profits *Never Say Never Again*
2003 $17,000,000 *The League of Extraordinary Gentlemen*

Awards and Nominations

1987   New York Film Critics   Best Supporting Actor   *The Untouchables*
1989   Golden Globe   Best Supporting Actor   *Indiana Jones and the Last Crusade*
1987   Hollywood Foreign Press   Best Performance by an Actor in a Supporting Role in a Motion Picture   *The Untouchables*
1993   National Board of Review   Honorary Award
1995   Golden Globe   Cecil B. DeMille Award
1999   European Film Academy   Best European Actor-People's Choice   *Entrapment*

Star on the Walk of Fame

Connery does not have a Star on the Walk of Fame at this time

Sean Connery and Kevin Costner in *The Untouchables* – Paramount Pictures, 1987

CHAD EVERETT

Vital Statistics

DOB: June 11, 1936 (Gemini) in South Bend, Indiana
Birth Name: Raymon Lee Cramton
Other Professional Name: Chad York
Hair: Dark Brown
Eyes: Blue
Physique: Athletic
Distinctive Feature: Deep Dimples in Cheeks

Biographical Sketch

Father
  Harry Clyde Cramton (Race car driver and racing mechanic)

Mother
  Virdeen Ruth (Housewife)

Sibling
  Deannie Elliot

Boyhood Years

Born in South Bend, Indiana but raised in Dearborn, Michigan, Everett attended and was the star quarterback at Fordson High School. He began acting in staged plays at age 14.

Chad Everett, Will Hutchins, and Diane McBain in *Claudelle Inglish* – Warner Brothers, 1962

Start of Career

Everett made the decision to become an actor after performing in a number of school plays while in high school. Continuing his education at Wayne University he received his degree in Mass Communications and Theater, after which he moved to Hollywood where he further honed his acting talent. The movie star handsome young man signed with talent agent Henry Wilson, known for his skill in furthering the careers of actors, Tab Hunter, Rock Hudson, and Troy Donahue, among others. Wilson arranged for his new client to sign a contract with Warner Brothers and created a name change as well.

Onscreen Persona

Deep dimples and charisma instantly captivated female hearts when Chad undertook the role of surgeon Dr. Joe Gannon in the television series *Medical Center* in 1969. After years of playing a variety of roles the actor hit his stride as the affable young doctor who held female viewers entranced each week for seven years. When the series concluded Everett went on to appear in *Centennial*, another well received series. His talent and charm wore well right up to his untimely death.

Personal Life

Marriage

Shelby Grant (actress) May 22, 1966 - June 25, 2011 (her death)

Children

Katherine
Shannon

Grandchildren

Six

Fast Facts

Chad Everett and Victoria Federova
in *Medical Center* –
CBS Television, 1969-1976

- Everett wrote a book of romantic poems that he dedicated to his wife, Shelby
- The couple renewed their wedding vows every seven years
- Addicted to alcohol for many years, Everett finally sought treatment by joining AA
- He attended meetings regularly even after he stopped drinking
- Lily Tomlin walked off the set of a taping of *The Dick Cavett* Show in 1972 when Everett referred to his wife as property in a joking manner.
- Played quarterback on his high school football team
- He was given an Alumni Arts Achievement Award in 1999
- Together with Shelby he contributed time to numerous charities including Children's Cancer Camp
- He was a longtime board member of The Muscular Dystrophy Association.

Salary

$250 per week while a contract player with Warner Bros. Studio

Date of Death

July 24, 2012 of lung cancer

Awards and Nominations

Golden Globe 1971 Best TV Actor -Drama   *Medical Center*
Golden Globe 1973 Best TV Actor-Drama   *Medical Center*
Laurel Awards 1966 3rd place New Faces-Male
TV Land Awards 2003 Classic TV Doctor of the Year   *Medical Center*
TP de Oro, Spain 1973 Best Foreign Actor   *Medical Center*

Star on the Walk of Fame

6922 Hollywood Blvd.

Chad Everett and Debbie Reynolds in
The Singing Nun – MGM, 1966

STEVE McQUEEN

Vital Statistics

DOB : March 24, 1930 (Aries) in Beech Grove, Indiana
Birth name: Terence Steven McQueen
Hollywood nickname: The King of Cool
Height: 5'9"
Hair: Sandy Blonde
Eyes: Blue
Physique: Slender and well-toned

Biographical Sketch

Father
   William (Stunt pilot with aerial circus)

Mother
   Julia

Boyhood Years

His father abandoned the family soon after McQueen was born. His mother left Steve with her parents until he was three moving on to live with an uncle in Skater, Missouri until the age of twelve when he joined his mother, who had remarried and moved to Los Angeles. According to rumor Steve openly disliked his stepfather. He became so incorrigible that his mother sent him to a home for rebellious boys when he was fourteen. She hoped the school would straighten him out. In 1947, at the age of seventeen, he managed to enlist in the Marines where he drove a tank while serving his country for three years.

Steve McQueen and Natalie Wood in
Love with the Proper Stranger –
Paramount Pictures, 1963

Start of Career

After being discharged from the service, McQueen used the G.I. Bill education program to study acting with Lee Strasberg in New York. He made his theatrical acting debut appearing in the Broadway production of *A Hatful of Rain* in 1955. Afterwards McQueen appeared in a number of unimpressive movies among them *The Blob*, a tongue in cheek horror film. In 1958 television opened up to the young actor in the western series *Wanted: Dead or Alive*, thrusting his career into high gear.

Onscreen Persona

Strong good looks shadowed by an appealing under layer of boyishness created a "bad boy" image that intrigued female audiences. Perhaps they thought he could be tamed with their love and understanding. Multi-talented, McQueen played a variety of roles convincingly throughout his career. No matter whom he was portraying on screen, the women in the audience made no effort to hide their adoration.

Personal Life

McQueen liked living on the edge, carrying that through in his pursuit of racecar driving as well as being a fervent motorcycle enthusiasm. He often did his own stunts in films and considered himself to be a professional race car driver, proving this by entering and nearly winning the impressive Sebring race in 1970. Off road motorcycle racing was a passionate pursuit that included entry into the impressive Baja1000 among other races. These pursuits led to his being inducted into the *Off-Road Motorsports* Hall of Fame in 1976.

Romances

While still married to his first wife, Niele Adams in the early seventies, McQueen began an ardent love affair with co-star Ali MacGraw during the filming of *The Getaway* on location. Their romance made Hollywood gossip columns sizzle with scandal. Eventually they divorced their respective spouses to marry each other.

Steve McQueen and Ali MacGraw
in *The Getaway* –
National General Pictures, 1972

Marriages

Neile Adams (actress) November, 1956-1972 (Divorced)
Ali MacGraw (actress) August, 1973-1978 (Divorced)
Barbara Minty (model) January, 1980 until his death

Children

Daughter Terry (with Adams) June 5, 1959. Deceased March 19, 1998.
Chad, (also with Adams) December 28, 1960

Grandchildren

Chase, 1995
Madison, 1997
Molly, 1988
Steven R. Chadwick, 1988

Fast Facts

- As a teenager McQueen worked as a towel boy in a brothel where it is rumored he also was educated in the ways of women and men.
- He followed a fixed daily two hour exercise routine
- In the fifties he raced motorcycles to supplement his income.
- It was rumored that McQueen may have been targeted by the notorious Manson Gang as he was close friends with Jay Sebring, one of Manson's victims.
- He was listed on President Nixon's Enemies List supposedly chosen by the image he displayed onscreen. In real life, McQueen was politically conservative and very patriotic.
- He was the inventor of a special race car seat
- He was one of three actors offered $4 million dollars to play *Superman* who also turned down the part.
- Rumor circulated that McQueen had a son named for him with a mystery woman
- In 1999 McQueen was posthumously inducted into the Motorcycle Hall of Fame
- He received an honorary membership in Stuntman's Association for his stunt work in th1971 film *Junior Bonner*
- His father died a few months before McQueen was able to locate his whereabouts. They never had the chance to reconcile.
- In 1974 he was the highest paid movie star in the world
- He owned a number of high end sports cars, among them a Porsche 917 and 9080
- His estate auctioned hundreds of items including his cars and motorcycles in a two day sale at the Imperial Palace Hotel and Casino in Las Vegas, Nevada in 1984
- The last car he ever drove in a movie and his favorite Ferrari were offered for auction in 2014 in Monterey, California

Salary

1974 $14,000,000 for *The Towering Inferno*

Date of Death

November 7, 1980 of cancer

In a much publicized fight to save his own life after being diagnosed with mesothelioma (a form of cancer reputed to be caused by exposure to asbestos) McQueen sought controversial treatment at a clinic located in Mexico. After months of undergoing treatment he had surgery to remove a metastasized tumor from his liver and suffered a fatal heart attack. He was just 50 years old.

Awards and Nominations

1964   Golden Globe Best Actor - Motion Picture, Drama *Love With The Proper Stranger*

1967 Golden Globe Best Actor - Motion Picture, Drama *The Sand Pebbles*
1970 Golden Globe Best Actor- Motion Picture Musical or Comedy *The Reivers*
1974 Golden Globe Best Actor- Motion Picture Drama *Papillion*
1967   Academy Award Best Actor in Leading Role *The Sand Pebbles*

Star on the Walk of Fame

6834 Hollywood Blvd.

Steve McQueen and Faye Dunaway in
The Thomas Crown Affair – United Artists, 1968

RYAN O'NEAL

Vital Statistics

DOB: April 20, 1941 (Taurus) in Los Angeles, California
Name at Birth: Charles Patrick Ryan O'Neal Jr.
Height: 6'1"
Hair: Blonde
Eyes: Blue
Physique: Athletic

Biographical Sketch

Father
  Charles O'Neal (Novelist and screenwriter)

Mother
  Patricia O'Neal (Theatrical actress)

Sibling
  Kevin O'Neal (Actor)

Boyhood Years

At the time of his father's transfer on assignment to Munich, Germany, O'Neal was in training as a boxer with an impressive record of amateur boxing 18 bouts with 13 knockouts while attending University High School in Hollywood. In Germany, O'Neal attended the Munich American High School until graduation.

Ryan O'Neal and Ali MacGraw in
Love Story – Paramount Pictures, 1970

Start of Career

It was inevitable with a mother who was an actress and a father a screenwriter that O'Neal should gravitate to acting as his life's career. Movies and television beckoned him however he began his acting career as a stand-in and stunt man. His first acting role was in *Tales of the Vikings*, produced in Germany.

Onscreen Persona

Boyishly handsome with a winning smile and a gleam in his eyes, O'Neal captivated female viewers holding them spellbound on 1964 with his initial appearance as the bad boy in *Peyton Place*, the first nighttime television soap opera. Guest roles in *Bachelor Father*, *The Many Loves of Dobie Gillis* and *Westinghouse Playhouse* led to the part that further catapulted the young actor into the hearts of young women everywhere. Having garnered the coveted male lead in *Love Story* his popularity soared even higher as the actor took claim to super stardom. He was the clean cut, boyishly handsome rogue who appealed to the secret desires of all young women.

Personal Life

Married in his early twenties to actress Joanna Moore (some years older), O'Neal sowed his wild oats while starring in *Peyton Place*. Rumors that he and Leigh Taylor Young, a new cast member, were romantically involved became a reality when the two married after his hasty divorce from Moore. Photos of the wedding in Hawaii showed the bride to be obviously pregnant. This was in the days before the latter was commonplace and it created newsworthy stirs. Nevertheless it did not dampen the enthusiasm of fans for this heartthrob. In the aftermath of the frenzy of popularity that followed the release of *Love Story*, the actor began to show signs of allowing success to go to his head. His behavior at Hollywood functions displeased reporters. One went so far as to write a scathing open letter to O'Neal in the pages of the magazine where she was on staff. All in all his inflated image of himself and combustible temper did not endear him to those within the community. His persona began to falter in popularity when some of his subsequent films were not well received at the box office or his peers. Nevertheless O'Neal commanded what was considered a substantial salary per film in those days.

Ryan and Tatum O'Neal in
Paper Moon – Paramount Pictures, 1973

In 1979, Ryan met and fell in love with actress, Farrah Fawcett; who was then married to Lee Majors (a close friend of O'Neal at the time). The friendship ended abruptly when Fawcett filed for divorce and moved in with O'Neal. During their seventeen years together Farrah and Ryan had a son, Redmond. However the relationship suffered a break in 1997.

In 2001 when O'Neal was diagnosed with leukemia, the former lovers reunited spending the rest of Farrah's life together. Not long afterward Fawcett was told by doctors that she had terminal cancer. This was the romance of the era as O'Neal remained devoted to the woman he loved until her death.

Romance

Farrah Fawcett actress, his partner 1979-1997, 2001-2009 her death

Marriages

Joanna Cook Moore (actress) 1963-1967 (Divorced)
Leigh Taylor Young (actress) 1967-1973 (Divorced)

Children

Tatum (with Moore)
Griffin (with Moore)
Patrick (with Young)
Redmond (with Fawcett)

Grandchildren

Three from Tatum
Three from Griffin
Two from Patrick

Fast Facts

- He was a lifeguard one summer
- He was rumored to be involved with Ursula Andress at one time
- Interviewed while starring in the *Peyton Place* series, veteran actress Ruth Warwick commented "O'Neal is so in love with himself, it is pitiful"
- A magazine writer who had established a professional rapport with the actor stated, "He was always friendly and cooperative even when I was on the set to interview someone else. But he changed after he was signed to do *Love Story*. He became very arrogant and rude."
- He was originally offered the part of Rocky Balboa in the first *Rocky*
- He was considered for the part of Michael Corleone in the first *Godfather* (1972)
- He has a number of assault charges leveled at him over the years
- Estranged from his actress daughter Tatum, they attempted numerous times to repair the rift including a reality show on television. The attempt at reconciliation did not take.
- Tatum, Griffin and Redmond have had serious drug use issues
- In 1972 O'Neal he was the second highest grossing actor in Hollywood
- Reputed to be a lothario, O'Neal's dating horizon has been peppered with Hollywood lovelies throughout the years. It was because Farrah learned that Ryan had strayed that she ended the relationship at that time.
- Farrah passed away before they could fulfill plans to marry
- He is left handed
- A contractor sued him for $61,000 when he would not pay his bill
- He is commended for always turning in a good performance no matter what the film
- He is a former Golden Glove Boxer
- As of this writing, his leukemia is in remission, but he has been reported to have prostate cancer.

- A woman who began stalking him after they met while vacationing in Greece was eventually hospitalized with psychiatric problems
- He joined the cast of *Bones* in a recurring role as Brennan's father Max in 2007
- He was not named in Farrah's will, a surprise to many.

Salary

$60,000   *Paper Moon*
$1,000,000   *The Main Event*
Net Worth $12 Million

Nominations & Awards

1971   Golden Globe Best Motion Picture Actor, Drama   *Love Story*
1974   Golden Globe Best Motion Picture Actor, Musical/Comedy *Paper Moon*
1988   Razzie Award Worst Actor, *Tough Guys Don't Dance*
1990   Razzie Award Worst Actor of the Decade, *Fever Pitch, Partners, So Fine, Tough Guys Don't Dance*
1990   Alan Smithe Award Worst Actor *Burn Hollywood Burn*
1971   Golden Laurel Best Dramatic Performance, Male   *Love Story*
2005   Razzie Award Worst Razzie Loser of First 25 Years
Won
1971   Golden Laurel Best Dramatic Performance Male *Love Story*

Star on the Walk of Fame

To date, he does not have a Star on the Walk of Fame

Ryan O'Neal and Barbra Streisand in
What's Up, Doc? – Warner Brothers, 1972

ROBERT REDFORD

Vital Statistics
DOB: August 18, 1936 (Leo) in Santa Monica, CA
Name at Birth: Charles Robert Redford, Jr.
Nickname: Bob
Height: 5'9"
Hair: Reddish Blonde
Eyes: Blue
Physique: Slender & Muscular

Biographical Sketch

Father
  Charles Robert Redford, Sr., (A one-time milkman who became an accountant for Standard Oil)

Mother
  Martha (Housewife)

Siblings
Younger half-brother, William

Boyhood Years

Robert Redford, Paul Newman, and Katherine Ross in *Butch Cassidy and the Sundance Kid* – 20th Century Fox, 1969

After the death of his mother when he was a young teenager, Redford's life took a turn for what was at the time, the worst. Stealing hubcaps and helping himself to the use of other peoples swimming pools by breaking into their backyards gained him a reputation as a delinquent By his own words he "was a failure at everything I tried; even fired from a job as a box boy in a supermarket." Fired again from a position at Standard Oil that was arranged for by his father who was then an accountant with the company, Redford was admittedly on a self-destructive path. An all-around athlete he excelled in baseball, football, and tennis. Following graduation from Van Nuys High School he attended The University of Colorado on a baseball scholarship.

As the pitcher for the school's baseball team Redford's unruly behavior did not sit well with the school board. Yet, he continued to act out a personal rebellion.

While student drinking was not new to the campus, Redford admits to being a bit too fond of alcohol at the time often referred to as "the campus drunk." His sudden departure from the University (whether at their request or by his own decision is vague) led to a move to Europe, Eventually settling in Paris. The Bohemian life appealed to Redford who eagerly absorbed the artistic, political and cultural aspects of the area. At the same time his interest in environmental causes was piqued. A year and a half later he returned to Los Angeles briefly before moving to New York where he continued with art classes at the prestigious Pratt Institute.

Start of Career

While at Pratt, a teacher, detecting something exceptional in Redford other than beyond art, suggested that he transfer to The American Academy of Dramatic Arts. His professional fate was sealed.

While appearing in the school's production of Chekhov's *The Seagull*, Redford realized that his real place in life was in films. He went on to appear in small theatrical and television roles until Hollywood and the world of eager fans discovered the Redford charm. Although he had once vowed never to live in Los Angeles again Redford had a change of mind when movies beckoned him. However he never permanently settled in Hollywood, making his home in other parts of the country far from the glamour scene.

Onscreen Persona

Put together a dazzling, charismatic smile, perfect timing, dedication, enthusiasm for his craft and the fervent approval of movie audiences, especially women, and you have the celebrated actor Robert Redford.

Robert Redford and Jane Fonda in
The Electric Horseman –
Columbia Pictures, 1979

From his early appearance in an episode of television's *Twilight Zone* to the well-received comedy *Barefoot in the Park* opposite actress Jane Fonda, Redford's foothold in all aspects of films has never faltered. Despite of, or perhaps because of, his boyish good looks Redford strove to create an image of himself as an actor who offered more than just sex appeal by choosing his films carefully. While not all of them were winners, most were. Portraying a variety of different character types with ease has kept him above the radar for almost fifty years.

Personal Life

Marriages

Shortly after his return to the States, twenty year old Redford met college student Lola Van Wagen who lived in the same apartment building in Los Angeles. Not long afterward they married and moved to New York together where Redford pursued a career in theater and television. He was barely twenty one; she was a few years younger. The marriage lasted close to thirty years.

In the early 1990's Redford met and fell in love with an artist fifteen years younger than him. She became his live in partner in Sundance, Utah. They lived a quiet life together on his ecologically designed ranch for ten years before marrying. The actor has always made an effort to keep his personal life as private as possible.

Lola Van Wagen   September 12, 1958-1985 (Divorced)
Sibylle Szaggars   July 2009

Children

Scott   1959   (died in infancy from SIDS)
Shauna   1960   (painter)
David James   1962   (screenwriter)
Amy Hart   1970   (actress)

Grandchildren

Seven

Fast Facts

- When asked about his greatest achievement in life, Redford is quick to reply "my children are the best things in my life."
- In the '90's son Jamie was diagnosed with ulcerative colitis and underwent two liver transplants during which time Lola and Bob emotionally supported one another as parents do when a child is ill. Despite their divorce they have maintained a close relationship.
- He is left handed
- He maintains a lean physique without dieting
- He was one of three actors who turned down an offer of 4 million dollars to play *Superman*
- His first movie *War Hunt* (1962) starred John Saxon
- He has made three films opposite Jane Fonda who freely admits to have once had a crush on him.
- Redford is ardently political, involved in environmental, Native American and art causes.
- He is a strong Democrat
- The film *The Way We Were* co-starring opposite Barbra Streisand, has joined the ranks of romantic tear jerker movies that women still longingly view on television.
- Ironically, The University of Colorado bestowed an honorary degree upon the actor in 1983 apparently forgiving his on campus behavior in the '50's.
- *Entertainment Weekly* voted him the 30th Greatest Movie Star of all time
- Recipient of Kennedy Center Honors 2005

- He seriously considered running for State Senator of Utah in 1970
- Founded Sundance in 1969
- #53 in *Empire Magazines* list of 100 Sexiest Movie Stars of all time.
- He and Paul Newman shared a close friendship and were rumored to be planning a new movie together at the time of Newman's death.
- He is a recipient of France's Order of Honor

Salary

1962	*War Hunt*	$ 500
1985	*Out of Africa*	$ 6,000,000
2001	*The Last Castle*	$11,000,000
Net Worth		$ 170 Million

Awards and Nominations

1963 Emmy Outstanding Performance by Actor *Alcoa Premiere*
1970 Golden Laurel Action Performance *Butch Cassidy and the Sundance Kid*
1994 Razzie Worst Actor *Indecent Proposal*
Won
1966 Golden Globe Most Promising Newcomer-Male for *Inside Daisy Clover*
1967 BAFTA Best Actor in Leading Role *Butch Cassidy and the Sundance Kid*
1969 BAFTA Best Actor in Leading Role *Downhill Racer* and *Tell Them Willie Boy is Here*
1996 Life Achievement Screen Actors Guild
2002 Lifetime Achievement/Honorary Oscar

Star on the Walk of Fame

Redford does not as yet have a Star on the Walk of Fame

Robert Redford and Barbra Streisand in *The Way We Were* – Columbia Pictures, 1973

Chapter Five
THE SEVENTIES

The seventies brought in a sense of elation and relief. After ten years of an intensely fought war in Vietnam, weary men returned home to rebuild lives that had been bruised and shattered physically and emotionally. Embracing peace, the American public "let it all hang out" in fashion trends, television series that emphasized comedy and a general feeling of relief that filled the air.

- The sum of $100 in 1970 translated into around $700 at the start of the new century.

- On April 7, 1970 movie icon John Wayne won his first and only Oscar for the lead role in
- *True Grit*.

- March 1, 1971 Richard Zanuck and David Brown joined Warner Bros.

- September 11, 1971 Donny Osmond's single *Go Away Little Girl* rose to #1 on the charts.

- A nostalgic look back at the fifties became a cult classic with the debut of *American Graffiti* on August, 1973 featuring a group of actors who went on later to make their mark in other films.

- The women's movement spurred on by Gloria Steinem took front and center as women fought for the right to be respected and treated as first class citizens. The sexual revolution encouraged women to enjoy physical freedoms of the kind that only men had taken before and do so without the stigma of judgment for the most part. Women chose to take forks in the road of life never before traveled by the distaff sex.

- July 31, 1975 the disappearance of Jimmy Hoffa, last seen in Detroit, Michigan, became an unsolved puzzle.

- The emergence of the macho man in real life and emulated On screen was predominant as men rebelled against giving up the position of power and control they held for centuries.

- On September 18, 1974 actress Doris Day won a $22 million malpractice suit from her former attorney who she accused of misappropriating her savings over the years.

- At first the women's movement found many women abandoning certain feminine aspects of their lives by not shaving their legs and underarms, presenting public faces devoid of makeup. By the close of the decade, women had forged an implacable path to recognition as persons in their own right, not to be subservient to men again, for the most part.

- Female movie fans clamored for the celluloid man who had strength of character tempered with the sensitivity to accept a woman on her new terms. Pretty boy looks were the exception. The heartthrob of the seventies was macho with strong features, still attractive but in an "all man" way. This heartthrob was sometimes conflicted in his behavior toward women.

- Women were confident of their ability to set and achieve goals of their own; ready to live life on their terms yet continue to nurture the family. It was a great responsibility, but women took it on with confidence realizing that they were carving out new and different lives for themselves. Tradition was wavering. Eventually women's rights were honored, but only after a long period of trial and error.

- The popularity of television brought the strong, taciturn tough guy into our homes. The men most women adored on the big and small screen exuded confidence but were not handsome in the traditional way. Nevertheless they stirred the hearts of female fans everywhere.

- Innovative producer Samuel Goldwyn died in his sleep in January 1974

- January 9, 1976 heralded the first of a chain of *Rocky* films starring Sylvester Stallone.

- A real life romance blossomed on television in the latter part of the decade when actress Marlo Thomas made a guest appearance on the highly popular Phil Donahue talk show. The two fell unabashedly in love before an entranced television audience of millions. They married after a much publicized courtship.

- In March, 1978 two men conspired to rob Charlie Chaplin's body from his grave.

- The cost of living escalated when a gallon of gas at the beginning of 1970 went from thirty five cents to ninety cents by the close of the decade. Average income in 1970 was $9,000 per annum, moving up to $17,550 by the end of 1979.

- The unparalleled resignation of President Richard Nixon rocked the nation as a first ever event.

- The pill gave women a choice of whether or not and when to have children while at the same time women had the opportunity to experience sexual freedom, once the domain of the male population.

- A new Dodge cost $3869

- Listening to music while driving was a luxury via an 8 track player in one's car.

- The waterbed, offering relief from back pain, gained in popularity.

- The microwave oven was a welcome innovation to the increased number of women now in the workforce outside of the home.

- Many families owned a color TV with shows such family oriented series as *The Waltons*, *The Brady Bunch,* and *Happy Days* entertaining families who watched them together at home.

- Disco took over the dance floor.

- Bell bottoms, hot pants, and platform shoes were the fashions of the era for women.

- Business men wore three piece suits opting for navy or gray along with boldly patterned ties.

- Other male fashion had a flamboyant flair.

- Children played outdoors until dusk without worrying their parents. Mealtime found the entire family seated at the kitchen or dining room table discussing the day's events, some of the meals that were served more than likely microwaved.

- It was a time of warm and cozy when political correctness had not yet intruded on our world.

- It was the era of the "take charge" man when the age of chivalry was not yet dead.

- The first Apple computer was offered for sale in 1977.

- The death of icon Elvis Presley at the age of forty two stunned millions of his fans, many of whom went into mourning for the singer.

- A new house at the beginning of the '70's cost under $24,000. By the end of 1979 it had gone up to $58,000.

- Average annual income in 1970 was $9,000 increasing by the end of the decade to $17.550

- Although the Vietnam War had finally ended, the Cold War continued.

- In late summer of 1972 a group of zealous Palestinian terrorists massacred eleven athletes from Israel after taking them hostage. This attack remains one of the most abhorrent acts of the 20th century.

- In the summer of 1974, President Nixon resigned in shame after a fiasco involving stolen tapes and The Watergate Hotel in Washington D.C.

- The celluloid heartthrob was not always traditionally handsome or possessed of 1930's perfect features, but had a strong, appealing face. The heartthrob of the seventies exuded confidence in himself and admiration for the opposite sex. He was respectful of women of all ages. Male chauvinism may have been a catch phrase in real life, but in reel life men did a little dance and sidestepped this label with sincere chivalry.

HARRISON FORD

Vital Statistics

DOB: July 13, 1942 (Cancer) in Chicago, Illinois
Birth name: Harrison Ford
Height: 6'1"
Hair: Brown
Eyes: Blue
Physique: Slender and toned
Distinguishing marks: Diagonal scar on chin

Biographical Sketch

Father
  Christopher (An advertising executive and part time radio actor)

Mother
  Dorothy Nidelman (Radio actress and homemaker)

Siblings
Terence, three years younger

Boyhood Years

The family lived an upper middle class life in Chicago suburbs of Park Ridge and Morton Grove. Ford was a quiet, shy young boy who was often bullied by his classmates. A "C" student he had little interest school beyond getting passing grades or in sports, Ford preferred to tinker with electronics and build things with his hands.

Although his father was Irish Catholic and his mother a Russian Jew the family did not follow an organized form of religion. Ford is an agnostic by choice.

Harrison Ford and Carrie Fisher in *Star Wars* – 20th Century Fox, 1977

Start of Career

As a dedicated Boy Scout, Ford earned the rank of Life Scout and was awarded a merit badge for Reptile Study. Before graduating from high school in Park Ridge, he adventured into broadcasting when the school acquired a new radio station. While at college Ford decided to take a drama class to help him raise his grade average and, by his own admission, as a means of meeting women. He soon became enthralled with the profession, deciding to pursue an acting career and in 1964 he and his soon to be wife drove to Los Angeles where Ford auditioned to do radio voiceovers.

When no acting jobs were forthcoming, Ford hired himself out as a carpenter to keep food on the table and pay the rent. Studying at the Laguna Playhouse he was eventually signed to a contract with Columbia Studios for $150 a week when he worked. It was his role in the now cult classic *American Graffiti* that brought Ford to the attention of movie producers who recognized his talent and star capability.

Onscreen Persona

Harrison Ford comes across on the screen as a dependable, no nonsense man on the rugged side. His appeal for women comes from a core of strength coupled with a subtle sense of humor that lets the ladies know he enjoys life and invites them to enjoy it with him, if only in a movie theater. Not handsome in the classic perfect profiles of actors from another era, Ford's rugged looks and versatile talent have captivated women fans from his first onscreen appearance in the early seventies. He is a man's man with plenty left over to command attention from the distaff side of moviegoers.

Personal Life

Romances

Lara Flynn Boyle (actress) 2000
Minnie Driver (actress) 2001-2002
Calista Flockhart (actress) 2003-2010

Marriages

Mary Marquardt 1964-1979 (Divorced)
Melissa Maarhison 1983-2001 (Divorced)
Calista Flockhart (actress) June 15, 2010

Harrison Ford, Melanie Griffith, and Sigourney Weaver in *Working Girl* – 20th Century Fox, 1988

Children

Benjamin   Sept. 22, 1967 (with Mary)
Willard   May 14, 1969 (with Mary)
Malcom Carswell March 10, 1987 (with Melissa)
Georgia June 30, 1990 (with Melissa)
Liam (Calista's son, adopted by Ford)

Grandchildren

Eliel 1993
Guiliana 1997
Ethan 2000

Fast Facts

- At the start of his career, Ford was told by a studio head that he would never make it.
- In the '90's Ford was the highest paid actor in Hollywood
- His films have been inducted into the National Film Registry
- He guards his privacy very carefully
- In 1997 Ford was #1 on Empire's list of Top 100 Movie Stars of All Time
- He was a member of Sigma Nu Fraternity while at college
- He has suffered from dyslexia and bouts of depression
- Ford is a staunch Democrat
- He lives in Wyoming in a modest farm style home when he is not working on a film
- He is a devotee of flying having obtained his pilot's license in 1977,
- He owns and pilots six different types of aircraft. His helicopter has been used to locate missing children.
- He says that flying is his passion
- A conscientious objector he did not serve during the Vietnam War
- He is dedicated to environmental causes
- He agreed to play the part in *American Grafitti* providing he didn't have to cut his hair.
- While filming *American Grafitti*, Ford was arrested and asked to move out of the motel in which he was living following his involvement in a bar fight.
- He was known as the Carpenter to the Stars when he supplemented his income by building furniture and making repairs for other actors.
- According to rumor Ford was expelled from college shortly before graduation. The reason varies, depending upon who gives it.
- George Lucas made the decision to cast Ford as Han Solo in *Star Wars* when Lucas heard Ford read with other actors auditioning for the part. The role gave Harrison Ford the push that launched him into super-stardom and heartthrob status.
- While filming *Indiana Jones and the Temple of Doom* in London, Ford suffered a herniated disc and was flown to Los Angeles for back surgery. He returned to work six weeks later.
- Chosen by *People Magazine* as the Sexiest Man Alive 1998

Salary

While attending Columbia's Talent School he was paid $150 per acting job
Ford was once the highest grossing actor in Hollywood earning $25 million plus 20% of the gross for The Widowmaker
Net worth $225 million

Awards and Nominations

Sour Apple Hollywood Women's Press Club 1982
Oscar Best Actor in Motion Picture Drama   1986-*Witness*
Golden Globe
   Best Performance by Actor in Motion Picture- Drama *Witness* 1986
   Best Performance by Actor in Motion Picture- Drama *Mosquito Coast* 1987
   Best Performance by Actor in Motion Picture, Drama *The Fugitive* 1994
   Best Performance by Actor in Motion Picture-Comedy/Musical, *Sabrina* 1996
Blockbuster Entertainment, Favorite Actor-Video *Air Force One* 1996
National Movie Award Best Performance-Male *Indiana Jones and the Kingdom of the Crystal Skull* 2008
People's Choice – *Indiana Jones and the Kingdom of the Crystal Skull* for Favorite On-Screen Match-Up (shared nomination) 2009
Favorite Male Icon-2012
BAFTA   1986-*Witness*
Awards
KCFCC   1986 Best Actor-*Witness*
Bambi   1997   *Air Force One*
Blockbuster Entertainment
   1994 Favorite Actor-Action The Fugitive
   1995 Favorite Actor-Action   *Clear and Present Danger*
   1999 Favorite Actor- Comedy/Romance *Six Days Seven Nights*
   2001 Favorite Actor - Suspense *What Lies Beneath*
   2002 Cecil B. DeMille Award
People's Choice
   1994   Box Office Star of the Century
   1998   Favorite Motion Picture Actor
   1999   Favorite All Time Male Movie Star
   2000   Favorite Motion Picture Actor

Star on the Walk of Fame

6801 Hollywood Blvd.

Harrison Ford and Kate Capshaw in
Indiana Jones and the Temple of Doom –
Paramount Pictures, 1984

RICHARD GERE

Vital Statistics

DOB: August 31(Virgo) 1949 in Philadelphia, Pennsylvania
Name at Birth: Richard Tiffany Gere
Height: 5' 11"
Hair: Brown
Eyes: Deep Set Dark Brown
Physique: Slender and toned
Outstanding attribute: Very soft spoken

Biographical Sketch

Father
   Homer (Insurance agent)

Mother
   Doris Ann (Homemaker)

Siblings
Five children in the family (Richard is the second child and eldest son. He has an older sister, two younger sisters, and a younger brother)

Boyhood Years

He was raised in a modest Methodist family.

Gere is an accomplished musician, excelling in trumpet and piano. As a boy he wrote music for school productions while also serving on the student council for gymnastics, lacrosse, and skiing. Gymnastics garnered him a scholarship to Amherst. Some say that Gere's college major in philosophy may have fostered his deep interest and eventual conversion to Buddhism. However he left Amherst after two years to devote himself to acting.

Richard Gere and Lauren Hutton in
American Gigolo –
Paramount Pictures, 1980

Start of Career

Learning his craft by studying at the Provincetown Playhouse for a season and then as a member of the Seattle Repertory Company, Gere headed for New York to work in the theater. In 1973 the part of Danny Zuko in the Broadway production of *Grease* bought him to the attention of studio heads who signed him to his debut film role in *Report to the Commissioner*. It was his role in *Yanks*, as the love struck American soldier stationed in London that brought him the attention of female fans and led to a series of impressive roles in the films that followed amid the twitters of enamored girls and women.

Onscreen Persona

A combination of brooding sensuality and quiet charisma comes across the screen to coax women into movie theaters. Soft spoken with an underlying tone of confidence, Gere had women champing at the bit from his very first starring role in *Yanks*, 1979.

Personal Life

Romances

Longtime partner Carey Lowell

Marriages

Cindy Crawford 1991-1995 (Divorced)
Carey Lowell November 9, 2002

Children

Homer James Jigme Gere (with Lowell)

Richard Gere and Debra Winger in *An Officer and a Gentleman* – Paramount Pictures, 1982

Fast Facts

- Gere is a Mayflower descendant
- He has been a Buddhist for ten years
- He trained for five months to do the tap dance routine in *Chicago*.
- He attended college on a gymnastics scholarship
- He is not a pure vegan, but has not eaten red meat for more than thirty years
- He was a Boy Scout
- He and wife Carey own The Bedford Post, an eight bedroom Inn located in Bedford, New York. The Inn has two restaurants, a yoga studio and a meditation center.
- He and his former wife, Cindy Crawford were named People Magazine's Sexiest Couple in 1993
- He composed and performed the piano solo in *Pretty Woman*, 1990
- President of the Gere Foundation (1991) serving in a nonprofit capacity focuses on International Humanitarian Issues, in particular that of Tibet.
- Voted Sexiest Man Alive, 1999

Salary

Intersection   1994 $7,000,000
Unfaithful   2002 $15,000,000
Sommersby   1993 $5,000,000
He now commands upward of $5-10 million per film
Net Worth $45 Million

Nominations & Awards

1993 Emmy Outstanding Supporting Actor in a Miniseries or Movie *And The Band Played On*
1982   Golden Globe Best Actor-Motion Picture Drama *An Officer and a Gentleman*
1990   Golden Globe Best Actor-Motion Picture Musical or Comedy *Pretty Woman*
2012   Golden Globe Best Actor-Motion Picture Drama *Arbitrage*
2002   Screen Actors Guild Outstanding Performance by a Male Actor in a Leading Role *Chicago*
Awards Won
1990   Golden Globe Best Performance by an Actor in a Motion Picture Comedy/Musical *Pretty Woman*
2002   Golden Globe Best Actor-Motion Picture Musical or Comedy   *Chicago*
2006   Hasty Pudding *Man of the Year*
2007   Hollywood Film Festival - Actor of the Year 2007
Gere has been nominated twice for a Razzie Award

Star on the Walk of Fame

The winner of a total of twelve awards in various categories, Gere does not, as yet, have a Star on the Walk of Fame

Richard Gere and Julia Roberts in
Pretty Woman – Touchstone Pictures, 1990

NICK NOLTE

Vital Statistics

DOB: February 8, 1941 (Aquarius) in Omaha, Nebraska
Birth Name: Nicholas King Nolte
Height: 6'
Hair: Blonde
Eyes: Blue
Physique: Muscular
Distinguishing attribute: husky/gravelly voice

Biographical Sketch

Father
   Franklin A. Nolte (Sold irrigation pumps, All American football star in his early years)

Mother
   Helen (Department store buyer)

Siblings
Nancy (older) executive at Red Cross

Boyhood Years

Nolte comes from a family of hard workers. His grandfather was a farmer; his father sold irrigation pumps and was also considered for All American status in football at Iowa State. Nolte was a shy boy who was very affected by watching his father confined to his bed from illness brought on by fighting in World War II. This so traumatized the young Nolte that he developed an abhorrence of war that carried through into his adulthood.

Nick Nolte and Susan Blakely in *Rich Man, Poor Man* – ABC Television, 1976

While playing on the football team at Westside High Nolte held the position of kicker. He was dropped from the football team of his first high school because of drinking during a practice session. An independent streak began in Nolte's youth along with a penchant for using his fists when provoked as well as for defying rules. He was considered a maverick to be reckoned with. He went on to attend Arizona State University where he played basketball, baseball and football, but was dropped by the University because of poor grades.

Start of Career

Chance led Nolte to a modeling career with the Eleanor Moore Agency in Minneapolis, Minnesota. Clairol promoted the young man in an ad for their Summer Blond shade of hair coloring. During his successful modeling career appearing in Clairol ads, Nolte was thought to be just another pretty boy. Determined to do more, Nolte moved to Los Angeles to pursue an acting career. He studied first at the Pasadena Playhouse and then enrolled in the Stella Adler Academy to hone his craft. Afterwards Nolte toured the country appearing in fourteen regional theaters in a self-imposed apprenticeship before making his first movie.

Onscreen Persona

Nick Nolte and Joanna Cassidy in *Under Fire* – Orion Pictures, 1983

Nolte was frequently cast as the charming bad boy. Roles that focused on characters that evoked sympathy especially from the women were his strong suit.

It was the part of rogue Tom Jordache in the television mini-series *Rich Man, Poor Man* 1976 that catapulted him to superstardom fame at the age of thirty five, a relatively late age for an actor to reach heartthrob status. Vulnerability combined with a vibe that clearly indicated he would not be beaten down paved the way for a loyal fan following. Female audiences admired the combination of soft center covered by an outer shell of strength and nonchalance that Nolte showed on screen. He received upwards of 2000 fan letters per week when the series aired. His popularity continued though the next decades, but it was his performance as Tom Wingo in *The Prince of Tides* (1991) that made women ardently clamor for more.

One adoring fan in describing his performance said, "He melted the cubes in my ice tray."

Personal Life

Romances

While filming *Cannery Row (*1982) Nolte and co-star Debra Winger had a torrid love affair.

Marriages

Sheila Page (actress) 1966-1970 (Divorced)
Sharon Haddad (dancer) 1978-1983 (Divorced)
Rebecca Linger 1984-1994 (Divorced)

Partner

Clytie Lane (current)

Children

Brawley (son) June 20, 1986 (with Rebecca)
Sophie Lane October 7, 2007 (with Clytie)

Fast Facts

- He has admittedly "made up" much of his biographical background. Whether this was to confuse the press and his public or just for the heck of it is not known.
- In 1965 he received a sentence of five years' probation for selling fake draft cards.
- While studying acting he earned his living as an iron worker.
- In 1968 he was sued for palimony (community property and support) by Karen Ecklund with whom he had lived for a number of years.
- Nolte battled with alcohol and drug addiction for many years.
- *People Magazine* named him Sexiest Man Alive in 1992
- According to friends, Nolte is essentially an introspective, unassuming man who seems to find inner peace through acting.
- Nolte's and Rebecca Linger's son Brawley is an actor who was prominently featured as Mel Gibson's kidnapped son in the film *Ransom*.
- In 2002 Nolte's addiction caught up with him when he was arrested for a DUI. This led to his admission that he had been taking GHB (the date rape drug) for a number of years. It was a much circulated, scary mug shot that made Nolte realize that he had to get his life back together. The first step was to enter a rehabilitation center on the East coast. That was followed by court ordered three years on probation, drug counseling, and random drug testing.
- In October, 2008, a computer printer sparked a fire that destoyed part of his Malibu, California home. Nolte escaped unharmed, but there was reportedly over $1.5 million in damage done.
- He is a devotee of Hemingway
- Today Nolte concentrates on taking care of his health by eating right, avoiding drugs and alcohol and striving to achieve the inner peace he has always longed for.

Salary

Rich Man, Poor Man (1976) $50,000
The Thin Line (1998) $1,000,000
The Prince of Tides (1982) $4,000,000
Net Worth $75 Million

Nominations & Awards

1991 Los Angeles Film Critics Association Best Actor *The Prince of Tides*
1991 Golden Globe Best Actor in a Motion Picture Drama *The Prince of Tides*

1998 New York Film Critics Circle Best Actor *Affliction*
1998 National Society of Film Critics Best Actor *Affliction*
2011 San Diego Film Critics Best Supporting Actor *Warrior*

Star on the Walk of Fame

As of this writing, Nolte does not have a Star on the Walk of Fame

Nick Nolte and Barbra Streisand in
The Prince of Tides – Columbia Pictures, 1991

BURT REYNOLDS

Vital Statistics

DOB: February 11, 1936 (Aquarius) in Lansing, Michigan
Birth Name: Burton Leon Reynolds Jr.
Nickname: Buddy
          Buddy Lee
Hair: Very Dark Brown (wears a toupee)
Eyes: Dark Brown
Physique: Athletic

Biographical Sketch

Father
  Burton Reynolds (Chief of police in Rivera, Florida)

Mother
  Fern (Nurse)

Siblings
Nancy (older sister)

Boyhood Years

Burt Reynolds in *Gunsmoke* – CBS Television, 1955-1975

The Reynolds family moved to Waycross, Georgia when Burt was young, later to Rivera Beach, Florida when Burt Sr. was hired as Chief of Police. Burt's father who was part Cherokee had been raised on an Indian reservation. He was a strict disciplinarian who didn't spare the rod when his son disobeyed the rules. A rebellious youth, Buddy did not take well to his father's rules and would frequently feel the sting of a strap as his father tried to impress the boy with the importance of behaving as expected. In time Buddy obeyed the rules at home, but outside of his home it was a different story. He reveled in being as wild as possible, getting into fist fights and in his teens driving as fast as possible. Many of the fights were due to the bullying he endured as boys at school taunted him with names 'Mullet' and 'Greaseball' because of his Indian and Italian heritage.

Going to the movies was a way to escape. His favorite film was one with an athletic theme, *Jim Thorpe-All American*. This ignited an interest in sports that led to his outstanding athletic prowess in high school.

In 1954 he entered Florida State on a football scholarship and quickly won acclaim and respect as a football hero. In 1955 a knee injury created a problem that kept him off the field for a while. The injury was exacerbated when Reynolds was further injured in a serious automobile accident ending his hope of a career in football.

Armed with the insurance settlement young Reynolds went to New York to hang out while he healed.

Start of Career

Burt Reynolds and Sally Field in *Smokey and the Bandit* – Universal Pictures, 1977

While in New York Reynolds was introduced to Conrad Hopkins, once the secretary of writer James T. Farrel Hopkins. This led to Reynolds first hint of where an acting career might take him. Hopkins, impressed with the young man's looks and demeanor, suggested that Reynolds give some thought to an acting career. He saw something in the young man that led him to believe Reynolds had what it took to make it to the big screen. Instead Reynolds returned to Florida enrolling in Palm Beach Junior College to earn enough credits to re-enroll in Florida State and resume his place on the football team since believing his injuries had fully healed.

While at Palm Beach J.C. he enrolled in an English Literature class taught by Professor Watson Duncan, who was also the drama coach. Always with an eye out for new talent, Duncan urged Burt to attend tryouts. The rest is history. Burt has often credited his English Professor with giving him a jumpstart on his acting career.

Onscreen Persona

He came across as a man's man with a strong appeal to women who were drawn to his good looks and quick wit. From 1972 thru 1982 Reynolds was the number one box office attraction. It was the film *Deliverance* that finally made Hollywood movie makers sit up and take notice. It also made Reynolds a super star, paving the way for better roles and more money. His versatility as an actor was evident in the variety of roles that followed showcasing his ability to play light comedy as well as serious drama. Most important was the actor Reynolds' onscreen connection with the women in the audience.

The infamous, daring Cosmopolitan Centerfold in (1972) did much to further draw on the fantasies of his feminine fans.

Personal Life

Romances

An eligible bachelor, Reynolds never lacked for female companionship. Among his actress girlfriends were Inger Stevens, Tammy Wynette, Adrienne Barbeau and Luci Arnaz. A romantic liaison with Dinah Shore (twenty years older than he) made the gossip columns sizzle with regular reports on the romantic duo. They were together for six years.

While filming *Smokey and the Bandit* opposite Sally Field, the two fell deeply in love. Fans followed reports of the romance with avid interest and were visibly saddened when the relationship ended after five years. Career differences were rumored to be the reason. Her career zigged with the release of *Norma Rae* while his zagged as his star status waned due to some less than popular films. The relationship apparently couldn't stand the strain.

Reynolds later had a romantic relationship with Pam Seals, a cocktail waitress, for four years. The relationship did not end amicably.

Marriages

Judy Carne (actress) 1963-1965 (Divorced)
Loni Anderson (actress) 1988-1993 (Divorced)

Children

Quinton Anderson, August 31, 1988 (adopted)

Fast Facts

- Reynolds signed a contract with Universal in 1958. A year later he was told that he couldn't act and released from his contact. However he had the last laugh on the nay sayers when his career began to zoom in the seventies and Reynolds was hailed as a super star.
- While being interviewed on the set of his television series *Dan August* in 1970 Burt told a writer that the one thing missing in his life was a son. Adopting Quinton was the highlight of his life.
- Burt's first impression upon viewing *Boogie Nights* was so negative that he fired his agent. The film and his performance went on to receive enthusiastic reviews from critics. He has been awarded honorary sheriff's badges from numerous small towns throughout the country.
- In 1955 he survived a serious operation receiving nine pints of blood and the removal of his spleen.

- He was once an avid autograph collector and has in his collection autographs from Clark Gable, Frank Sinatra, Bette Davis and Barbara Stanwyck that he treasures.
- A great admirer of Spencer Tracey, he was befriended by the actor when both were filming at the same studio. The two formed a solid friendship often spending time together discussing sports and acting.
- From 1978 to thru 1982 Reynolds was reported to be the highest paid actor in Hollywood.
- His son is named for Quint Aspen, the half breed blacksmith Reynolds portrayed in the television series *Gunsmoke*.
- During the mid '90's Reynolds health deteriorated and he became addicted to medication taken to ease his pain and to help him sleep.
- He was close friends with Charles Nelson Reilly and an inseparable friend of Dom De Luise
- He has worn a hair piece for many years. It has been reported that he once paid $12,000 for a hair piece.
- He bought a 180 acre ranch in Florida for his parents that once belonged to Al Capone
- In 1983, he received a blow while doing his own stunts filming *City Heat* that resulted in a broken jaw. Riddled with pain for months Burt sought relief by taking pain killers. When he tried to wean himself off of the drugs he fell into a coma for eight days. Reynolds recalls having an out of body experience during this time.
- In 1996 Reynolds filed for Chapter 11 Bankruptcy brought about by failed films and a much publicized costly divorce from Loni Anderson. He was also having difficulty getting jobs at the time because studio heads felt he was no longer bankable.
- He was honored in 2000 with the Children at Heart Award for his contribution and humanitarian work with children who were injured in the Chernobyl nuclear fallout in Russia.
- In 2009 he checked himself into a rehab center due to an addiction to pain medication following back surgery.
- The next year he had quintuple bypass surgery.
- Reynolds has made a number of come backs from ill health, a chaotic and expensive divorce and mistakes in judgment from failed movies, but he has always landed on his feet.
- He is admired for his resiliency.
- His favorite films in which he starred are: *Starting Over*, *The End*, *Smokey and the Bandit* and *Deliverance*.
- He has received The People's Choice Award for Favorite All Around Motion Picture Actor six years in a row.
- He is the founder of The Jupiter Playhouse in Jupiter, Florida and has often directed productions.
- He was much admired by Frank Sinatra

- During his early days as an actor Reynolds was often mistaken for Marlon Brando who he greatly resembled.
- Reynolds has done many of his own stunts throughout his film career.
- It has been rumored, as this is being written, that his multimillion dollar home in Hobe, Florida is being foreclosed due to nonpayment of his mortgage. Reynolds has indicated his surprise at this. He has been trying to sell the property for years but in the slow market has had to lower the price a number of times to no avail.
- In 2007 Burt was pleased to accept a prestigious honor at the World Stuntman Award. Banquet. Arnold Schwarzenegger who presented him with the Taurus Lifetime Achievement plaque said of Reynolds, "he is the greatest of the great."
- Early in the decade he could be seen in commercials for Miller Lite Beer.

Salary

Angel Baby (1961) $15,000
City Heat (1984) $4,000,000
Net Worth $12 Million

Awards and Nominations

Golden Globe 1971, 1975, 1980, 1991, 1993
1998   Oscar Best Actor in a Supporting Role *Boogie Nights*
1992   Primetime Emmy *Evening Shade*
1991   Razzie
1998   Golden Globe Best Performance by Actor in Supporting Role Motion Picture *Boogie Nights*
1991   Primetime EmmyLead Actor Comedy series *Evening Shade*
1994   Razzie Worst Actor *Cop and a Half*

Burt Reynolds and Dolly Parton in *The Best Little Whorehouse in Texas* – Universal Pictures, 1982

Star on the Walk of Fame

6838 Hollywood Blvd.

JOHN TRAVOLTA

Vital Statistics

DOB: February 18, 1954 (Aquarius) in Englewood, New Jersey
Name at Birth: John Joseph Travolta
Nickname: Little Bone (he was very skinny as a youngster and teenager)
Hair: Black
Eyes: Blue mixed w green & gray
Physique: Athletic

Biographical Sketch

Father
  Salvatore, a semi pro football player, later a tire salesman

Mother
  Helen, member of Sunshine Sister, a vocal group on radio and a high school drama teacher

Siblings
Joey, Sam, Ellen, Ann, and Margaret

Boyhood Years

John Travolta, Ron Palillo, Robert Hegyes, Lawrence Hilton-Jacobs, and Gabe Kaplan in *Welcome Back, Kotter* – ABC Television, 1975-1979

Travolta was the youngest in a family of six children

Encouraging his children to express their music and acting abilities, Travolta's father helped them build a theatre in the basement of the basement of their home. John quickly realized that his love of the music especially that of The Beatles and a penchant for dancing could lead to an acting career and set about perfecting his craft. He learned to play the guitar, entered and won a Twist dance competition in school and followed through his admiration of actor James Cagney by enrolling in an Actor's Workshop was he was 12. He went on to take tap dancing lessons from Gene Kelly's brother Fred improving on himself by watching the TV show *Soul Train* and adapting new dance steps into his repertoire. Travolta was immersed in show business.

His parents agreed to let him drop out of high school at the age of sixteen so he could pursue his acting career. Moving in with his older sister Ann who lived in New York, Travolta held a number of jobs to support himself taking whatever theatrical jobs off Broadway he was offered. As his experience grew so did his talent and soon he was being offered parts in TV. In 1975 the doors opened wide as Travolta won the role of the tough, cocky Vinnie Barbarino in the television series, *Welcome Back Kotter*.

Within a short time of its debut, the show had made him a star and the hero of young girls who huddled around their television sets ever week to see what cool and self-assured Barbarino was up to. When movie roles came along, John had a built an adoring following who were happy to plunk down the price of a ticket to see their idol on the big screen. The decade of the Seventies became his time to shine.

Start of Career

Travolta took odd jobs to sustain him during the lean days while doing summer stock and waiting for his "break." Recognition came when he joined the touring company of the off Broadway musical, *Grease* leading to the part of Doody in the film when he was barely out of his teens.

At the start of the decade, Travolta appeared on television in a few minor roles including an ad for the army. When *Welcome Back, Kotter* was being cast for television his career was launched in the role of gang leader 'Barbarino.' Within a short time after it was aired in 1975, the confident, very cool character played by Travolta was recognized as a bright new talent as well as the focus of enthusiastic female fans.

The stellar role of dancer Tony Manero in the classic disco-focused *Saturday Night Fever* brought John further into the world of adoring fans and won him a place among super stars of the era. He hasn't faltered since.

Onscreen Persona

His trademark strut, the flashing smile and striking good looks came across the screen with ease. With the release of *Saturday Night Fever* young Travolta suddenly became a household name as women clamored to see his films while young men attempted to emulate his onscreen brash moves as a way to attract girls. Disco raged with a fierce intensity as dance fever became the dedicated social venue of the decade. In his white suit, the deep cleft in his chin lending a vulnerability to his looks and the flashing eyes, John Travolta shone on screen.

John Travolta and Karen Lynn Gorney in *Saturday Night Fever* – Paramount Pictures, 1977

While filming *The Boy in the Plastic Bubble* in 1976, twenty-four-year-old Travolta fell in love with his so-star Diana Hyland, sixteen years his senior. The romance was fodder for Hollywood gossip columnists. Readers of fan magazines and viewers of Hollywood news on television were titillated by all of the reports of the romantic twosome. Sadly, the relationship was a brief one as Diana lost a fight against breast cancer a year after they met. It has been reported that she died in John's arms. Her death so devastated the actor that he withdrew for several months going into a self-imposed dating hibernation. It took years before Travolta opened up his heart to love again following Diana s death. He eventually made the dating scene again and let love into his heart when he met Kelly Preston in 1987.

Returning to his career Travolta wanted more of a challenge and went on to appear in a variety of roles. However nothing matched the fervor of his Tony Mareno. When the actor originally slated to play the part of Vincent Vega in *Pulp Fiction* dropped out and John Travolta stepped in to play the cold and cruel criminal partner to Samuel Jackson a different side to the actor surfaced. A new facet of his career emerged to the delight of his fans.

Marriages

Kelly Preston (actress) September, 1991

Children

Jett April 13, 1992 (died January 2, 2009 of a seizure)
Ella Blue April, 2000
Benjamin Hunter Kaleo November 23, 2010

Fast Facts

- Both John and Kelly are practicing Scientologists. Travolta became interested in the controversial religion when he read *Dianetics* during the filming of *The Devil's Run*
- He owns and flies a jet.
- When Oprah Winfrey gave the studio audience of her first show in September, 2010 an all-expense paid trip to Australia, Travolta piloted the plane that flew them there.
- He was the first male cover of *McCall's* magazine in July, 1978
- *Entertainment Weekly* voted Travolta as the 64th Greatest Movie Star of All Time
- Princess Diana asked him for a dance when they attended the same White House party and of course he obliged.
- He and Forest Whitaker are good friends. The two appeared in *Phenomenon* together.
- He worked on his disco dancing skills for nine months during the filming of *Saturday Night Fever*.
- He was close friends with Robin Williams
- A childhood problem with insomnia resurfaced during the filming of *Blow Out*, an intense film.
- Playing the violin helps calm his nerves
- His career floundered in the 1980's but was revived in the '90's.
- He says that regular marriage counseling is helpful to his marriage

- He was offered the lead in the film version of *Chicago* but was advised to turn it down. It went to Richard Gere who won an award for this role in the movie.
- Travolta has recorded a number of singles over the years adding singer to his resume

Salary

$140,000   *Pulp Fiction*   (1994)
$8,000,000   *Phenomenon*   (1996)
$17,000,000   *Primary Colors* (1998)
He currently receives $20,000,000 per picture
Net Worth $160 Million

John Travolta and Olivia Newton-John in *Grease* – Paramount Pictures, 1978

Awards and Nominations

1995 Academy Award Nomination Best Actor in a Leading Role *Pulp Fiction*

1978 Academy Award Nomination Best Actor in a Leading Role Saturday Night Fever
1998 Saturn Award Best Actor Face/Off
1997 American Cinematheque Award
1996 American Comedy Award Funniest Actor in a Motion Picture Leading Role Get Shorty
2013 American Film Festival Career Tribute
1995 BAFTA Nomination Best Actor Pulp Fiction
1998 BAFTA Britiannia Award for Excellence in Film
1999 Blockbuster World Artist Award
1998 Chicago International Film Festival Lifetime Achievement Award
1998 Golden Apple Award Male Star of the Year
1978 Golden Apple Award Male Star of the Year
2008 Golden Globes Nomination Best Performance Supporting Actor Hairspray
1999 Golden Globes Nomination Best Actor in a Motion Picture Comedy/Musical Primary Colors
1996 Golden Globe Award Best Actor in a Motion Picture Comedy/Musical Get Shorty
1995 Golden Globe Nomination Best Actor Motion Picture Drama Pulp Fiction
1979 Golden Globe World Film Favorite Male
1979 Golden Globe Nomination Best Actor Motion Picture Comedy/Musical Grease
1978 Golden Globe Nomination Best Actor Motion Picture Comedy/Musical Saturday Night Fever
1981 Harvard Hasty Pudding Man of the Year

Star on the Walk of Fame

6901 Hollywood Blvd.

Chapter Six
THE EIGHTIES

1980 ushered in the decade of "ME" focusing on the pursuit of status. Who had the most luxurious home, the most expensive car, a wardrobe of designer labels and the most prestigious lifestyle was what it was all about. Status was the watchword that seemed to propel the nation as the Eighties debuted. The rich and famous took center stage. Spend, spend, spend was the theme song of the Yuppies (young and upwardly mobile). Reticence was a thing of the past as the era opened with the voice of the people shouting their views on everything from politics to personalities.

- Nineteen-year-old kindergarten teacher, Diana, the new Royal Princess was a virgin whispered to be a necessary qualification for the bride of the future King of England. Diana, a member of the aristocratic Spencer family, quickly captured the hearts and admiration of not only the UK but the world over with her demure sweetness. The couple first met in the summer of 1980. Following a six month courtship Prince Charles proposed, Lady Diana said yes and plans for the fairy tale wedding began. The televised ceremony was held in London's St. Paul's Cathedral on July 29, 1981 and viewed by 750 million people throughout the world. The date of the wedding was later declared a national holiday in the UK.

- *Dynasty*, nighttime soap opera series about wealth, intrigue, and social mores debuts on January 12, 1981.

- Hollywood icon Ingrid Bergman dies of cancer on her birthday, August 29, 1982.

- *Fatal Attraction* premieres on September 11, 1987 creating a stir among married people who may be thinking about having an affair.

- February 29, 1983 the final episode of the long running army film *M*A*S*H* gathers fans around television sets to say farewell.

- Saturn and her rings of beauty was photographed by spaceship Voyager 2 creating a new interest and curiosity about the vastness of the Universe. Another wonder astonishing us is as an adventurous man who flew a plane propelled only by solar power. He managed to stay up in the air for over five hours. It was a powerful indication of what harnessing the energy of the sun could accomplish.

- Highlighting the year was the nomination by President Ronald Reagan of the first woman to sit on the Supreme Court. Sandra Day O'Connor gave credence to feminine power with this recognition by serving her country and her sex with honor.

- Rubik's Cube, a toy that challenged the mind debuted in 1981 with sales well over ten million dollars.

- The medical and technological fields introduced the miracle of the mechanical heart. Although he lived only one hundred and twelve days after receiving the Jarvic-7, sixty one year old Barney Clark was able to leave his bed and walk for the first time in months soon after the breakthrough heart surgery.

- All around entertainer Michael Jackson showed us his Moonwalk that continues to entertain

- In March, 1981 John Lennon was assassinated in broad daylight. Shocked fans throughout the world went into deep mourning.

- President Reagan survived an attempted assassination by John Hinckley Jr. as he walked to his limousine surrounded by secret service men.

- On September 18, 1983 Vanessa Williams became the first Black American to be crowned Miss America.

- *E.T.,* a lovable visitor from outer space enchanted movie audiences.

- The Vietnam Memorial was erected in Washington, D.C.

- In August, 1984 *Red Dawn* (starring actor Patrick Swayze) was the first movie to be given the label of PG13.

- George Clooney made his television debut on September 21 1985 when he became a regular on *The Facts of Life*.

- October 2, 1988 icon Rock Hudson was the first celebrity actor to publicly succumb to AIDS. He was 59.

- In the United States movies were as popular as ever as 20 million people per week escaped their everyday lives in the comfort of a darkened theater where imagination held court.

- Actors on the big screen were a compelling combination of youthful good looks and sophistication. The small, more intimate television screen brought Hollywood hunks into the comfort of people's homes in dramatic series and made for television movies.

- The competition between the two mediums was constant and fierce.

TOM CRUISE

Vital Statistics

DOB: July 3, 1962 (Cancer) in Syracuse, New York
Birth Name: Thomas Cruise Mapother, IV
Height: 5' 7"
Hair: Dark Brown
Eyes: Brown
Physique: Six pack abs, also described as rippling.
Outstanding Feature: Winsome Smile

Biographical Sketch

Father
  Thomas Cruise Mapother, III, (Electrical engineer)

Mother
  Mary

Siblings
Lee Anne
Marian
Cass

Boyhood Years

Cruise has said that his father was a bully who beat him often. The family lived modestly in Canada until Cruise was twelve when his mother took her four children and left the man the actor describes as a merchant of chaos.

Tom Cruise and Rebecca DeMornay in *Risky Business* – Warner Brothers, 1983

Because of his small stature young Cruise withstood years of bullying from classmates. However he went on to became a dedicated floor hockey player who played the game mercilessly with no concern for his personal safety. This zealousness cost him an injured knee and a chipped front tooth. His single minded dedication to hockey went on to serve Cruise well in other areas of his life.

While attending Henry Munro Middle School, Cruise played the lead in a school production shaping his ambition to become an actor. Prior to that Cruise spent a year studying to become a monk in a Franciscan seminary on a church scholarship.

Start of Career

Abandoning the idea of entering the priesthood, Cruise focused on acting that he felt was his true calling. Upon graduating from high school he decided to go for broke and headed for New York to get a toe hold in the acting profession by performing in a number of theatrical productions. Eventually he traveled to the West Coast where he made his first appearance on screen in a small part in the 1981 production of *Endless Love*.

His career spiraled upwards after the release of the movie *Risky Business* in 1983, a movie well ahead of its time in theme and very well received by smitten females in the movie theater audience.

Onscreen Persona

Clean cut and boyish looking, Cruise captivated the opposite sex not only with his pleasing countenance, but because he projected a look of friendliness and appeared to be a very likable guy.

Tom Cruise and Demi Moore in *A Few Good Men* – Columbia Pictures, 1992

Personal Life

Cruise has a reputation among his peers of being one of the nicest actors in town.

Romances

Relationship with actress Rebecca De Mornay 1983-85
Brief dating friendship with Heather Locklear
Relationship with Penelope Cruz 2001-2004

Marriages

Mimi Rogers	1987 - 1990 (Divorced)
Nicole Kidman	1980 - 2001 (Divorced)
Katie Holmes	2005 - 2012 (Divorced)

Children

Isabella and Connor (adopted while married to Kidman)
Suri 2006 (daughter with Katie Holmes)

Fast Facts

- Everyone within the Hollywood community speaks highly of Cruise.

- "Nothing ends nicely. That's why it ends." A favorite personal quote of his, perhaps a reflection of his life experiences.
- Cruise campaigned along with other actors to encourage young people to vote in the 2008 elections.
- Most of his films have been blockbusters bringing in millions at the box office.
- He was ranked #1 on the Hot List of *Entertainment Tonight* in 2006.
- In 2007 he was #14.
- He proposed to Katie on top of the Eiffel Tower
- It has been said that Cruise was introduced to Scientology by first wife, Mimi Rogers, during their courtship days.
- He dealt with dyslexia for much of his life, attributing his cure to L. Ron Hubbard founder of Scientology.
- In 1990 *People Magazine* voted him The Sexiest Man Alive
- In 2006 *Forbes Magazine* listed Cruise as the world's most powerful celebrity
- He has a pilot's license and owns a WWII P-51, Mustang, and Pitts Special S-2B Stunt Plane.
- He has been quoted as saying that he loves kids and wanted to have a large family with Katie
- Because of the strained relationship with his father, Cruise is very close to his children, who he says are the most important part of his life.
- He has referred to daughter Suri as his fountain of youth
- Upon the death of Paul Newman, he said "The world has lost an icon. I have lost an idol."
- He believes in aliens, stating that it is arrogant to think that we are alone in the Universe.
- Cruise was honored by Mentor L.A. for his work on behalf of children throughout the world.
- In May, 2011 he received the Simon Wiesenthal Humanitarian Award
- He is only the fourth actor to receive the Entertainment Icon Award from the Friars Club
- It has been rumored that he and Penelope Cruz had reached the point of discussing marriage but she ended the relationship because she felt she couldn't embrace Scientology for herself.

Salary

1983 *Risky Business* $75,000
2001 *Minority Report* $25,000,000 + 30% of box office profits
Net Worth $ 250 million dollars

Awards and Nominations

Academy/Oscar
1990   Best Actor in Leading Role *Born on the Fourth of July*
1997   Best Actor in Leading Role *Jerry Maguire*

2000 Best Actor in Supporting Role *Magnolia*
Golden Globe/Nominated
1984 Best Performance by Actor in Motion Picture-Comedy/Musical *Risky Business*
1993 Best Performance by Actor in Motion Picture-Drama *A Few Good Men*
2004 Best Performance by Actor in Motion Picture-Drama *The Last Samurai*
Golden Globe/Won
1990 Best Performance by Actor in Motion Picture-Drama *Born on the Fourth of July*
1997 Best Performance by Actor in Motion Picture-Comedy/Musical *Jerry Maguire*
2000 Best Performance by Actor in Supporting Role in Motion Picture *Magnolia*

Star on the Walk of Fame

6912 Hollywood Blvd.

Tom Cruise and Indra Ove in
Interview with the Vampire –
Geffen Film Company, 1994

TED DANSON

Vital Statistics

DOB: December 29, 1947 (Capricorn) in San Diego, California
Name at Birth: Edward Bridges Danson, III
Height: 6' 2 1/2"
Hair Brown
Eyes: Brown
Physique: Athletic
Outstanding feature: Strong Square jaw

Biographical Sketch

Father
  Edward (Archeologist and museum director)

Mother
  Jessica

Siblings
Jan

Boyhood Years

Ted Danson and Shelley Long in
Cheers – NBC Television, 1982-1993

As a youngster, Danson's friends were the Hopi and Navajo who lived on an Indian reservation near Flagstaff, Arizona, where the Danson family lived during Ted's formative years. Athletic and sports minded Danson played high school basketball. When he was just twelve the curator at the Museum of Northern Arizona engaged the impressionable youngster in a game he called billboarding. Danson took part with a friend in destroying hundreds of outdoor advertising signs in the name of the environment. This so impressed Danson that he undertook advocating for environmental causes and as an adult has been instrumental in a number of organizations dedicated to protecting the environment ever since.

Start of Career

A chance audition that led to his transferring to Carnegie-Mellon University in his sophomore year where he enrolled in the drama department.

Onscreen Persona

An excellent sense of timing and an appealing smile combined to create the image of a cool, nonchalant stud whose carefree style and good looks were a challenge to female audiences. In *Cheers* Danson exemplified a combination of handsome with not too swift in the intelligent arena and women lapped it up.

Personal Life

Romance

During the filming of the comedy *Made in America* opposite Whoopi Goldberg, the two began a much publicized romantic relationship. It lasted a short time.

While on a canoe ride together during a break in filming of *Pontiac Moon* co-stars Danson and Mary Steenburgen fell deeply in love.

Marriage

Randall Lee Gosch August, 1979-1977 Marriages (Divorced)
Cassandra Coates July, 1977-1993(Divorced)

Mary Steenburgen (actress) October 1995

Children

Kate 1979
Alexis 1985 (adopted)
Lilly and Charlie McDowell (Stepchildren with Steenburgen)

Ted Danson and Whoopi Goldberg in *Made in America* – Warner Brothers, 1993

Fast Facts

- Enjoys tap dancing for fun.
- Has had his photo on the cover of *GQ* three times.
- While filming *Living with the Dead,* a mini-series about the life of psychic James Praagh, Danson was united with his deceased father through the psychic. It made a believer of the actor. He is convinced that in years to come contacting those who have passed on will be routine in what he calls *Common Sense 101*.
- He admits to having a faulty social memory and often calls people by the wrong name.
- He and Steenburgen have a friendship with former President Bill Clinton dating back many years. They visited The White House on a number of occasions while Clinton was in office and always slept in The Lincoln Bedroom.
- The couple attended Chelsea Clinton's wedding.

- Danson is very involved in environmental and philanthropic causes. He is the founder of the American Ocean Campaign (1986) dedicated to preserving our oceans and marine wildlife.
- He always waits until his wife falls asleep before he falls asleep himself. It's a ritual he is said to find endearing.
- He is a sculptor.
- He follows a vegan diet but does eat fish.

Salary

1993   Season of *Cheers* $450,000 per episode
1994   *Getting Even with Dad* $4,000,000
CSI $225,000 per episode
Net Worth $60 million

Nominations & Awards

Nominations Emmy Best Actor in TV Comedy Series Nine Times
Awards Golden Globe Best Actor in TV Comedy Series 1989, 1990
Emmy Best Actor in TV Comedy Series 1990, 1993

Star on the Walk of Fame

7021 Hollywood Blvd.

Ted Danson and Terry Ferrell in
Becker – CBS Television, 1998-2004

MICHAEL DOUGLAS

Vital Statistics

DOB: September 25, 1944 (Libra) in New Brunswick, New Jersey
Name at Birth: Michael Kirk Douglas
Height: 5'10"
Hair: Sandy Blonde
Eyes: Blue
Physique: Athletic
Distinguishing Attribute: Husky Voice

Biographical Sketch

Father
  Kirk Douglas (Actor)

Mother
  Diana Dills (Actress)

Siblings
Joel   (younger half-brother)
Peter (younger half-brother)
Eric   (younger half-brother, deceased July 2004)

Boyhood Years

The divorce of Douglas' parents when he was six kept him and his father apart for most of the time, with the exception of the holidays. Michael's formative years were spent at Eaglebrook School in Massachusetts. Although younger than his classmates, he kept up scholastically.

Michael Douglas and Karl Malden in
The Streets of San Francisco –
ABC Television, 1972-1977

His father's caution that acting was an emotionally erratic career and he preferred his children not to consider it did nothing to change Michael's mind. He was determined to make acting his career from his early teens. To that end Michael studied acting with Wynn Handman at The American Place Theatre in New York before going out on casting interviews.

Start of Career

Because he was labeled the next Kirk Douglas the fledgling actor chose his movie roles very carefully to avoid being identified with his father's macho image on screen. In time he was more recognized among his peers and movie audiences as a skilled actor in his own right. Although he made his acting debut in the television series *The Streets of San Francisco* starring Karl Malden, Douglas didn't reach heartthrob status until the '80's.

When *The Streets of San Francisco* ended in 1977, he concentrated on making movies, emerging soon afterwards a full-fledged heartthrob.

Onscreen Persona

Striking good looks and an obvious talent drew throngs of female audiences into theaters whenever one of his films was shown. Women were intrigued by the sensitivity and humor Douglas displayed on screen. He was young, good looking and talented enough to portray a variety of characters on screen convincingly.

Michael Douglas and Glenn Close in *Fatal Attraction* – Paramount Pictures, 1987

Personal Life

Meeting Catherine Zeta-Jones in 1999 is said to have completely changed his life for the better. Their marriage is considered to be one of the most successful in Hollywood. Together they have dealt with a serious stalking issue (2004) by taking legal action against the woman who was sending letters threatening Catherine's life for over a year, leading her to the verge of a collapse. The woman behind the letters was prosecuted and sentenced to three years in prison.

In August 2010, Douglas was found to have stage-four Throat Cancer. A series of chemotherapy and radiation treatments resulted in remission. Having lost a great deal of weight after months of treatment Douglas went on a weight gain diet when he was pronounced in remission.

Romances

Brenda Vaccaro 1962-1968
Kathleen Turner 1983

Marriages

Deandra Douglas March, 1977-June, 2000 (Divorced)
Catherine Zeta-Jones November 18, 2000

Children

Cameron Morell December 13, 1978 (with Diandra)
Dylan Michael August 8, 2000 (with Catherine)
Carys Zeta April 20, 2003 (with Catherine)

Fast Facts

- Branching out to producer, Douglas's first effort was *One Flew Over the Cuckoo's Nest*, a film based upon a book that his father purchased and gave to Michael. The movie went on to win more awards than any other film to that date.
- He takes his position as an actor seriously and tries to infuse a message of peace into each of his films.
- The assassination of John Lennon, who lived just a few blocks from Douglas at the time, left him shaken for a very long time.
- He advocates for nuclear disarmament
- A skiing accident in 1980 halted his career for three years
- In September, 1992 Douglas entered the Sierra Tucson Center for alcohol and drug addiction where he was successfully treated.
- He received an honorary Doctorate of Letters in 2006 from the University of St. Andrews in Scotland
- Douglas holds citizenship in both the USA and Bermuda (by virtue of his mother) and owns homes in New York and Bermuda
- He underwent knee surgery
- He and Catherine, share the same birth date although he is twenty five years her senior

Salary

Basic Instinct   (1992) $15,000,000
The American President (1995) $15,000,000
A Perfect Murder   (1998) 20,000,000
Net Worth $ 200 Million

Michael Douglas and Annette Bening in
The American President –
Columbia Pictures, 1995

Awards and Nominations

Douglas has been nominated numerous times for Golden Globe Award, Emmy and Oscar as well as other prestigious acting awards.
1988 Academy Award Best Actor in a Leading Role *Wall Street*
1988 Golden Globe Best Performance by an Actor in a Motion Picture Drama *Wall Street*

Star of the Walk of Fame

As of this writing, Michael Douglas does not have a Star on the Walk of Fame

HARRY HAMLIN

Vital Statistics

DOB: October 30, 1951 (Scorpio) in Pasadena, California
Name at Birth: Harry Robinson Hamlin
Height: 5' 10"
Hair: Dark Brown
Eyes: Brown
Physique: Slender & Well Toned
Outstanding Feature: Sensual Mouth

Biographical Sketch

Father
   Chauncey Jerome Hamlin (Rocket scientist involved in the space program in 50's and 60's.)

Mother
   Bernice (Socialite-housewife)

Siblings
Older brother
Younger half brother

Boyhood Years

Harry Hamlin in *Clash of the Titans* – MGM, 1981

Growing up in a family of privilege, Hamlin attended private schools as a youngster. Although his parents were conservative for the most part, they surprised him with a gift of a subscription to *Playboy Magazine* the Christmas he was eleven.

When he was thirteen Hamlin's mother took him to New York where they attended a performance by Richard Burton in *Hamlet*. Afterward Harry caught a glimpse of Burton being met in a limousine in which the beautiful Elizabeth Taylor was waiting. The story goes that an impressionable young boy was so fascinated by this display of celebrity lifestyle that he decided then and there that he would become an actor.

Start of Career

While attending The Hill Street boarding school in Pennsylvania Hamlin appeared in a number of musicals and plays as well as participating in the sports of lacrosse and soccer. Deciding to study for an acting career, Hamlin went on to graduate from Yale with a BA in Drama, then attended the American Conservatory Theatre's Advanced Actor training Program emerging from his studies with a Master of Fine Arts degree in acting.

Onscreen Persona

Having made an entre' into the world of the thespian aided by both his good looks and talent Hamlin was cast in a pivotal role in the film *Clash of the Titans*. Young and sensually appealing the newbie actor immediately caused feminine hearts to beat faster and he was soon heralded as a major heartthrob.

Personal Life

Romances

Long term live-in relationship with actress Ursula Andress, fifteen years his senior (1978-1982)

Marriages

Laura Johnson (actress) 1985-1989 (Divorced)
Nicolette Sheridan (actress) 1991-1993 (Divorced)
Lisa Rinna (actress) 1997

Harry Hamlin, Jill Eikenberry, and Corbin Bernsen in *L.A. Law* – NBC Television 1986-1994

Children

Dimitri 1981 (with Ursula Andress)
Delilah June 1998 (with Lisa Rinna)
Amelia June 2001 (with Lisa Rinna)

Fast Facts

- The television series *Studs Lonigan* further established his heartthrob status
- Chosen People's Sexiest Man Alive (1987)
- Member and one time President of Delta Kappa Epsilon Fraternity
- He and his wife own a women's boutique in Sherman Oaks, California called Bella Gray
- He was awarded a Fulbright Scholarship for acting in 1976 but returned the money choosing to accept a role in *Movie Movie* instead.
- His aunt, Martha Visser, was a renowned artist whose works were exhibited at the Museum of Art in New York City
- Grandson of Chauncey Jerome Hamlin, founder of the Buffalo Museum of Science, Buffalo, New York
- He is considered to be highly intellectual, sociable and gracious

- He and Lisa appeared in a red carpet type commercial for Silhouettes, a product of Depends for women.
- He was a contestant on *Dancing with the Stars* in 2006
- In a candid interview Hamlin discussed the "drink" from the film *The Crash* that was referred to in real life as wakeup juice. According to Hamlin his father became addicted to this drink that purportedly contained speed. At the time the ingredient was kept under wraps. Hamlin stated that it was distributed among those in the space program, that President Kennedy sampled the concoction as well. At the time it was considered innocuous except for the burst of energy that resulted from drinking it. A book about Max Jacobson entitled *Dr. Feelgood* was supposedly written about the German doctor who was said to have distributed this wonder drink.

Awards and Nominations

Golden Globe 1978 Best Motion Picture Acting Debut /Male- *Movie Movie*
Golden Globe 1988 Best Performance by an actor in a Television Series, *L.A. Law*
Golden Globe 1989 Best Performance by Actor in TV Series Drama, *L.A. Law*

Star on the Walk of Fame

As of this writing, Harry Hamlin does not have a Star on the Walk of Fame.

Harry Hamlin and Jason Robards in
Laguna Heat – HBO, 1987

TOM SELLECK

Vital Statistics

DOB: January 29, 1945 (Aquarius) in Detroit, Michigan
Name at Birth: Thomas William Selleck
Nickname: Tom
Height: 6' 4"
Hair: Dark Brown
Eyes: Green
Physique: Athletic
Distinguishing Feature: Prominent Mustache
　　　　　　　　　　　　Warm Smile Displaying Deep Dimples
　　　　　　　　　　　　Deep, Easily Recognized Voice

Biographical Sketch

Father
　Robert (Real estate manager and investor who managed Selleck Properties at the time of his death in 2001)

Mother
　Martha (Homemaker)

Siblings
Robert One year older
Daniel Five years younger

Boyhood Years

Tom Selleck and Dana Delaney in *Magnum, P.I.* – CBS Television, 1980-1988

The family moved to Sherman Oaks located in the San Fernando Valley just outside of Los Angeles proper. Here Selleck and his brothers enjoyed a happy childhood. At Grant High School, Tom excelled in sports. This resulted in a basketball scholarship to USC where he joined the Trojan team. During his college days he earned pocket money by modeling for print ads later moving into TV commercials.

With a strong interest in architecture Selleck planned on majoring in business and architecture at college but, as he explains it, he arrived late at enrollment and found those classes filled. The next table offered openings in drama, so Selleck signed on. This was the fortuitous occurrence that ultimately led him to his true lifetime career. It wasn't long before he found that he was happy with this accidental choice and with the encouragement of his drama teacher he focused on making acting his life's work.

A member of the Sigma Chi Fraternity Selleck considers the friendships made at college to be significant.

Start of Career

Pursuing his ambition further Selleck studied with Milton Kastselas at The Beverly Hills Playhouse. His modeling experience gave him an edge as he was comfortable in front of the camera and was soon getting small parts in television.

Onscreen Persona

Although Selleck's looks shouted matinee idol, his first appearance before a television audience was as a contestant on the popular *Dating Game TV* show. Next came a series of small parts in various venues of comedy, drama, and westerns. His big break came with the lead in *Magnum, P.I.* It was this series that show cased Selleck's appeal to television audiences, especially women, and established him as a heartthrob. Ruggedly handsome with a good humored demeanor Selleck created a character that completely mesmerized women viewers for eight seasons.

Along came the movie *Three Men and a Baby*, the highest grossing film of 1987. Selleck's calm yet commanding presence once again captivated the female audience who were clearly in awe of him. He was a man's man who produced an extra beat in the hearts of his female audience.

Personal Life

Romances

Mimi Rogers (actress)

Marriages

Tom Selleck and Paulina Porizkova in *Her Alibi* – Warner Brothers, 1989

Jacqueline Ray (model) 1971-1982 (Divorced)
Jillie Mack 1987

Children

While married to first wife Jacqueline, Selleck adopted her son Kevin from a previous marriage. He has remained close to his adopted stepson.

Hannah Margaret Mack December 16, 1988 (with Jillie Mack)

Fast Facts

- He has appeared in a number of westerns, naming the *Jess Stone* series among his favorites.
- Selleck owns an avocado farm that he works and lives on between movie and television roles. He is the recipient of an honorary doctorate from Pepperdine University given to him because of his outstanding character and ethics.
- As a member of the California National Guard Selleck's unit was activated during the Watt's riots in Los Angeles.
- *People Magazine* chose him as one of the fifty most beautiful people in the world in 1998.
- He is actively involved in the NRA.
- Has always had a close, devoted relationship with his parents.
- Selleck is a on the Board of The Joseph and Edna Josephson Institute of Ethics, a nonprofit organization.
- He appeared on Broadway in a production of *A Thousand Clowns* in 2011 until the play was shut down due to the terrorist attack of 9/11.

Salary

Net Worth $22 Million dollars

Awards and Nominations

Tom Selleck, Steve Guttenburg, and Ted Danson in *Three Men and a Baby* – Buena Vista Pictures, 1987

Golden Apple 1982   Male Star of the Year
Golden Apple 1983   Male Star of the Year
Emmy 1984 Outstanding Lead Actor in a Drama Series *Magnum P.I.*
People's Choice 1984 Favorite Male TV Performer
People's Choice 1985 Favorite Male TV Performer, Drama
People's Choice 1985 Favorite All-Round Male TV Performer
Golden Globe 1985 Best Performance by an Actor in a TV-Series-Drama
He was inducted into the National Cowboy and Western Heritage Museum Hall of Great Western Performers in 2010

Star on the Walk of Fame

6925 Hollywood Blvd

JIMMY SMITS

Vital Statistics

DOB: July 9, 1955 (Cancer) in Brooklyn, New York
Name at Birth: Jimmy (not James) Smits
Height: 6'3"
Hair: Very Dark Brown
Eyes: Brown
Physique: Slender & Firm

Biographical Sketch

Father
  Cornelius (Manager in a screen printing factory)

Mother
  Emilina (Nurse)

Siblings
Yvonne
Diana

Boyhood Years

Devout Catholics, the Smits lived in a working class neighborhood, but Jimmy also spent a good deal of his formative years in Puerto Rico where his mother has her roots.

Start of Career

Jimmy Smits, Corbin Bernsen, Blair Underwood, and Harry Hamlin in *L.A. Law* – NBC Television, 1986-1994

A Bachelor of Arts in Theatre from Brooklyn College in 1980 led to travel throughout the States with a repertory troupe. Off Broadway experience led to notice from movie and television casting directors, and the role of 'Eddie Rivera,' partner of Don Johnson in *Miami Vice*. A number of movie roles followed although Smits did not continue on the series after the pilot aired. In the mid 80's Smits was cast in the role of 'Victor Sifuentes' on the series, *L.A. Law* and soon won over the hearts of female fans of the show.

Onscreen Persona

Fiery good looks coupled with an engaging smile quickly won women over. Smits exuded a quiet confidence and charm that female fans adored.

Personal Life

Romances

Long term relationship, actress Wanda de Jesus 1986-present

Marriages

Barbara 1981-1987 (Divorced)

Children

Taina 1973   (with Barbara)
Joaquin 1983   (with Barbara)

Fast Facts

Jimmy Smits and Kim Delaney in *NYPD Blue* – ABC Television, 1993-2005

- He is very committed to supporting and serving the Hispanic Community
- Turned down the role of Finn in *NYPD Blue*, but joined the series in 1994 after David Caruso's departure
- In 1991 he was named "King of Brooklyn" in a Welcome Back to Brooklyn Festival
- He was given the Horizon Award in 1997, a Congressional recognition given to
- U.S, citizens who have set an exceptional example for young people by their personal successes.
- When first told that their son planned on studying drama, Smits parents thought he meant to teach high school drama after getting his degree. They were surprised when he explained.
- TV Guide ranked him #17 on their list of fifty Sexiest TV Stars of All Time
- He and Jennifer Lopez are co- owners of a Latin nightclub in Los Angeles
- He roots for the New York Knicks

Salary

$150,000 per episode on *Outlaw*
Net Worth $130 Million

Awards and Nominations

Golden Globe 1990 Best Performance by Actor in TV Series Drama *L.A Law*

Star on the Walk of Fame

Smits does not have a Star on the Walk of Fame.

DENZEL WASHINGTON

Vital Statistics

DOB: December 23, 1954 (Capricorn) in Mount Vernon, New York
Birth Name: Denzel Hayes Washington, Jr.
Nickname: D
Height: 6' 1//2"
Hair: Black
Eyes: Brown
Physique: Athletic

Biographical Sketch

Father
   Denzel (Pentacostal minister)

Mother
   Lennis (Beautician, former gospel singer)

Siblings
Lorice
David

Boyhood Years

Denzel grew up in an integrated neighborhood in the Bronx, New York. In school he excelled in athletics. His mother believed in discipline by way of way of setting limits and lovingly encouraged her son to participate in groups with values such as the local Boys Club. Having developed a positive work ethic early, at the age of twelve he was helping out part time at his mother's business establishment.

Denzel Washington in *Mo' Better Blues* – Universal Pictures, 1990

When he was fourteen, the news of his parents divorcing left Washington devastated. His mother had great concern for the son who has always been sweet and even tempered when Denzel became disruptive and rebellious. Although she understood the reasons for the change in his behavior Mrs. Washington grew even more alarmed when Denzel turned away from his religion as that had always been an integral part of the family lifestyle. She decided to enroll Denzel in a private preparatory school in upstate New York.

Here, Denzel worked off his vast store of energy by involving himself in a number of athletic activities; football, basketball, baseball, and track were great outlets for this all-around athlete. He joined the Last Express, playing the piano in the all black band.

In 1972 he enrolled in Fordham University where he planned to take a pre-med course. However poor grades led to his dropping out to take on a variety of jobs. One summer while working at a camp he was cajoled into performing a recitation in a camp talent program. The applause and compliments he received for his performance was enough to make Denzel enroll in a theater workshop. Returning to Fordham, he changed his major to journalism. However after appearing on stage in *The Emperor Jones* and *Othello* he took on a double major, graduating with a degree in both drama and journalism.

Start of Career

Acting won out and Denzel moved to San Francisco to study for a year at the prestigious American Conservatory Theater before moving on to Hollywood where he made the rounds auditioning for parts in movies and television. There was little hesitation in offering him roles as it was apparent that Washington was not only handsome and virile visually but was multi-talented and capable of playing a variety of parts from comedy to serious drama.

Onscreen Persona

Carbon Copy (1981) with George Segal showed the humorous side of his acting ability. In 1982, he was given the choice role of 'Dr. Chandler' in the medical series *St. Elsewhere* on NBC. It brought him before a television audience of enthralled women viewers for six years. Women watched the show on their televisiOn screens each week mesmerized by the new star on the horizon with his enigmatic smile and subtle sensuality.

Denzel Washington and Boaz Yakin in *Remember the Titans* – Buena Vista Pictures, 2000

Having reached heartthrob status as 'Dr. Chandler', Washington hit his stride even further in the next decade as he appeared in a number of highly acclaimed movies. Each one giving audiences a different view of his acting talent. Washington has been compared to the prestigious actor Sidney Poitier for his talent and dedication to his craft.

Personal Life

Marriage

Pauletta June 1983 (The couple met in 1977 when both were filming the television movie, *Wilma*)

Children

John David July 28, 1984
Katia 1987
Malcom and Olive, twins 1991

Fast Facts

- He and Julia Roberts are good friends
- Tom Hanks has been quoted as saying that working with Denzel Washington in *Philadephia* 1983, was like going to film school.
- He credits Jim Brown and Gayle Sayers as his youthful role models
- He was #39 on a list of the Greatest Movie Stars of All time by *Premiere Magazine*
- In 1996 *People Magazine* chose Washington to be their Sexiest Man Alive
- He is only the second African American to win an Oscar. The other actor is Sidney Poitier.
- He was honored at the 31st Kennedy Center in December, 2008
- Has worked with Spike Lee numerous times
- Although Washington made a name for himself in the eighties, it was not until the nineties that his salary reflected his super star status.
- Spokesperson for Boys and Girls Clubs of American
- Donated $1 million to Save Africa's Children in 2006
- He and his wife renewed their wedding vows while visiting South Africa
- Was his own stuntman for fight scenes in *The Book of Eli* (2010)
- Would like to work with Al Pacino and Robert DiNero
- A fan of the television series *Monk* with Tony Shaloub and Washington worked with Shaloub in 1981 on *The Siege*
- Visited Israel with a delegation of African Americans on the occasion of her 60th anniversary in 2008

Salary

Virtuosity $7,500,000
Courage Under Fire (1996) $10 million dollars
American Gangster (2007) $40 million dollars
Net Worth $140 million

Awards and Nominations

Denzel Washington and Lymari Nadal in *American Gangster* – Universal Pictures, 2007

1989 Academy Award Best Supporting Actor *Glory*
2001 Academy Award Best Actor *Training Day*
2010 Tony Award Best Male Lead in a Play *Fences*

Star on the Walk of Fame

As of this writing, Denzel Washington does not have a Star on the Walk of Fame

Chapter Seven
THE NINETIES

The ninth decade of the twentieth century came to be known as the age of electronics. The Internet reigned supreme as computers and people at their computers became the focus of business and personal communication. The art of letter writing was surpassed by the quickly typed e mail. Statistics indicate that three million of us were on the "net" by 1994 from buying merchandise to paying our bills online. One could easily establish a relationship be it business or personal with the click of the keys on the computer typing out our message to a faceless contact. Real intimacy took a step backward in our lives and cell phones became a necessary commodity and another form of distancing in our relationships.

- Minimum wage was $5.15 per hour in mid-decade with the average teacher's annual salary at $39,347.

- Women were expected to live to the age of 79 while men had a life expectancy of 73 years. However this had no bearing on the movies made in this decade. The audience Hollywood played to were teenagers, with money crowding their wallets and purses, and who went to the movies two by two on date nights and in small groups of enthralled young women eager to watch their favorite heartthrob on the screen.

- December 23, 1993 marked the debut of the first major film with AIDS as the theme. Tom Hanks and Denzel Washington headed the brilliant cast of *Philadelphia* that brought the poignancy of the disease to the public in a sensitive and informative way that movie goers applauded.

- March 4, 1995 Hollywood and his many fans mourned the death of lovable actor John Candy

- Comedian George Burns put out his final cigar at the age of 100 on March 9, 1997.

- Paul McCartny was knighted by Queen Elizabeth on March 11, 1997 for his service to the music industry and genre.

- Actress Ginger Rogers died on April 25, 1995

- September 6, 1997 millions of people throughout the world somberly watched the televised funeral of Princess Diana.

- On January 5, 1998 longtime favorite Sonny Bono was killed in an unusual skiing accident.

- James Cameron's long awaited film, *Titanic*, brought in a record-breaking $600 million box office total as of August 31, 1998.

- The emerging celluloid heartthrob began to change as teenagers dominated ticket sales at the box office. He was cute and sweet with a look bordering on innocence. These were the young men who titillated teenage girls eagerly gravitating to them on screen, freshly shaven youth who often appeared to be barely out of puberty. Young women wanted to feel safe even in a climate of uncensored sexuality and freedom to make choices. Boyish looking heroes were non-threatening, therefore safe.

- Teenagers were not the only feminine devotee of the on screen heartthrob. The young matron and her mother had to be pleased as well. This led to a mixture of both types of heartthrobs with someone for everyone.

BEN AFFLECK

Vital Statistics

DOB: August 15, 1972 (Leo) in Berkeley, California
Name at Birth: Benjamin Geza Afleck-Boldt
Height: 6'2"
Hair: Dark Brown
Eyes: Brown
Physique: Bulked Up and Buff

Biographical Sketch

Father
  Timothy (Social worker)

Mother
  Christina (School teacher)

Siblings
Casey younger brother, actor

Boyhood Years

Raised in Cambridge, Massachusetts, in an upper middle class home Affleck was much like other boys his age except for his decision at a very young age to become an actor. To that end his mother enrolled him in drama classes where he formed a close friendship with Matt Damon, a fellow student who also had aspirations to become an actor. The two not only took acting classes together but played Little League baseball as well as encouraging each other in their chosen profession. They became lifelong friends.

Ben Affleck and Matt Damon in
Good Will Hunting – Miramax Films, 1997

Start of Career

At the age of eight Affleck caught the attention of the viewing public and those behind the scenes when he appeared in a PBS mini-series, *The Voyage of the Mimi* (1984). He continued to gain recognition in his teen years appearing in TV movies. The break Affleck had been waiting for came with his appearance in the movie *Dazed and Confused* (1993). Afterwards he went on to appear in a number of independent films. It was the movie *Chasing Amy* (1997) that finally brought the handsome young actor recognition at the Sundance Film Festival.

In the interim Affleck and Damon worked on a movie script of their own hoping to have control over the production so they could make a film that they thought was right for the times. After a little struggle for this independence of creativity, a friend showed the script to the head of Miramax Pictures and the duo were off and running as co-producers with complete control of how the film would be made.

The rest is movie history. *Good Will Hunting* brought rave reviews not only for the storyline, but for the superb acting.

Personal Life

Romances

Dated actress Gwyneth Paltrow 1998-99
Engaged to former co-star/actress/singer Jennifer Lopez November 2002-2004

Marriage

Jennifer Garner   June 29, 2005

Children

Violet Anne December 1, 2005
Seraphina Rose Elizabeth January 5, 2009
Samuel Garner February 27, 2012

Ben Affleck and Jennifer Lopez
in *Gigli* – Columbia Pictures, 2003

Fast Facts

- Affleck believes in giving back whenever possible He supports the non-profit organization A-T Project that offers assistance to young people afflicted with the rare progressive disease ataxia-telangiectasia. He gives of his time as well as his money attending benefits whenever possible and advocating the charity before Congress.
- He surprised a car attendant once with a tip of $100
- He has maintained a close friendship with actor Matt Damon since the age of ten.
- Took his mother to the Oscars in 1997 and agreed to let her keep the Oscar he won for *Good Will Hunting* until she became a grandmother.
- His (then) addiction to gambling is said to have been the cause of a breakup with Jennifer Lopez in 2003. They made up briefly before breaking up for good.
- He has numerous tattoos on his back and shoulders.
- He bites his nails.

Salary

Chasing Amy 1997 $7,000
Jersey Girl 2004 $10,000,000

Gigli 2003 $12,500,000
Daredevil 2003 $11, 500,000 plus percentage of gross
Good Will Hunting 1997 split $600,000 for writing script with co-writer Matt Damon
$2,800,000 per film at latest report
Net Worth $65 million

Awards and Nominations

Nominations for Acting
1998 Saturn Award Best Supporting Actor *Armageddon*
1999 MTV Movie Award Best Male Performance *Armageddon*
2001 Teen Choice Actor in Adventure/Drama for *Pearl Harbor*
2004 MTV Movie Award Sexiest Hero *Daredevil*
Awards for Acting
2000 Blockbuster Entertainment   Favorite Actor Drama/Romance *Bounce*
1999 Blockbuster Entertainment   Favorite Actor Comedy/Romance *Force of Nature*
1998 Blockbuster Entertainment Favorite Supporting Actor Sci Fi *Armageddon*
Peoples Choice Award (2nd place) Toronto Film Critics Association Award
2001 Teen Choice Best Actor *Pearl Harbor*
2006 Golden Globe Best Performance by an Actor /Supporting Role *Hollywoodland*
1999 Best Male Performance *Armageddon*

Star on the Walk of Fame

Affleck does not have a Star on the Walk of Fame as of this writing

Ben Affleck and Charlize Theron in
Reindeer Games – Dimension Films, 2000

GEORGE CLOONEY

Vital Statistics

DOB: May 6, 1961 (Taurus) in Lexington, Kentucky
Name at Birth: George Timothy Clooney
Height: 5' 11"
Hair: Dark Brown
Eyes: Brown
Physique: Muscular
Outstanding features: Prominent square jaw, twinkling eyes and expressive smile

Biographical Sketch

Father
  Nick Clooney (Journalist, anchorman and game show host)

Mother
  Nina (Former beauty pageant queen)

Siblings
Adeline "Ada", older

Boyhood Years

Although the Clooneys are among one of entertainment's elite families, they lived modestly in numerous towns throughout Kentucky and Ohio when George was a youngster due to his father's occupation. The family finally settled in Kentucky in August, 1974, moving into a large Victorian home.

The family was a close one gathering together at the dinner table to hold lively discussions. Nick Clooney made a point of always being home for dinner and encouraged in depth conversation of worldly events.

George Clooney, Kim Fields, Nancy McKeon, and Lisa Whelchel in *The Facts of Life* – NBC Television, 1979-1988

Clooney's world turned dismal when he was stricken with Bell's Palsy as a young teenager, causing him much distress as he became the butt of verbal bullying from his schoolmates. He eventually recovered.

Start of Career

Having been in the Hollywood realm via family in one way or another since childhood, Clooney moved to heartthrob status by way of several failed TV pilots and appearing in numerous B movies. In the latter days of the hit series *The Facts of Life* Clooney's screen appearances as 'George,' the handyman, elicited enough of a feminine following to bring him to the serious attention of casting directors. He was given a leading role in the popular TV series, *ER* in 1994 and feminine hearts have not stopped fluttering since for this irresistible actor.

Onscreen Persona

The name George Clooney has definite sigh appeal. It's love at first sight and forever after for this handsome, debonair actor with the mischievous glint in his eyes. Prior to *ER* he intrigued the younger female set with his enigmatic smile that not only lit up his handsome face, but sparkled from his soft brown eyes. Whether he is playing the part of a wise cracking handyman, a clever criminal, a romantic suitor, or a dedicated hero, Clooney stands apart from the crowd. Talk show host Kelly Ripa has referred to him as a modern day Cary Grant. To his adoring female fans Clooney exudes a charm that is uniquely his. The young, and the not so young, flock to see his movies.

Personal Life

Romances

Clooney is probably the most watched bachelor actor in the business as eager fans devour copy from the gossip columns in various publications, hanging onto every word said about his love life. His romantic liasons rarely last more than two years. When the lady of his choice brings up the subject of marriage a warning bell goes off in Clooney's heart that is the defining moment for the end of a Clooney romantic relationship.

George Clooney and Julianna Margulies in *ER* – NBC Television, 1994-2009

Lisa Snowdon   model   5 years
Sarah Larson   2007-2009
Elizabeth Canalis   2009 -2011
Stacey Keibler (former wrestler) 2011-2013

Marriage

Talia Balsam (daughter of actors Martin Balsam and Joyce Van Patten) 1989-1992

Author's Note: News that surprised us all was Clooney's engagement in late April to humanitarian attorney Amil Alamuddin. Amil turned the actor down a few times before consenting to go on a date. Her rumored reason, she didn't want to date an actor.

Fast Facts

- He has been named the sexiest man alive twice (1997 & 2006) by *People Magazine*

- He owned a pig named Max from 1988 until 2006 when it passed away
- In 2003 he topped the list of *TV Guide's* Sexiest Stars
- Before he decided upon acting as a career Clooney seriously considered baseball and tried out for the Cincinnati Reds.

Salary

Sisters 1991 $40,000 per episode
One Fine Day 1996 $ 3,000,000
The Perfect Storm 2000 $8,000,000
Oceans Eleven 2001 $15,000,000
Net worth $155 million

Star on the Walk of Fame

As of this writing, George Clooney does not have a Star on the Walk of Fame.

George Clooney and Elle MacPherson in
Batman and Robin – Warner Brothers, 1997

JOHNNY DEPP

Vital Statistics

DOB: June 9, 1963 (Gemini) in Owensboro, Kentucky
Name at Birth: John Christopher Depp, III
Height: 5'10"
Hair: Dark Brown
Eyes: Dark Chocolate Brown
Physique: Trim and Muscular
Outstanding Feature: Sensual lips, high cheekbones

Biographical Sketch

Father
  John (Civil engineer)

Mother
  Betty (Part-time waitress)

Siblings
Debbie half sister
Danny half brother
Christine
Elisa

Boyhood Years

The family lived in a number of different locations due to his father's job. When he was seven the Depps settled into a motel in Miramar, Florida, while his father checked out jobs. The youngest of four children, Depp hated the family's living accommodations. He became withdrawn. This led to some odd behavior on Johnny's part, such as compulsively turning off the light switches twice.

When his mother gifted him with a guitar twelve year old Johnny turned his focus on music. For a time he considered music to be his future career. The divorce of his parents when he was barely sixteen had a strong effect on Depp. Rebellious and unhappy he took to smoking, experimented with drugs and eventually dropped out of school to pursue his dream of becoming a rock star. To that end Depp became part of a popular garage band called *The Kids*.

Johnny Depp and Winona Ryder in
Edward Scissorhands –
20th Century Fox, 1990

Start of Career

The band traveled to Hollywood in hope of scoring a record contract. When that didn't happen they broke up. By then Depp had married Lori Anne Allison, the sister of a band member who had aspirations of becoming an actress. Having become acquainted with actor Nicolas Cage, Lori introduced the two men. It was Cage who encouraged Depp to think seriously about becoming an actor, recognizing latent talent in the young man.

Although his movie career was launched in the mid-eighties with a role in the horror classic, *ANightmare on Elm Street*, it wasn't until the films *Edward Scissorhands* and *Cry Baby* in 1990 that he embraced the full scope of heartthrob by appearing in the two very diverse roles. After *Nightmare,* he enrolled in acting classes to fine hone his craft. Teenagers soon discovered the magic of Depp on the small screen when he starred in the television series, *21 Jump Street*, but it was in the decade of the nineties that he embraced the full scope of his female audience from young to mature.

Onscreen Persona

Johnny Depp and Penelope Cruz in *Pirates of the Caribbean: On Stranger Tides* – Walt Disney Studios Motion Pictures, 2011

On screen Depp is a chameleon. Taking on a variety of roles, audiences never know who is going to show up on the screen from film to film. No matter what the personality of the character Depp is portraying on screen, there is a very effective hypnotic pull between him and his female audience. Solemn and sincere, he comes across as appealing even when going for a slightly humorous approach to his onscreen character.

He is known for his penchant to stretch his talent. It's difficult to pin point the actual effect this uniquely talented actor has on his audience. Playing young and innocent, confused and determined or sensual and romantic can all be used to describe his onscreen self. Whichever comes across on the movie screen has women clamoring for more.

Personal Life

Romances

Depp's love life was actively varied after his divorce at the tender age of twenty two.
Engaged to actress Jennifer Grey
Romantic liaisons with actress Sherilyn Fenn 1986-1988
British model Kate Moss 1994-1998
From 1989 -1993 Depp was so deeply involved with Winona Ryder that he had her name and the tag word "Forever" tattooed across his right forearm. After their breakup the tattoo was reduced to read "Wino Forever."

In 1998 he fell in love with French singer-actress Vanessa Pardis. The two live together but have never married.

Marriages

Lori Anne Allison (he was twenty, she was twenty five) 1983-1985

Children

Lily-Rose Melody 1999 (with Pardis)
Jack 2002 (with Pardis)

Fast Facts

- He ranked among *People's Magazine's* Fifty Most Beautiful People in the World.
- He was #1 I *Empire Magazine's* List of 100 Sexiest Move Stars of All Time.
- In 2003 he was chosen The Sexiest Man Alive by *People Magazine*.
- He turned down the role opposite Angela Jolie in *Mr. and Mrs. Smith*. The part went to Brad Pitt and changed the course of lives. One can only wonder how the scenario might have played out if Johnny Depp had taken the role when it was offered.to him first.
- It was his portrayal of 'Toby' in the movie *This Boy's Life* that brought Depp recognition from the prestigious New York Film Critics and the National Society of Film Critics. This led to a nomination for Best Supporting Actor by both groups. It was also the start of an emerging heartthrob status.
- He smokes.
- He is very private.

Salary

2010 $91 million for *Pirates of the Caribbean: Dead Man's Chest*
Net Worth $350 million

Nominations & Awards

2003 Academy Award Nomination Best Actor in a Leading Role Pirates of the Caribbean: The Curse of the Black Pearl
2004 Academy Award Nomination Best Actor in a Leading Role Finding Neverland
2007 Academy Award Nomination Best Actor in a Leading Role Sweeney Tood: The Demon Barber of Fleet Street
2003 BAFTA Nomination Best Actor in a Leading Role Pirates of the Caribbean: The Curse of the Black Pearl
2004 BAFTA Nomination Best Actor in a Leading Role Finding Neverland
1990 Golden Globe Nomination Best Actor Motion Picture Musical/Comedy Edward Scissorhands

1993 Golden Globe Nomination Best Actor Motion Picture Musical/Comedy Benny & Joon
1994 Golden Globe Nomination Best Actor Motion Picture Musical/Comedy Ed Wood
2003 Golden Globe Nomination Best Actor Motion Picture Musical/Comedy Pirates of the Caribbean: The Curse of the Black Pearl
2004 Golden Globe Nomination Best Actor Motion Picture Drama Finding Neverland
2006 Golden Globe Nomination Best Actor Motion Picture Musical/Comedy Charlie and the Chocolate Factory
2006 Golden Globe Nomination Best Actor Motion Picture Musical/Comedy Pirates of the Caribbean: Dead Man's Chest
2007 Golden Globe Award Best Actor Motion Picture Musical/Comedy Sweeney Todd: The Demon Barber of Fleet Street
2010 Golden Globe Nomination Best Actor Motion Picture Musical/Comedy Alice in Wonderland
2010 Golden Globe Nomination Best Actor Motion Picture Musical/Comedy The Tourist

Star on the Walk of Fame

South Side of 7000 Hollywood Blvd.

Johnny Depp and Kate Winslet in
Finding Neverland – Miramax Films, 2004

LEONARDO DiCAPRIO

Vital Statistics

DOB: November 11, 1974 (Scorpio) in Los Angeles, California
Birth Name: Leonardo Wilhelm DiCaprio
Nickname: Leo
Height: 5' 11"
Hair: Sandy Blonde
Eyes: Blue
Physique: Toned/firm, broad shoulders

Biographical Sketch

Father
  George (Comic book distributor)

Mother
  Irmelin (Legal secretary)

Boyhood Years

DiCaprio is an only child. Following the divorce of his parents when he was just a year old, he lived in Echo Park, an area that was somewhat unsavory. DiCaprio has described it as Hollywood slums. Recognizing her son's visual appeal, his mother made the rounds of agents certain that he had a career in television ahead of him.

Leonardo DiCaprio, Kirk Cameron, and Tracey Gold in *Growing Pains* – ABC Television, 1985-1992

Start of Career

Although he was decidedly a cutie, he was also a bundle of energy and mischievous. This led to some difficulty on the set of *Romper Room*, Leonardo's first major screen gig. While it was *Titanic* that launched a very young DiCaprio into superstardom and heartthrob status, his first on screen appearance was in the horror flick, *Critters 3*. Actor Robert De Nero chose DiCaprio out of 400 boys who auditioned for the part of his son in *This Boy's Life* garnering the young actor critical acclaim.

Onscreen Persona

In *Titanic* where DiCaprio first titillated feminine hearts, the young actor with the smooth face and look of innocence continued to display a major talent as he had in previous films. But there was something special in his portrayal of the poor youth who successfully romanced the beautiful, wealthy young woman lustfully portrayed by Kate

Winslet. It was the role that opened up a new acting vista for the actor earning him entre into the select world of Hollywood heartthrob.

Versatility is the acting style that continues to keep him at the top of the zone.

Personal Life

Romances

DiCaprio's romantic history is not only varied but so whirlwind as to make one wonder, is he shying away from marriage much like bachelor around town, George Clooney, or is he just fickle?

Leonardo DiCaprio and Kate Winslet in *Titanic* – Paramount Pictures, 1997

Since the outpouring of female appreciation with the release of *Titanic*, Leo has been on an almost nonstop dating marathon starting with actress Juliette Lewis in 1993.

Other beauties he has squired around town with some overlap are:

1994 model Bridget Hall
1994 actress Brittany Daniels
1995-1998 actress/Spice Girl Emma Bunton
1995-1996 actress Claire Danes
1997 actress Alicia Silverstone

In 2000, Leo and model Gisele Brindschen began a five year relationship resulting in their being named Most Beautiful Couple by *People Magazine*. As yet not on the path to marriage, DiCaprio continues to be seen around town with some of Hollywood's loveliest happily at his side.

Fast Facts

- His hobby is bird watching
- He has a charitable Foundation*
- Purchased an island in Central America near Belize on which he plans to build an eco-friendly resort.
- He donated $1 million to the Clinton Bush Haiti Fund after the devastating earthquake that left so many homeless and destitute.
- A deeply principled man, the actor bowed out of a film actor Mel Gibson was to direct after hearing an audio about Gibson who was alleged to have abused a former girlfriend both physically and verbally.
- He is actively involved in environmental issues.

- The DiCaprio Foundation is dedicated to conserving wildlife.
- He owns a tortoise with a life span of eighty years.
- He is considered to be gracious and kind.
- DiCaprio and his mother aided in the restoration of the Los Feliz branch of the Los Angeles Public Library in the area of his boyhood home with a donation of $35,000 in the mid 1990's. The original library was destroyed in the Northridge earthquake in 1994.
- He and actor Tobey Maguire's friendship that began at an audition in 1990 continues to flourish.

Salary

Titanic $2.5 million
2010 $28 million per film
Net Worth $200 million

Awards and Nominations

Leonardo DiCaprio and Carey Mulligan in *The Great Gatsby* – Warner Brothers, 2013

1994 Golden Globe Best Performance by an Actor in a Supporting Role Motion Picture *What's Eating Gilbert Grape*
1998 Golden Globe Best Performance by an Actor in Motion Picture Drama *Titanic*
2003 Golden Globe Best Performance by an Actor in Motion Picture Drama *Catch Me If You Can*
2001 Razzie Worst Actor *On the Beach*
1994 Academy Award Best Actor in Supporting Role *What's Eating Gilbert Grape*
2005 Academy Award Best Performance by Actor in Leading Role *The Aviator*
2007 Academy Award Nomination Best Performance by Actor in Leading Role *Blood Diamond*.

Star on the Walk of Fame

As of this writing, Leonardo DiCaprio does not have a Star on the Walk of Fame.

COLIN FIRTH

Vital Statistics

DOB: September 10, 1960 (Virgo) in Grayshot, Hampshire, England, UK
Name at Birth: Colin Andrew Firth
Height: 6' 1"
Hair: Light Brown
Eyes: Referred to by fans as the most beautiful brown
Physique: Firm
Outstanding Physical Attribute: A fan once described Firth as having a face chiseled out of marble

Biographical Sketch

Father
   David (History teacher and lecturer at Winchester University College)

Mother
   Shirley (Lecturer on comparative religions)

Siblings
Younger brother Jonathan (actor)
Younger sister Kate voice coach

Boyhood Years

Colin Firth in *Pride and Prejudice* – BBC One, 1995

Growing up as the son of two intellectuals created an atmosphere for learning for Colin. Rather than follow in the professional footsteps of his parents, Firth chose another path. He gravitated toward expressing himself as an actor that began in early childhood. When the family returned to England after living in Africa for some years Firth discovered the attraction of acting when a pantomime at the performed at age of five that brought him accolades. By age fourteen, after four years in a drama workshop, Firth was certain that an acting career was his destiny.

Colin's parents moved to Nigeria when he was an infant returning to England when he was around four. He and his siblings were raised in an atmosphere of culture and academia due to both parents being noted teachers. The family's original roots were in India tracing back to his paternal grandfather who did missionary work as an Angelican priest and his maternal grandparents who were missionary ministers.

Firth recounts his youth as one of privilege not because the family was wealthy but due to the fact that their home was abundant with a variety of culture as it was often filled with company from India where the culture was vastly different from that in England.

Because his father's teaching job afforded the family the diversity of travel, the family moved around a bit even settling in St. Louis, Missouri, for a short period of time. Recounting that aspect of his life Firth recalls it as "the most hideous memory" of his youth. He remembers himself as a precocious brat, decidedly displeased with what he was being taught in school because it was of no interest to him.

As a result he did not do well academically, often failing exams and finally opting out of formal education when he was legally of age to do so.

He admits to being a happy adult whereas his childhood and youth were not.

Start of Career

Having decided at the age of fourteen to become an actor Firth went on to study acting at the London Drama Centre. Honing his craft six days a week for three years during which the young actor played a variety of intense roles. .

Colin Firth in *The King's Speech* – Momentum Pictures, 2010

While attending the Drama Centre Firth was discovered by a scout while playing *Hamlet*. This led to his first film co-starring with Rupert Everett in *Another Country* 1984. Afterwards his career began to move up steadily with a part in the television series *Camille* opposite Greta Scacchi.

In 1995, Firth attracted a great deal of female attention with his portrayal of Darcy in one of the television productions of *Pride and Prejudice*.

He has gone on to titillate feminine hearts since often starring in movie roles of the romantic genre that have women clamoring for more.

Onscreen Persona

He personifies the proper English gentleman much like that of Olivier who commanded attention just by appearing on screen. Firth can be described as a late blooming heartthrob. He was in his mid-thirties when the miniseries *Pride and Prejudice* aired on the BBC, elevating him to heartthrob status.

Personal Life

Romances

An intense five year relationship with actress Meg Tilly 1989-94
Jennifer Ehle actress, dated for about a year

Marriage

Livia Gluggioli (Documentary film producer) June 21, 1997

Children

William Firth 1990 (with Meg Tilly)
Luca   March 29, 2001 (with Livia)
Mateo   August 2003   (with Livia)

Colin Firth, Pierce Brosnan, and Stellan Skarsgard in *Mamma Mia* - Universal Pictures, 2008

Fast Facts

- His first non-acting job was as a dustman.
- *People Magazine* listed him on their 50 Most Beautiful people list in 2001.
- He speaks fluent Italian.
- He thinks he is getting too old to be sexy, but his female fans say otherwise.
- He and Meg lived in Canada in a log cabin during the five years they were together.
- He is actively involved in a number of causes among them Survival International, the Refugee Council and Oxfam.
- Firth and a few colleagues have formed The Friends of Drama Centre London to raise funds for an independent trust that supports the school dedicated to encourage those who want to be involved in some phase of the acting community.

Awards and Nominations

2001 Emmy Outstanding Supporting Actor in Miniseries or Movie *Conspiracy*
2010 WAFCA Best Actor   *The King's Speech*
Venice Film Festival, Independent Spirit, Los Angeles Film Critics Association, People's Choice Award, Screen Actors Guild, and more.

Star on the Walk of Fame

6714 Hollywood Blvd.

JUDE LAW

Vital Statistics

DOB: December 29, 1972 in Lewisham, London
Birth Name: David Jude Heyworth Law
Height: 6'
Hair: Light Brown
Eyes: Green
Physique: Slender & Muscular
Outstanding Feature: Kiss inviting lips

Biographical Sketch

The family lived in Backheath, England where Law attended public school until his parents realized that the climate of violence and bullying among the students was having an adverse effect on their son and enrolled him in a private school where he flourished until he chose to drop out to pursue an acting career.

Father
  Peter (Teacher)

Mother
  Maggie (Teacher)

His parents now own a theatre company in France.

Siblings
Older sister Natasha (a photographer)

Boyhood Years

Jude Law and Gwyneth Paltrow in *The Talented Mr. Ripley* – Paramount Pictures, 1999

Realizing Jude's interest in acting at an early age his parents took him to the theater often, discussing the play in depth afterwards thus fostering the impressionable boy's ambition. By the age of twelve he was enrolled in the National Youth Music Theatre and appeared in a couple of theatrical productions. At age of seventeen he quit school by- passing the usual teenage interests to focus on his life's ambition and soon had a solid reputation as an actor. After establishing success in the theater, he migrated to Hollywood and the Silver screen. It was in the film The *Talented Mr. Ripley* that he gained female attention. Though it was not a big role, Law was a big presence causing women in the audience to take notice.

He has chosen to play diversified roles in an effort to overcome the singular appeal of his outstanding good looks alone.

He often chose to portray a character without redemption as that of a hit man in *The Road to Perdition* to that purpose.

Despite every effort by the makeup department to make Law into an unappealing assassin, his female fans remained adoring and loyal.

Onscreen Persona

His stunning good looks and soft spoken British accent is prime woman appeal. A smile from Jude Law could instantly defrost a refrigerator. Women fans clamored for more and studio decision makers listened attentively casting him in potential box office hits as often as possible. Joining his fans in their open admiration for this talented heartthrob are some of Hollywood's top actresses.

Naomi Watts has called Law one of the most beautiful of men. Gweneth Paltrow proclaimed Law to be most charming. While he is admired for his standout good looks, his innate talent continues to bring him accolades.

Personal Life

Romance

Engaged to actress Sienna Miller, 2010

Marriage

Sadie Frost, actress 1997, divorced 2003

Jude Law and Cameron Diaz in
The Holiday – Columbia Pictures, 2006

Children

Rafferty 1996 (with Sadie Frost)
Iris October, 2000 (with Sadie Frost)
Rudy September 10, 2002 (with Sadie Frost)
Sophia September 22, 2009 (with Samantha Burke)

Fast Facts

- Named Sexiest Man Alive by *People Magazine* 2004.
- He dropped out of high school in his junior year to pursue a career on British television.
- He is devoted to his children.
- He learned to play the saxophone for his role in *The Talented Mr. Ripley*.

- He was an accomplished stage actor, but his first films were a box office disappointment.
- He shocked and disappointed his female public when it was revealed that he had an affair with his children's nanny. It ended his engagement to Miller.

Salary

1999 *The Talented Mr. Ripley* $745,000
2009 *Sherlock Holmes* $9,000,000

Awards and Nominations

2001 Best Performance by Actor in Supporting Role, Motion Picture *Artificial Intelligence*
2003 Best Actor *Cold Mountain*
2009 Best Performance by Actor in a Motion Picture *The Talented Mr. Ripley*

Star on the Walk of Fame

6931 Hollywood Blvd.

Jude Law and Robert Downey, Jr. in
Sherlock Holmes – Warner Brothers, 2009

BRAD PITT

Vital Statistics

DOB: December 18, 1963 (Sagittarius) in Shawnee, Oklahoma
Name at Birth: William Bradley Pitt
Height: 5'11"
Hair: Blond
Eyes: Blue
Physique: Washboard Abs

Biographical Sketch

Father
   William Hill Pitt (Manager of a trucking firm)

Mother
   Jane Etta

Siblings

Douglas, younger brother
Julie, younger sister

Boyhood Years

Pitt was an all-around athlete at Kickapoo High School, on the debating team and displayed an interest in the theater by appearing in school musicals. At the University of Missouri he majored in journalism with an emphasis on advertising. While at college Pitt occasionally appeared in school musicals. It is a bit of a mystery as to why he left just two college credits short of graduating and moved to Hollywood.

Brad Pitt and Kirsten Dunst in
Interview with the Vampire -
Geffen Film Company, 1994

Once in Hollywood, while pursuing an acting career Pitt supported himself doing a variety of odd jobs, ie: limo driver for strippers, refrigerator installer for an appliance store and once advertised a local El Polo Loco fast food restaurant by dressing as a giant chicken and standing outside of the eatery cajoling people to dine inside.

Start of Career

One of the strippers for whom Brad ran errands had acting aspirations, and one day Pitt went along with her to an acting class taught by Coach Roy London. That was the turning point that determined a definite choice of career for Brad.

Onscreen Persona

Despite portraying a very unsavory character in an early film, *Too Young to Die* opposite Juliette Lewis, Pitt made enough of an impression on the powers that be to cast him in his signature role of the bare chested hitchhiker stud in *Thelma & Louise* (1991). The movie catapulted the young, sensually appealing Pitt into instant sex symbol. So much so that female fans tore at his clothes whenever he appeared in person.

Although he has a look of innocence about him, Pitt's sensual appeal comes across the screen in whatever role he is playing.

Personal Life

Romances

Soon after the picture wrapped Juliette Lewis and Pitt lived together for a number of years. Gwyneth Paltrow and Pitt fell in love at first sight according to both. They dated exclusively for two and a half years, but broke it off suddenly after a seven month engagement. Pitt and Jennifer Aniston began dating in 1998.

Brad Pitt and Geena Davis in *Thelma and Louise* – MGM, 1991

Marriages

Jennifer Aniston
Following their wedding on July 29, 2000 at a rumored cost of $1 million dollars, the newlyweds became known as the Golden Couple of Hollywood, thrilling fans with news of their life together that was reported on an almost daily basis.

In 2005 while filming *Mr. and Mrs. Smith* opposite Angelina Jolie sparks between the on screen couple became a torrid real life romance. The marriage of Aniston and Pitt ended after five years in October, 2005. Afterwards Pitt / Jolie became the fodder of the tabloids and columnists throughout the world. At first many friends and fans alike took sides about the breakup of his marriage creating a furor of gossip, eventually coming to accept the new relationship was a permanent one. In time the couple was dubbed Brangelina by the press.

Although they have not yet married, the couple has lived together since 2005 and became officially engaged in April of 2012.

Children

The Pitt/Jolie family consists of six children. Maddox, adopted by Jolie prior to her relationship with Pitt, Zahara, (2005) adopted by Jolie at the age of six months.
In 2006 adoption by Pitt was finalized and both Maddox and Zahara were legally granted surnames of Jolie-Pitt.
Shiloh, the natural daughter of the two was born on May 27, 2006.
Son Pax was adopted by Jolie on March 15, 2007at the age of three.
Pitt adopted Pax in the U.S on February 21, 2008.
In May, 2008 Jolie revealed that she and Pitt were expecting twins. Knox and Vivienne were born on July 12, 2008.

A total of six children within a span of three years made the Jolie-Pitt household a lively one. Jolie has commented that Brad is not only a hands-on father who has embraced the role completely, but that he has been an especially supportive partner during her pregnancies.

Fast Facts

- In January 1999 a nineteen year old fan entered his home during the night through an open window, found and dressed in Pitt's clothes and sat in the house for several hours. When apprehended, a restraining order was issued for the fan to stay at least 100 yards away from the actor for three years.
- Of Pitt, Jolie says "I'm very lucky to have him." Of her, Brad states, "She is the Eighth wonder of the world."
- Twice named Sexiest Man Alive by *People Magazine*, 1995 and 2000
- Pitt has become actively involved in social and philanthropic issues since the relationship with Jolie began.
- In 2007 while attending a Film Festival in Italy of his newly released film *The Assassination of Jesse James,* Brad experienced the nightmare of every actor, an unwelcome and frightening demonstration of adoration from a fan who somehow broke through security to ardently fling her arms around his neck. As security officers led her away she remarked that she only wanted to hug him.
- He is left handed
- He has a terrific sense of humor
- In September, 2006 Angelina and Brad formed the Joie-Pitt Foundation that supports worldwide humanitarian causes. Among charitable causes to which the foundation contributes: Civil Rights, World Poverty & Hunger, and Underprivileged Children.
- Although photos of their children have been sold for publication, the proceeds were donated to various charities the couple supports.
- It is rumored that Pitt posed semi-nude for a calendar while in college. No further facts have been revealed however.
- The Chinese government has banned him from the country for life because of his role in *Seven Years in Tibet*.

- He supports same-sex marriage and has stated in an interview that he and Jolie will marry when everyone in this country is legally allowed to marry.

Salary

First starring role 1988 *The Dark Side* $1,523 per week for seven weeks.
Thelma & Louise (1991) $6,000
Mr. and Mrs. Smith (2005) $20,000,000
Moneyball $20,000,000
Net Worth $170 million

Awards and Nominations

Nominations
Five times for an Oscar
Five times for a Golden Globe
Pitt has additionally been nominated for numerous awards within the industry

Awards
Golden Globe Best Supporting Actor *Twelve Monkeys* 1995

Star on the Walk of Fame

As of this writing, Brad Pitt does not have a Star on the Walk of Fame.

Brad Pitt and Angelina Jolie in
Mr. and Mrs. Smith –
20th Century Fox, 2005

Chapter Eight
2000 -2010
21st CENTURY

In Hollywood the year 2000 introduced the scruffy look. As the decade wore on more and more celluloid heartthrobs sported stubble and the appearance of men of the untamed West. The reinvented look of the brawny frontiers man of yesteryear with his unshaven face, tumbled hair, and rugged appearance sparked a response in female fans.

Actors sporting full beards, goatee and/or mustaches dominated the screen and their everyday lives.

The persona of the heartthrob was varied, on the one hand there was the ripped body and sensual vibes that tantalized the sophisticated female into the theater. On the other there was the vulnerable, clean shaven sensitive youth who enticed with his gentle, sexually non-threatening ways.

A firm body superseded the perfect profile and the slim, toned physique of prior years. Strong, muscular bodies and strong facial features were the norm among heartthrobs as the new century progressed. Obvious virility was in for the over twenties.

- The Kodak Theatre official home of the Academy Awards opened on November 9, 2001.

- On March 24, 2002 the first Oscars ceremony was held here with Whoopi Goldberg presiding. Oscars for best picture went to *A Beautiful Mind* with Halle Berry garnering the Best Actress Oscar for her role in *Monsters Ball* and Denzel Washington awarded an Oscar for his role in *Training Day*. This event was a first of its' kind as two black actors walked off with an Oscar for the first time in movie history.

- Greek actress Nia Vardolos made Hollywood sit up and take notice as she took home the Best Original Screenplay Oscar on April 19, 2002, *My Big Fat Greek Wedding*, based in part on Vardolos' life experiences, went on to earn $240 million dollars and a very appreciative audience.

- Iconic actress Katherine Hepburn passed away on June 29, 2003 at the age of ninety six.

- Charles Bronson, long time tough guy of movies, died on August 30, 2003.

- Multi-talented, beautiful actress Halle Berry good humoredly accepted the Razzie for *Cat Woman* in February, 2005.

- On March 7, 2010 the Oscar for Best Director was awarded to a woman for the first time in Academy history. Kathryn Bigelow was handed the symbolic statue by Barbra Striesand for directing the stunning film *Hurt Locker*.

- The sudden death of idol Michael Jackson from cardiac arrest on June 24, 2009 caused a furor that continued well beyond the close of the decade.

- Many gay celebrities proudly emerged from the closet.

- Average cost of a move ticket was $5.34

The economy was headed for the dumpster. Nevertheless the movies beckoned and we went, hoping that the images and story unfolding on the screen would make us forget for a while that our world was in disarray.

BRADLEY COOPER

Vital Statistics

DOB: January 5, 1975 (Capricorn) in Philadelphia, Pennsylvania
Name at Birth: Bradley Charles Cooper
Nickname: Coop
Height: 6' 1"
Hair: Curly Dark Brown
Eyes: Hypnotic, the color of pale blue denim
Physique: Six Pak Abs

Biographical Sketch

Father
  Charles J. Cooper (Stockbroker)

Mother
  Gloria (Homemaker)

Siblings
Holly (older sister)

Boyhood Years

The family settled in Jenkintown; a suburb of Philadelphia, where Cooper received his primary education at Germantown Academy before moving on to graduate with honors from Georgetown University in 1977with a degree in English. Having mastered the French language, Cooper spent several months as an exchange student in Aix-en-Provence further honing his language skills.

Bradley Cooper and Scarlett Johansson in
He's Just Not That Into You –
New Line Cinema, 2009

"People thought that I was a girl," is how Cooper recalls his childhood. "I looked like one," he added in a 2010 article appearing in Details publication.

Start of Career

Deciding upon an acting career early on, Cooper attended the Actors Studio Drama School at The New School in New York City before setting out to auditions. In 1999 he appeared on the television series *Sex and the City* later making his film debut in *Wet Hot American Summer*, a lesser known film in 2001.

Guest star roles followed generating great interest in the young, clean cut actor among the women in the audience. It was the film *The Hangover* that put the actor over the top at last earning him a Hollywood Comedy Award (October, 2009). The movie opened doors to a number of offers and his heartthrob career was finally launched. The film also gave birth to two more *Hangovers*.

Onscreen Persona

Blue eyes with a decided twinkle that sets female hearts a flutter, a smile that brightens the screen, and a great sense of comedic timing equals Bradley Cooper heartthrob. He has subsequently shown a depth of acting ability that earned him accolades and an Oscar nomination.

Entertainment Weekly predicted major stardom for the talented young actor.

Personal Life

While Cooper is not exactly a playboy he does have a flair for the ladies. Cooper appears to favor blondes though not exclusively and has been seen around town with one or another lovely on his arm from time to time.

Bradley Cooper and Sandra Bullock in *All About Steve* – 20th Century Fox, 2009

Romances

Renee Zellweger 2009-2011
Zoe Saldana 2011-2013
Cameron Diaz

Cooper also appears to favor women a few years his senior, who of course do not look their age. He has on occasion dated against the advice of others in the business, but being a man of his own convictions, Cooper goes where his heart tells him.

Marriage

Jennifer Esposito December 2006- May 2007

Fast Facts

- His father passed away after a long illness, leaving the actor devastated.
- He then invited his mother to live with him. This gesture has endeared the actor to his female fans who admire his concern and devotion to his mother.
- He wears his father's wedding ring on the ring finger of his right hand.

Salary

2010 $15,000,000

Awards and Nominations

2009 Satellite Award Nomination *The Hangover*
2009 Hollywood Film Award Comedy of the Year *Silver Linings Playbook*
2010 MTV Movie Award Best Comedic Performance *The Hangover*

In the ensuing years Cooper has been nominated for and won numerous awards including the prestigious Golden Globes.

Star on the Walk of Fame

As of this writing, Bradley Cooper does not have a Star on the Walk of Fame.

Bradley Cooper and Julia Roberts in
Valentine's Day – Warner Brothers, 2010

PATRICK DEMPSEY

Vital Statistics

DOB: January 13, 1966 (Aquarius) in Lewiston, Maine
Name at Birth: Patrick Galen Dempsey
Height: 5' 10"
Hair: Curly Black
Eyes: Blue
Physique: Toned

Biographical Sketch

Father
    William (Insurance agent)

Mother
    Amanda (School teacher)

Siblings
Two older, Dempsey has chosen not to name them as a way of ensuring their privacy

Boyhood Years

Patrick Dempsey and Amy Adams in *Enchanted* – Walt Disney Studios Motion Pictures, 2007

Living what he describes a normal, uneventful childhood in Buckfiled, Maine. Dempsey exhibited an interest in entertainment as a youngster of eleven when he became adept at juggling and performing acts of magic.

Start of Career

At seventeen Dempsey abandoned high school to seek an acting career.

He gained fame as a teenage heartthrob in the 80's, but almost faded into the Hollywood background afterwards until he was signed on to play a neurosurgeon in the highly rated TV

Onscreen Persona

Female devotees of *Grey's Anatomy* soon bestowed the nickname of 'Dr. McDreamy' on the middle aged, but very sexy actor. He has since become the epitome of on screen doctors in the tradition of others in previous decades (*Medical Center*, *Ben Casey*, *Marcus Welby*, and *Dr. Kildare*). 'Dr. McDreamy' is the physician women would most like to take their pulse.

Personal Life

Marriages
Rocky Parker 1987-1994 (Divorced)

Jillian Fink 1999

Children

Tallula 2002 (with Jillian Fink)
Twin sons, Darby Galen and Sullivan Patrick February 1, 2007 (with Jillian Fink)

Patrick Dempsey and Ellen Pompeo in
Grey's Anatomy –
ABC Television, 2005 to present

Fast Facts

- As a teenager Dempsey was Maine State Champion downhill skier.
- Voted #13 in *Elle Magazine's* Fifteen Sexiest Men, June 2007.
- He was diagnosed with dyslexia at the age of twelve. Today he has to memorize scripts instead of reading them off of the pages.
- Delving into his "medical" knowledge as a top ranking surgeon in the TV series, Dempsey offered a bit of advice to doctors attending his daughter when he took her to the hospital when she sustained a bad cut son her chin. Dempsey suggested that the wound be closed with medical glue rather than stitches. The doctor did as he suggested. The wound healed without leaving a scar.
- Dempsey's passion after acting is race car drivingIn 2010 he teamed up with Avon Cosmetics to develop a line of men's fragrances

Salary
Grey's Anatomy   2007-2008 $225,000 per episode
Freedom Writers   2007 $500,000
Made of Honor   2008 $4,000,000

Awards and Nominations

Primetime Emmy Awards
2001 *Once and Again* (Strangers and Brothers)
2008 Teen Choice Award Actor in Drama Action Adventure
Golden Globe
2007 *Grey's Anatomy* Series-Drama

Star on the Walk of Fame

As of this writing, Patrick Dempsey does not have a Star on the Walk of Fame.

ZAC EFRON

Vital Statistics

DOB: October 18, 1987 (Virgo) in San Luis Obispo, California
Name at Birth: Zachary David Alexander
Nickname: Zacqurista
Height: 5'8"
Hair: Dark Brown
Eyes: Brilliant Blue
Physique: Athletic/Muscular

Biographical Sketch

Father
　David (Electrical engineer)

Mother
　Starla (Secretary)

Siblings
Younger brother, Dylan

Boyhood Years

The family settled in Arroyo Grande, nearly two hundred miles north of Los Angeles, a community in the college town of San Luis Obispo. The family was, as Zac describes them, middle class and normal.

Start of Career

Zac Efron and Vanessa Hudgins in *High School Musical* – The Disney Channel, 2006

Recognizing their eldest son's beautiful singing voice, his parents gave him voice lessons. This led to his auditioning for parts in Little Theater musical productions. At the age of eleven he landed a part in a Performing Arts production of *Gypsy*. Efron soon became addicted to the laughter and applause. His love of the craft soon evolved into what he considers to be his destiny as an actor.

Onscreen Persona

Clean cut with a look of sweet innocence about him, Zac went to open auditions and won the lead in the Disney Cable production *High School Musical*. As the young man in the lead role Efron quickly moved into the hearts of adoring adolescent girls. From an open audition to a genuine overnight success, Zac zoomed to the top of the charts. His popularity was so phenomenal that it became necessary for the family to obtain a private phone number soon after the musical was aired.

During the first decade of the new century Efron's appeal was mostly to the starry eyed teenagers who flocked to see his films, but the tone of these began to change as Zac moved away from portraying the naïve young boy to that of a young man revealing his sensual side in movies such as *The Lucky One* (2010.). An appealing strength exuding from the actor created a wider feminine fan base.

Personal Life

Romances

A close relationship developed with Vanessa Hudgens his co-star in *High School Musical* 2006-2010. The two claimed they were comfortable with one another as friends and actors. But in 2009 they visited Brazil together while rumors spread that the relationship had become more than friendship.

Zac Efron and Taylor Schilling in *The Lucky One* – Warner Brothers, 2012

Fast Facts

- He has said that he likes his women chunky the same way he likes peanut butter.
- What has astonished many people in the business is the fact that Efron has remained level headed throughout his astonishing rise to the top. As one observer put it "There have been no public scandals, no drunken outbursts or bad behavior on the set."
- A few people have commented on the fact that it isn't easy to keep your feet on the ground when you are floating in the air of adulation, especially when you are very young as Zac was.
- "I didn't start out with the idea of being a star. Acting is something I love to do. It's fun for me. I've made it a rule to never forget that, It's never been about money but more of what I enjoy doing," is how he put it in an interview some time ago.
- Next came a part in the screen version of the Broadway hit, *Hairspray*. Efron was off and running up the ladder of stardom.
- In the years ahead movie audiences will be treated to actor Zac Efron in a variety of different roles as he stretches his talent. No longer a wide eyed young man, he has grown into a sophisticated, multi-talented actor while still remaining grounded in his personal life.
- He chose to preserve the image of clean cut boy next door by refusing to do sex scenes during the time he was under contract to Disney.

- A foreign newspaper erroneously reported him as having died creating a lamenting wail among his young and ardent fans.
- By his own admission dancing is not something that comes easily to him. He attributes that to having focused on sports as a youngster making it difficult to get dance movements right. This has proven stressful in attempting to perform dance routines in the musicals. But he has never backed down.
- He is the consummate professional.
- In *The Lucky One* Efron shed his former acting self to play a young man with the usual response to the woman he loves. The sexy scenes in this first non-innocent film has led to even more female adulation as his fan base continues to grow. Continuing to stretch himself as an actor, Efron has the admiration of all who work with him.
- No untoward behavior such as temperament, or too much drinking, no scandals or any other kind of inappropriate behavior has ever been attributed to the young man who assures his family and friends "I've been lucky, but what you do with that luck afterwards is what defines you if you."

Salary

2007 *Hairspray* $100,000
2008 *High School Musical* $3,000,000
2009 *17 Again* $1,000,000

Nominations and Awards

2007 Young Artist Award   *High School Musical*
2008 Favorite International Personality or Actor *High School Musical*
2008 Best Kiss MTV shared with Hughes
2008 Favorite Star Under 35 People's Choice
2009 Favorite Movie Star Blimp Award *17 Again*
2007 Fave Movie Actor Blimp Award *17 Again*
2009 Teen Choice *High School Musical 3: Senior Year*
2009 Sho West Convention Breakthrough Performer of Year

Zac Efron and Matthew McConaughey in *The Paperboy* – Millennium Films, 2012

Star on the Walk of Fame

As of this writing, Zac Efron does not have a Star on the Walk of Fame.

HUGH JACKMAN

Vital Statistics
DOB: October 12, 1968 (Libra) in Sydney, Australia
Name at Birth: Hugh Michael Jackman
Height: 6' 3"
Hair: Dark Brown
Eyes: Brown
Physique: Ripped
Outstanding Attribute: A warm, wonderful smile

Biographical Sketch

Father
   Christopher John (Accountant)

Mother
   Grace (Housewife)

Siblings
Older brothers Ian and, Ralph
Older sisters Sonya and Zoe

Boyhood Years

Jackman's parents emigrated from England to Australia in 1967 under the Ten Pound Poms act. Their marriage had been sanctified early on by Evangelist Billy Graham when the couple converted to Christianity. Jackman was the baby of the family and the second child to be born into the family in Australia.

Hugh Jackman and Halle Berry in *Swordfish* – Warner Brothers, 2001

When he was eight the family was divided by the divorce of his parents with Mr. Jackman raising his three sons while Mrs. Jackman returned to England with their daughters.

As a youngster Hugh spent as much time as he could out of doors enjoying the beach and camping. Being infused with wanderlust he traveled throughout Australia whenever he could, devouring atlases at night to satisfy his curiosity about the world he lived in.

His first ambition was to become a chef, believing that it was a perfect job for him as he had sampled food on board planes in his travels and thought that the food was prepared in a galley on board the planes.

After graduating from Public School he was enrolled in the all-boys Knox Grammar School in Sydney. It was here that he had his first acting experience starring in the school's production of *My Fair Lady* in 1985.

Start of Career

Although Jackman originally chose journalism as his life's work, he gravitated toward the study of drama at the Western Australian Academy of Performing Arts having decided acting was what he really preferred a career.

Hugh Jackman and Famke Janssen in *X-Men: The Last Stand* – 20th Century Fox, 2006

By a stroke of luck he was offered a choice role in an ABC production before he could begin pounding the pavements. Starring in the prison drama *Correlli* (1995) opposite an attractive actress named Deborra Lee Furness completed the lucky break as the two fell in love and eventually were married.

Jackman soon found himself with a promising career and the woman with whom he planned to build a life. After *Corelli* there were guest spots and musical productions in his native Australia until he was cast in the coveted role of *Wolverine* in the 2000 film *X-Men*. After that there was no stopping this affable, multi-talented actor.

Onscreen Persona

Intense and virile the actor sends appealing vibes to his women fans. Although most of the roles Jackman portrays on screen are heavy rather than lightly romantic there is an intangible essence about his screen presence that pulls entranced women in each time he appears in a scene.

Personal Life

Marriage

Deborra-Lee Furness 1996

Childen

Oscar Maximillian (adopted in 2000)
Ava Elliot (adopted in 2005)

Fast Facts

- He is involved in a number of philanthropic venues, among them The Bone Marrow Institute of Australia that he and his wife serve on as patrons.
- He has a Twitter account.
- Jackman is very open about his devotion and admiration for his father who he refers to as his rock.
- A brilliant song and dance man Jackman enthralled both his peers seated in the audience and the millions of television viewers of the 81st Academy Awards he was hosting in February, 2009 when he stepped out on stage in a captivating routine.
- 2000-2004 named one of *People Magazine's* Most Beautiful People in the World.
- Has won numerous awards for appearances in theatrical productions.
- Family is of utmost importance to him.
- He has hosted the Tony Awards twice to date.
- Co-starred with actress Halle Berry in four films.
- He is left handed.
- Although he enjoyed acting classes and theater, the idea that acting could be a full time job rather than a hobby did not surface until he was in his early twenties.
- He openly admits that he was probably the worst student in drama school.
- He designed their wedding rings bearing the Sanscript inscription translated "we dedicate our union to a greater source".
-
- He has a French bulldog named Peaches.
- He has a great sense of humor.

Hugh Jackman and Anne Hathaway in
Les Miserables –
Universal Pictures, 2012

Salary

2009 *X-Men Origins: Wolverine* $20,000,000
2011 *Butter* $2,000,000
2011 *Real Steel* $9,000,000

Awards and Nominations

2002 Golden Globes Best Performance by an Actor in Motion Picture-Musical or Comedy *Kate & Leopold*
Other Nominations thru 2010
AFI Award, Empire Award, People's Choice, Saturn Award, SFX
Awards Won
Primetime Emmy, Saturn, AFI International, People's Choice

Star on the Walk of Fame

6931 Hollywood Blvd.

SHEMAR MOORE

Vital Statistics

DOB: April 20, 1970 (Taurus) in Oakland, California
Name at Birth: Shemar Franklin Moore (The name Shemar is a combination of his father and mother's first names)
Height: 6' 0"
Hair: Head Shaved (Brown)
Eyes: Brown
Physique: Ripped

Biographical Sketch

Father
  Sherrod Moore (Died when Shemar was eight)

Mother
  Marilyn (Business Consultant)

Siblings
Kosheno
Sheburra
Shenon
Romeo

Boyhood Years

Shemar Moore and Victoria Rowell in
The Young and the Restless –
CBS Television, 1973-present

Until the age of two, the year of his parents' divorce, Shemar lived in The Netherlands. Because his mother spoke only Dutch to him, it became his first language. His father wasn't around much so Moore did not speak English until he moved to Bahrain, England where his mother taught mathematics. Her work took her to Greece and Africa affording Shemar a cosmopolitan upbringing of sorts until they settled in Chicago then later moved to Northern California where she worked in a clinic. Eventually they settled Palo Alto, California where Moore was active in a number of sports while attending Henry M. Gunn High School. Scouts actively showed interest in the young man who was known for pitching a baseball at ninety four mph.

His mother discouraged Shemar from accepting offers to play professional baseball fearful of the injury factor. Nonetheless he went on to Santa Clara University on a partial baseball scholarship where he majored in communications with a minor in Theater Arts while continuing to play varsity ball. A minor medical situation created a problem for Moore on the pitcher's mound and he decided then to concentrate on an acting career.

Because of his imposing presence he was able to secure enough modeling jobs to help pay for expenses not covered by his scholarship.

Start of Career

Shemar Moore and Ashley Scott in
Birds of Prey –
Warner Brothers Television, 2002-2003

A lucrative modeling career helped subsidize Moore's college education. Soon afterward Moore moved to Los Angeles where he invested his savings in himself by taking acting lessons in preparation for his plan of an acting career. An audition for a part in the popular daytime soap opera, *The Young and the Restless* led to the role of 'Malcolm' on the series. Titillating female viewers for eight years the talented, hunky actor made a total of seven pilots before garnering the role of 'Derek Morgan' in the outstanding 'cerebral 'detective' series, *Criminal Minds*.

Onscreen Persona

Smoldering is the best adjective to describe Moore's presence on the screen. Feminine hearts race shamelessly at the sight of this strong, forceful yet sensitive actor who has captured their adoration. When he refers to the character of 'Penelope' as 'baby girl' one can almost see thousands of women viewers swooning in front of their television sets.

Personal Life

Romances

Toni Braxton; who he met soon after graduating from Santa Clara University. The two sizzled together for a long while.

Halle Berry; Moore states frankly that he fell hard for Halle who was newly divorced from David Justice at the time. He refers to their relationship as "a necessary experience."

Fast Facts

- His early days in Los Angeles found Shemar spending whatever money he earned on acting lessons while he spent his nights sleeping on a friend's couch.
- He is very appreciative of his fans and stays in touch via his personal Facebook page and ShemarMoore.com website.

- He enjoys working out and is faithful to a regimen of four days a week of biking, lifting weights and hiking. That body does not just happen.
- He is very close with his mom, crediting her for his values in life that include chivalry and respect for the emotions and feelings of a woman.
- He is frank about Halle Berry with whom he had a romantic relationship that both tried to keep secret for personal reasons.
- Following his mother's diagnosis of Multiple Sclerosis, Moore became actively involved in helping to raise funds for MS research. Fellow cast members have joined him in various fund raisers.
- Although Moore is not involved in a romantic relationship at this writing he is frank about wanting to marry and have children one day in the near future.
- In an interview published in *Essence Magazine*, Moore reflected on the wisdom of his grandmother who advises him not to rush or force it, that the right woman will show up. To which Moore responds "So I'm waiting on her."

Salary

$100,000 per episode for TV series *Criminal Minds*

Shemar Moore and Joe Mantegna in
Criminal Minds –
CBS Television, 2005 to present

Nominations and Awards
1996 Daytime Emmy Outstanding Young Actor in a Drama Series *The Young and the Restless*
1997 Daytime Emmy Outstanding Young Actor in a Drama Series *The Young and the Restless*
1998 Soap Opera Digest Hottest Male Star *The Young and the Restless*
1999 Soap Opera Digest Hottest Male Star *The Young and the Restless*
2005 BET Comedy Outstanding lead Actor in a Theatrical Role Diary of a Mad Black Woman
Additional nominations for Image Awards, 1997, 1998, 1999 Outstanding Actor in a Daytime Drama Series, *The Young and the Restless*
2000 Daytime Emmy Outstanding Actor in a Daytime Drama Series *The Young and the Restless*
Additional Image Awards 1998, 1999, 2000, 2001, 2002, 2005, 2006 for Outstanding Actor in a Daytime Drama Series *The Young and the Restless*

Star on the Walk of Fame

As of this writing, Shemar Moore does not have a star on the Walk of Fame.

ACKNOWLEDGEMENTS

My sincerest appreciation goes to my research team. There are too many to list here, but thanks.

To Judith Moose; who first recognized the interest this book could generate and kept encouraging me to continue writing it.

To members of my family who were so supportive, especially my Aunt Mona and Uncle Jerry who gave me the first push into writing about Hollywood. To my son; Barry for believing in me and my daughter-in-law; Adrienne who spurred me on when I faltered.

My gratitude to my friend; actress Linda McCulough who gave me a heads up whenever I needed it.

And a big Thank You to Alex Joyce, my computer tech for his invaluable help when there were glitches with my computer and a word program that went awry. For his help in putting it together. He knows what that means.

Special thanks to Bryan and Domingo, just because.

Finally, my loving thanks to my grandson Scott who patiently made himself available at odd hours when I contacted him in exasperation. You are a genius.

ABOUT THE AUTHOR

Sylvia Safran Resnick

In the world of entertainment, celebrity popularity rises and falls faster than an elevator, but one thing that remains the same is society's desire to learn more about their favorite stars and what makes them tick. Gossip columnists and entertainment journalists walked among the stars every day and gave the public "the scoop" on who did what with whom. Sylvia Safran Resnick spent the better part of 33 years as one of the most respected entertainment journalists in the industry.

Her accomplishments in the field of entertainment journalism are as impressive as the celebrities she frequently covered week after week. From 1964 to 1973, Sylvia's byline could be found coast to coast in publications including Movie Stars, Photoplay, TV Radio Mirror, Modern Screen, and TV Star Parade. She worked with the mega-giant Sterling Publications, with her specific area of expertise focused on in-person interviews with an assortment of film and television stars. For three years Sylvia wrote the columns Las Vegas Go-Round and TV Star Parade.

Moving up the corporate ladder, Sylvia soon found herself serving as the associate editor for what was perhaps the most famous celebrity magazine of the 1970s; Rona Barrett's Hollywood. Aside from her duties as associate editor, she maintained the same stringent work ethic she always had and produced columns related to Daytime television and film reviews. Keeping within the industry that she's spent her life loving, Sylvia was often sought out to cover an assortment of Hollywood premieres, parties and any entertainment journalist's dream; she covered The Golden Globe Awards and The Emmy Awards ceremonies.

In 1973, Sylvia's attention was captured by another industry. From a journalistic perspective, the Beauty Industry was just as interesting as the entertainment field, but also proved to be very similar. The beauty magazines were built on emulating the styles projected by Hollywood legends and Hollywood's glamour girls were constantly drawn to the pages of beauty magazines. Sensing that this was the perfect niche, Sylvia became the beauty editor of Best Ways Magazine, featuring interviews and spreads on celebrity lifestyles. Never having completely left the entertainment field, from 1977 until 1991, Coronet, Pageant, Ladies Home Companion, Big Valley and In The Know magazines readers were treated to columns dealing with the current "hot" topics of the day.

With 33 years of journalism under her belt, Sylvia soon heard another project calling. This one would be special. Instead of sharing a tidbit or two about someone, she'd give the public an insider's glimpse at the life of a celebrity. Her first celebrity novel was *An Unauthorized Biography of Burt Reynolds* (published by St. Martin's Press) and was quickly followed with *A Biography of Kristy McNichol, The Partridge Family Cookbook* (Curtis Publications) and *The Walton Family Cookbook* (Bantam).

Under pen name Sheri Paul, Sylvia released an additional two genres of literary projects. The first was a trilogy series of mysteries titled *Debbie Preston, Teenage Reporter* (New American Library Publishers). The second and third endeavors were erotic stories named *Heat Wave* and *Summer of Love*.

By now you may find yourself asking what Sylvia Resnick is doing today. The answer is quite a few things and slowing down is definitely not one of them! Sylvia is in the process of writing four more books – one of each – Entertainment, Romance, Erotica, and Mainstream Fiction.

www.ingramcontent.com/pod-product-compliance
Lightning Source LLC
Chambersburg PA
CBHW082108230426
43671CB00015B/2632